PARENTING OUT OF CONTROL

MARGARET K. NELSON

Parenting Out of Control

Anxious Parents in Uncertain Times

NEW YORK UNIVERSITY PRESS

New York and London

NEW YORK UNIVERSITY PRESS
New York and London
www.nyupress.org

Library of Congress Cataloging-in-Publication Data

Nelson, Margaret K., 1944–
Parenting out of control : anxious parents in uncertain times /
Margaret K. Nelson.
p. cm.
Includes bibliographical references and index.
ISBN-13: 978–0–8147–5853–3 (cl : alk. paper)
ISBN-10: 0–8147–5853–3 (cl : alk. paper)
1. Parenting—United States. 2. Parent and child—United States. I. Title.
HQ755.8.N453 2010
649'.10973—dc22 2009048944

New York University Press books are printed on acid-free paper,
and their binding materials are chosen for strength and durability.
We strive to use environmentally responsible suppliers and materials
to the greatest extent possible in publishing our books.

Manufactured in the United States of America

10 9 8 7 6 5 4 3 2 1

For my grandchildren, Maya Ruth Nelson and Sadie Klein Nelson

◈ CONTENTS

Acknowledgments ix

Introduction: No Playpen 1

I Parenting Styles
Introduction to Part I: Anxious and Engaged 17

1 Looking toward an Uncertain Future 23
2 Looking Back: Are the Good Times Gone? 48
3 Clear and Present Dangers 70
4 How They Parent: Styles, Satisfactions, and Tensions 87

II Parenting and Technology
Introduction to Part II: Do You Know Where Your Children Are? 107

5 Staying Connected 113
6 Constraining Practices 128
7 What They're Hiding: Spying and Surveillance 142

8 From Care to Control 163
Conclusion: The Consequences of Parenting Out of Control 174

Appendix A: Methods 187
Appendix B: Data Analysis 195
Notes 201
Bibliography 233
Index 247
About the Author 257

◈ ACKNOWLEDGMENTS

It is always a delightful moment to turn to this part of a manuscript. Not only is this an indication that yes, at last, the process of writing is almost complete, but it is also a time to offer thanks rather than simply to accumulate debts. And so, with a great sense of relief, I thank the following people and institutions.

My first thanks go to the many men and women who agreed to be interviewed for this project. Without their willingness to take time out of busy lives, to look inside themselves, and to provide candid answers to probing questions, this book could not have come into being. They are, of course, nameless here. My second thanks is to the interviewers who took time out of their busy lives to ask those probing questions. And these I can name: Paul Barnwell, Katie Edwards, Kate Elias, Adam Fazio, Jenny Harris, Liz Kofman, Mary Mendoza, Ana Rita Pergolizzi, Susan Reagan, Dena Simmonds, Susan Wargo, and Lauren Ziegler.

I have received significant financial support from Middlebury College in conjunction with the A. Barton Hepburn Chair. I appreciate each and every penny. I appreciate as well the support from a Mellon Grant for a course reduction as this project was getting under way and the encouragement and flexibility of Carol Rifelj, who was the dean for faculty development at that time.

I have had wonderful student assistants at various stages of the project, including Katie Hylas, Kristin Haas, and Julia Szabo. Val Benka—long past being my student—did her usually magnificent job of editing as I was putting on the final touches.

During the past couple years, a group of colleagues have offered all sorts of vital support. Laurie Essig (with help from Lynn Owens and Rebecca Tiger) invented the title. Rebecca Tiger made sure that I was not off-base in my discussion of "control." Karen Hansen knocked sense into my head when in response to my muttering that this project was maybe too hard she said, "They're all hard. They're just hard in different ways." Naomi Gerstel and Anita Garey both read drafts at crucial stages and offered invaluable advice. I take responsibility for my own errors; I credit Naomi and Anita with saving me from far more numerous ones.

My editor at NYU Press, Ilene Kalish, supported this project from the start. At the same time, she sent me back to the drawing board more than once. Though I did not always show my appreciation of her critiques at the time, I'm happy to acknowledge that she was right. As the manuscript moved into production, Aiden Amos, Despina Papazoglou Gimbel, and Andrew Katz played important roles.

On a daily basis I rely on a number of wonderful friends and family members, including Emily Abel, Charlene Barrett, Jane Chaplin, Sonja Olson, Burke Rochford, and, especially, Bill Nelson. I am grateful that I have these people in my life.

◈ INTRODUCTION

No Playpen

When I was raising my children in the 1970s, there were no baby monitors to help me hear them cry in the middle of the night, no cell phones to assist me in keeping track of their whereabouts at every moment, and no expectation that I would know any more about their educational successes or failures than they, or a quarterly report card, would tell me.[1] Indeed, although I thought of myself as a relatively anxious parent, I trusted a girl in the third grade to accompany my five-year-old son to and from school, and when he was in the first grade, I allowed him to walk that mile by himself. Moreover, although I thought of myself as a deeply engaged parent, I did not believe I needed to know what my children were doing at every moment once they had reached their teen years. And although I was as status conscious as anyone else and deeply interested in seeing my children get into "good" colleges, I never called a teacher to find out about a homework assignment or contested an assigned grade. In retrospect, and from the vantage point of watching my younger friends and colleagues with their children today, my parenting style seems, if not neglectful, certainly a mite casual.

I'm not alone in feeling that something about the parenting of young children has recently shifted in profound ways. The other day I ran into a woman I've known for years but hadn't seen for some time. We compared notes. "Grandchildren?" I asked. "Yes," she answered, "and moving back to live near me." As I expressed envy because mine live four hours away, she expressed hesitation. She wondered whether she could participate in the rearing of those grandchildren according to the style her daughter, a successful attorney in her own right, had chosen. "No playpen," I joked. "Right," she said, "no playpen."

Personal experience aside, contemporary popular culture is replete with descriptions of a new style of parenting that appears to prevail especially among elite parents who, supposedly, worry all the time about the safety of their children and who, it is said, hover over and monitor them more closely than ever before, even if they are likely to eschew artificial constraints such as playpens. Parenting books, journalists, and academics comment on this phenomenon that some have dubbed "hypervigilance" and occasionally offer advice about how best to cope with it.[2]

I'm also not alone in feeling that the intensity that characterizes parenting today does not seem to let up when children enter late adolescence or even early adulthood. At the sixty-fifth birthday party of a colleague, I chatted with a woman who worked in career counseling at a nearby university. I asked her how her job had changed over the past thirty years. Her answer came swiftly: "They're now so immature when they graduate, and they have to consult their parents about everything." She added, "But that's not the worst of it. The parents call all the time too, demanding to know just what it is I am doing for their children."

Although this career counselor might have been overstating the degree to which the undergraduate students at her university sought parental advice and the degree to which the parents managed to intervene in the lives of those twenty-one-year-olds, hers is a common overstatement. Wikipedia defines a "helicopter parent" as a "mother or father who 'hovers' over a student of any age."[3] Put this term into a Google search and scores of references pop up.[4]

Moreover, it turns out that both the notion that this hovering is intense and the notion that this hovering is welcomed by young adults may not be exaggerations at all. The National Survey of Student Engagement, which "obtains, on an annual basis, information from hundreds of four-year colleges and universities nationwide," reported in 2007 that 86 percent of first-year college students had "frequent" (defined as "very often" or "often") electronic contact with their mothers, and 71 percent had "frequent" electronic contact with their fathers; these rates are about the same for college seniors too.[5] Moreover, 13 percent of first-year and 8 percent of senior students reported in the survey that a parent or guardian "frequently intervened on their behalf to help them solve problems they were having at the college," and "another quarter of first-year and 21 percent of senior students said their parent or guardian *sometimes* intervened."[6] Another recent study reports that parents of college-age children communicate with those children an average of more than ten times per week through a sum of all forms of communication, such as cell phones, email, and letters.[7] This study further suggests that intensive communication is initiated relatively equally by both parents and children and that both parents and children desire it:

> Students reported that the contact was more often initiated by parents than by themselves, although only slightly more so. Parents reported that initiation of contact was roughly equal. Moreover, the vast majority of students expressed satisfaction with the frequency of communication, and 29 percent of those surveyed would have preferred more communication with their fathers. None of the parents surveyed wanted less communication than they had, and 13 percent would have preferred more.[8]

Much commentary about this new style of parenting notes that it appears to be accompanied by, enacted through, and perhaps even rests on a series of technological developments.[9] In addition to the common baby monitors and cell phones, it turns out that parents can buy a GPS tracking device to put in a car to monitor adolescent driving practices, attach a transponder to a child's wrist to ensure that they can locate children who venture farther than a preprogrammed distance, purchase a drug testing kit to use at home, place a program on their computers to record their children's every keystroke, and install a piece of software to prevent access to designated Internet sites.[10] Parents can also activate the blocking capacity of the V-chip that is now mandatory on larger televisions. Some of these devices rely on the cooperation of children; this is true, for example, of cell phones. But it also turns out that parents can implement controls, spy on their children, and monitor their children's behavior, especially their driving, from a distance without the active participation of their children at all.[11]

Studying Parenting Styles

Curious about the hovering and curious about its possible link to new technology, I designed a research project that would allow me to explore and explain the roots, dynamics, and class location of a style of child rearing that I have come to call "parenting out of control" as it affects attitudes toward and behaviors directed at adolescent children. This book represents the results of that research. I both holistically examine parenting in the contemporary United States amid social, cultural, and technological changes and focus particularly on the contrast between parenting out of control and a different style of care—found within a different social milieu—that I call "parenting with limits."

I draw on intensive interviews that my research assistants and I conducted with a total of ninety-three parents (of whom three-quarters were mothers). These interviews took place in respondents' homes in thirty-seven different locations in eleven different states representing seven of the nine major regions of the country: New England (Connecticut, Massachusetts, Vermont), the Middle Atlantic (Pennsylvania, New Jersey, New York), the South Atlantic (North Carolina), East South Central (Kentucky), West North Central (Missouri), West South Central (Texas), and the Pacific West (California). The vast majority of the parents with whom we spoke had at least one teenage child at the time of the interview. (A complete discussion of the methods and sample can be found in appendix A.)

In what follows, I compare the parenting styles of what I refer to as the "professional middle-class" parents with those from the "middle" and "working" classes.[12] Since class status is in some ways an arbitrary designation, let me take a moment to address how I define it and why I use the awkward term "professional middle class." Because social class has material, cultural, and social elements, no way of designating the social class position of an individual is perfect. Relying on just income as a measurement of class status taps into the material component of social class but often misses the cultural and social elements, especially insofar as these are reflected in (or components of) occupational position and the activities of daily life. Although an individual's job constitutes an important determinant of daily life, relying on it as an indicator of social class is an especially unsatisfactory approach for women who may be staying at home with their children and who may have deferred or halted career aspirations and opportunities to care for a family. Moreover, elite jobs that build on professional training do not always yield high incomes (and thus cannot invariably be identified as upper middle class or upper class); academics can testify to that fact, as can lawyers and doctors who put public interest above financial gain. Education often offers a better measure than income for assessing cultural issues and, because of the strong association between education and occupation, for explaining those issues of job flexibility and authority connected to occupational status. Education, through its association with occupation and income, can also determine to a great extent the milieu in which one lives, whom one takes as a reference group, and the kinds of values one holds.[13] These are all important determinants of what one defines as good parenting.

Consequently, education is the key to how I identify class status in this study. I define the "professional middle class" as people with educational credentials beyond a bachelor's degree and, when employed, as people holding professional occupations: this grouping includes such individuals as an Asian American college professor from Berkeley, California, a white attorney in a Boston suburb, and a white woman with a PhD who is, by self-definition, a "stay-at-home mom." The people in the middle class with whom I spoke have a bachelor's degree, but nothing higher; usually they are in what have been referred to as "semiprofessional" positions. This group includes a Latino policeman from San Antonio, Texas, and a white high school teacher from Louisville, Kentucky. None of the working-class respondents have a bachelor's degree, although many of them have attended some college (including occasionally having received an associate's degree); they hold a vast range of occupations. Among the working-class individuals are a white man employed as a sheet-metal worker, a first-generation immigrant from Italy who lives on Staten Island, New York, and is a stay-at-home mom, and an African American woman who works as a teacher's aide in Philadelphia.

In general, I make no distinction between working-class and middle-class parents. Throughout the comparisons, it should be remembered that these inclusive groupings—of all three social classes—contain within them individuals who deviate from the general patterns of parenting I ascribe to each group. Moreover, because my central focus in this study is the professional middle-class parents who have adopted the style I call "parenting out of control," middle- and working-class parents who follow what I call "parenting with limits" often serve as a touchstone rather than an equal focus of analysis.[14]

For well over a decade my own research has been with people less privileged than myself and with those in vulnerable positions. This is the first time I have focused on individuals close to me in background, occupation, and interests. Indeed, a few of the people my research assistants and I interviewed I count as friends and colleagues; some of them are one step removed—the friends and colleagues of friends and colleagues. The spotlight I turn on the professional middle class may be all the more self-conscious, and maybe even harsher, for my awareness that, were I somewhat younger than I am, I too might well be "parenting out of control."

The spotlight through which I examine parenting styles can be thought of as having four lenses that are sometimes overlapping and sometimes distinct.

One lens simply reveals the major features of the professional middle-class style and how it differs from that of the less privileged parents. A second lens seeks to uncover some of the root causes of the professional middle-class style. A third lens examines how these styles are enacted in conjunction with technologies. And finally, yet another lens links parenting out of control to other contemporary theoretical (and social) currents.

A Descriptive Lens: The Importance of Class

When I compared parenting styles among the professional middle-class respondents with those of their less privileged peers, I found quite distinctive differences. Among the former, parenting includes a lengthy perspective on children's dependency without a clear launching point for a grown child, a commitment to creating "passionate" people who know how to find a "proper" balance between working hard and having fun, personalized and negotiated guidance in the activities of daily life, respectful responsiveness to children's individual needs and desires, a belief in boundless potential, ambitious goals for achievement, and an intense engagement with children who in previous generations might have been encouraged to begin the process of separation. Privileged parents also put child rearing front and center: even in the midst of extremely busy lives, they highlight the significance and meaning they find in this activity, and they avoid shortcuts (such as playpens) that could make their job easier. Parents who view themselves as being much alone in the task of raising children and as having sole responsibility for their children's safety and psychological well-being readily embrace these burdens.

As the following chapters show, in some ways these characteristics make for an approach to parenting that is filled with tensions and enduring dilemmas. For example, professional middle-class parents want both to protect their children from growing up too quickly and to push them to high achievement at an early age. The latter impulse often leads to treating their children as peers and to claiming that those children can be trusted to make decisions on their own; the former impulse often leads to hovering and to concealed surveillance. And while the contemporary style of parenting rests on an approach that has been found among privileged parents for some time—an emphasis on being permissive rather than authoritarian or even authoritative, a reliance on internalized constraint rather than punishment and external control—the intense negotiation that often results from a commitment to loose reins and to trust takes place along with what appear to be relatively new patterns of vigilance and connection.[15] All of this makes for the much noticed distinction between the current parenting style and that which characterized child rearing among the elite as recently as twenty or thirty years ago. This distinction is commented on by the parents interviewed for this study who see themselves as forging a new model.

By way of contrast, the working-class and middle-class parents assume that higher education will prepare their children to live on their own; they are more concerned with skills that will ensure self-sufficiency than they are with passion and fun. Working-class and middle-class parents are also less interested in intimacy and engagement than they are in clear rules of authority within the family. While they too find satisfaction in raising children, they do not believe they need to be involved in making every decision about their children's lives, and they welcome shortcuts that can ease their burdens. And although they too view themselves as having sole responsibility for their children's safety, limited resources of time and money shape day-to-day decisions and strategies. Finally, middle-class and working-class parents experience fewer internal contradictions in their parenting approach, and they are less conscious of carving out a new mode of parenting that differs radically from that of their own parents. Although they understand that more isolation for individual families and what are seen to be greater dangers might require more intense vigilance, they refer more often to continuity than to difference. Both attention to external constraints and attention to having children who obey family rules are central to my dubbing this approach "parenting with limits."

An Analytical Lens: Finding Causes

It would be thrilling to announce that I had found a single reason for the new approach to rearing children among the professional middle class. But no *single* cause could possibly explain such a complex shift in orientation toward parenting; moreover, particular aspects of this new approach in all likelihood have multiple and overlapping causes. These realities frame my analysis of how the differences between the groups of parents can be linked to the diverse ways adults in different social classes envision the future, remember their own histories, and evaluate present concerns. I search for explanations rather than *the* explanation; I explore the manner in which many different strands of influence feed into specific elements of the new distinctive style of parenting out of control.

I start with a consideration of how parents think about their children's futures. I argue that parents from all social backgrounds worry about contemporary conditions of acute economic uncertainty.[16] But, not surprisingly, the content of the worries and the responses to these concerns are different among the more privileged than they are among those with fewer resources at their disposal. Anxious to secure their children's competitive advantage in a world that is marked by increasing anxiety about college acceptance and increasing economic inequality (and perhaps shrinking options for elite status), professional middle-class parents seize opportunities for educational success and enroll even their very young children in a dazzling array of "extracurricular" activities. They assume that their children are, if not perfectible, blessed with boundless potential. In response, they nurture children to become the best they can possibly be; they also provide them with the "best" social, cultural, and economic capital.[17] However, because contemporary professional middle-class parents do not know which skills will be most appropriate and useful in a rapidly changing world, they hope to encourage a broad range of skills and the readiness to be flexible. The delayed launching of children into adulthood may well be tied to concerns about not settling too soon in a world undergoing major transformations. The professional middle-class parents are also well aware of the personal costs of their own success: most have sacrificed a fair degree of leisure to get where they are; many also have sacrificed their youthful idealism. These are pains from which they hope to protect their own children as they guide them toward the future. These pains are also reason for parents to find in their children companionship that they do not otherwise experience in their busy lives. From a different social and economic milieu, and out of both economic necessity and inclination, middle- and working-class parents envision a shorter educational future, clearer career goals, and an earlier launch.

Understandings of the past are also relevant to how parents make choices about child-rearing strategies. Some professional middle-class parents who adopt the new approach of a high degree of connection with their adolescent children do so not just in response to something missing in their lives but also in response to what they regard as problems with how they were treated during their own teenage years and to what they recall as having been an essential distance between parents and children. This is true of those who experienced authoritarian parenting. It is also true of those raised in the more permissive mode advocated by Dr. Spock.[18] Ironically, some of the loudest claims for the beauty of intimacy between parents and teens come from a generation of parents who themselves once proclaimed that it was foolishness to trust anyone over thirty. Over and over professional middle-class parents told me, with pride in their voices, that it was now very different in their homes—that an adolescent child was their "best friend." Less privileged parents also told me that they saw reasons to be more vigilant than their parents had been, but they also said that they knew well the difference between being a parent and being a friend.

The professional middle-class parents who hold their adolescent children close are not just responding to and reversing the lessons of the past or anticipating future concerns. They are simultaneously responding to what they see as the threats to their children's present well-being. These perceived threats include what they describe as media images of violence and, what they speak of with even more urgency, as media images of sex. Over and over professional middle-class parents told me—in this case less with pride than with anxiety—that they want to protect their children from too much exposure to the images around them and from growing up too fast. Professional middle-class parents have additional daily concerns that stem from the actions they have taken to prepare their children for the future and to help them compete on a daily basis with their peers. Having purchased devices such as cell phones and laptop computers so that their children will not be left behind in the race to the top, and having encouraged their children to participate in scheduled activities from morning to night, elite parents then worry that they have overindulged, overscheduled, and overpressured their children. Some of the hovering they do is thus to keep track of the consequences of patterns of child rearing they have created. Middle-class and working-class parents also said they were concerned about what it was their children were exposed to in the media, but they stressed even more concrete dangers in their neighborhoods and schools. Over and over these parents told me that they worried about their capacity to keep their children safe from physical harm.

The Lens of Technology: Enacting Parenting Styles

When I began this research, I assumed naively that the hovering professional middle-class parents would opt for all the help technology could offer to help them keep track of and even spy on their children. In fact, I began this project in part because I thought that it would allow me the fun of exploring novel technologies such as GPS tracking systems for teen drivers and their use within the home.[19]

As I show in part II of this book, I was wrong. The elite parents I interviewed do opt for some of these technologies, and, in particular, they purchase both baby monitors and cell phones. These devices are viewed as desirable by professional middle-class parents because they fit well with the style of parenting they have adopted: these devices enable parents to be aware of and intimate with their children. But the professional middle-class parents decidedly do not seek out technologies that offer either constraint (such as child locators) or surveillance (such as GPS tracking systems in cars). Indeed they appear to find some of these morally repugnant. Why, they say, would I want a machine to tell me where my child is? Why would I want them to track their driving? I *trust* them, they say.

This professional middle-class resistance to new technologies that could assist hovering turns out to be a complex phenomenon because it hinges on the technology itself and not on the practices of either constraint or surveillance. In fact, the professional middle-class parents who make significant claims of trusting their children actually forgo neither constraint nor surveillance. Rather, they engage in quite thorough and quite careful attempts to limit and monitor their children's daily activities. They *do* hover. But instead of relying on technological assistance (beyond baby monitors and cell phones) for these practices, they rely on their own presence and on the intimacy that is a hallmark of their parenting. As a result, both constraint and monitoring are highly individualized and subject to negotiation. Thus, what the psychologist Barbara Hofer has called the "electronic tether"—the cell phone and email that connects parents and children at a distance—proves to be quite elastic, and often quite unpredictably so.[20]

The situation is quite different among middle-class and working-class parents. These less privileged parents prefer clear rules and the assistance of more technology. Hence, rather than lurking in a doorway to sneak a look at what a teenager is doing on the computer, as a professional middle-class mother might do, a working-class mother installs a piece of commercial software that blocks unwanted Internet sites. Or, rather than watching videos with a teenage son to ensure that images of violence are subject to detailed discussion, as a professional middle-class father might do, a working-class father simply activates the V-chip on the television. The less elite parents, then, rely on limits rather than subtle control.

The Lens of Theory: Parenting Out of Control

My findings of intimacy and hovering combined with elastic constraint and covert surveillance are central to my dubbing the professional middle-class approach "parenting out of control." Clearly intimacy and hovering lay the groundwork for control in the commonsense meaning of the word: parents are carefully guiding, shaping, and determining the contours of their children's actions. Because so much of teenage children's daily lives is subject to observation, discussion, and negotiation, those who are subject to this kind of parental oversight may experience their parents as being "out of control." And the parents who implement these strategies may feel that the time required to raise children has gotten "out of control." Indeed, if the jury is still out on the effects these strategies will have on the independence and autonomy of young adults, a considerable body of evidence (including this book) suggests that the new parenting style consumes the lives of the *parents* who adopt it, often at the expense of other meaningful relationships.[21] This is another way that parenting has gotten "out of control."

The phrase "parenting out of control" is also linked to a more nuanced meaning. In the abstract world of social theory, a distinction has emerged between strategies that shape individuals by relying on disciplinary techniques and strategies that accomplish those ends through mechanisms of control. French social theorist Michel Foucault is the premier authority on the former approach. In his groundbreaking study of discipline, Foucault analyzes the structure of a prison that was designed like a panopticon with an always-present, elevated guard whose presence was apparent but whose direct gaze was concealed from the prisoners.[22] Because the inmates would always be visible but would not know when they were being watched, Foucault argues, they would come to obey the rules, to discipline themselves. That is, self-discipline emerges from uncertainty about whether one is being watched at any given moment. As the contemporary theorist of surveillance David Lyon says, "[This uncertainty] creates the desire to comply with whatever is the norm for the institution in question. Through the process is developed an inner compulsion to 'do the right thing' as prescribed by the organization, which produces the desired 'docile bodies.'"[23] Here, then, is a model of shaping that relies on clear constraint, on hierarchy, on overt judgments about what is and is not appropriate, and on acknowledged surveillance. This is also a model that assumes that at some point the guard is no longer necessary because the subjects have become "docile." And this is the model assumed to be in use in the full range of contemporary institutions, including the school and the army, each of which is "producing" its own distinctive product: in the school one becomes a student; in the army, a soldier. This also is the model used in the family by parents who emphasize hierarchical authority and clear limits.

By way of contrast, what can be called a strategy of control relies less on enclosure and confinement than on constant communication, less on clear rules than on shifting possibilities, less on hierarchy than on intimacy, less on acknowledged surveillance than on the denial that it is necessary (because of trust), and less on the finished product than on the ongoing processes of shaping "inmates."[24] Indeed, in this model, there is no "finished product" or launch into self-discipline. This new model of shaping corresponds well to what I see going on within the professional middle-class families. And, as has been implied, this model is quite different from the (older, disciplinary) approach to child rearing found in middle- and working-class families who understand and experience the past, present, and future quite differently than do the more privileged parents.

Most investigations of the new model of control, and especially of its uses within the fields of criminal justice, refer to the state or occasionally the community as a smaller unit of analysis.[25] However, I suggest that these concepts of control and discipline might be an interesting medium through which to contrast parenting practices in different social classes. In so doing I link family "styles" to broader cultural trends and suggest that the family is not all that different—or distant—from other institutions with authority over, and involvement in the shaping of, contemporary subjects, including the criminal justice system.[26]

Brief Overview

I divide this investigation of parenting strategies into two parts. In part I, I demonstrate how parenting out of control emerges from the ways in which professional middle-class parents make sense of their position in the world. I show that although parents from the working and middle classes share some concerns with parents from the professional middle class—especially about safety issues and parental isolation—the more privileged parents have a quite distinctive (and sometimes inconsistent) approach to child rearing. In part II, I begin with a brief discussion of how the family has been ignored in discussions of surveillance technologies and then turn to how parents in different social classes enact child rearing in response to the new range of technologies for connecting to, constraining, and spying on their children. Once again, I demonstrate that in spite of some shared interests in new technologies, the professional middle-class parents approach these in ways that are quite different from their less privileged peers. The last two chapters offer some final thoughts. In chapter 8, I review the sources and dimensions of the two parenting styles discussed in the book, and I demonstrate how care can shade into control; in the conclusion, I consider the consequences of different ways to approach the care—and control—of teenagers.

Coda

These days as I walk across the opulent lawns of the private, liberal arts college where I teach, most students passing by have a cell phone, seemingly glued to one ear. They are so deeply engaged in their conversations that they barely notice anyone around them, and they are startled when I call out a greeting. Often, it seems from the words I overhear, those conversations concern plans to meet a friend for lunch, for a study date, or to go for a run. But at least as often, it seems from the words wafting in the wind, these are conversations with "mom" or "dad." How did it happen, I wonder, that college students became so willing to talk with their parents that they would call—or answer calls—en route to classes and the gym? This certainly wasn't the case for the members of my generation, who dutifully made a call but once a week, and whose parents rarely, if ever, called us. Unraveling this mysterious new behavior—and the mysteries surrounding other forms of connection, as well as those of constraint and surveillance, found within the milieu in which my elite students were hatched—is what this book is about.

PART I

Parenting Styles

◈ INTRODUCTION TO PART I

Anxious and Engaged

Scholarly and ad hoc explanations for the new overanxious parent suggest a variety of immediate causes. Some argue that since events such as Columbine and especially 9/11, the world has become—or appears to be—a more dangerous place. Consequently, parents are "simply" responding to that new danger—or to a perception of danger.[1] Many point to a new "culture of fear" and especially to widely publicized stories of kidnapping, Internet pornography, and sexual predators.[2] Some note that more parents are having just one child, and therefore a larger proportion of all parents are "new" parents who are more anxious than those who are more experienced.[3] In a similar vein, it is argued that as parents have fewer children, each child becomes ever more precious.[4] Finally, some point to the "erosion of adult solidarity" and a feeling on the part of parents that they cannot rely on others to help them with the activities associated with the daily task of raising their children.[5]

From a somewhat different perspective, another set of scholars point to the rise of a more generalized "anxiety" and the emergence of a "risk society." Many of these ideas come from the sociologists Anthony Giddens and Ulrich Beck.[6] Giddens, for example, notes that although the world has not necessarily become more hazardous, the absence of tradition leads to a preoccupation "with the future (and also with safety)."[7] When dangers are redefined as risks and thus "viewed as the product of human action and decision-making rather than of fate," individuals might hold themselves ever more responsible for ensuring the safety of themselves and of those who are dependent on them.[8] In conjunction with this approach, a growing body of empirical research notes that as the dangers facing children are interpreted as risks to be managed, parents come to limit the mobility of their children, leading ultimately to a more circumscribed existence.[9] Additionally, scholars suggest that as the state has retreated from responsibility for its citizens, all individuals bear greater burdens for ensuring the security of themselves and members of their family.[10]

Each of these explanations is convincing in its own way, and each finds resonance in the responses of the parents, from among all socioeconomic classes, who were interviewed for this study. Parents do talk about the rise of terrorism as a source of anxiety and as an issue of attention as they teach their children to be aware, even as they want to make their children secure in the world. Parents also talk about predators—in the neighborhood and on the Internet—who might snatch or harm their children. Parents do hold themselves responsible for the well-being of their children and, indeed, look to themselves rather than some broader community of family or neighborhood (or even the state) to secure that well-being. And parents describe being more anxious about their firstborn and becoming less so with subsequent children.

Even so, there are several questions that remain. First, because these arguments often treat anxiety as an undifferentiated and global phenomenon, they do not distinguish among different groups of parents. Public Agenda, which describes itself as "a nonprofit, nonpartisan organization working to strengthen our democracy's capacity to take on tough issues," reports that the vast majority of parents worry "some" or "a lot" about such issues as "protecting your child from drugs and alcohol," "someone physically harming or kidnapping your child," and "the negative influence of other kids on your child."[11] But Public Agenda also reports that a higher proportion of low-income parents than of high-income parents worry "a lot" about these particular issues. These class differences are significant. They are ignored, however, when an assumption is made that all parents make decisions about child rearing from the same set of concerns.

Moreover, theories assuming that concerns about risk and danger are exaggerated fail to take into account the fact that although some of these anxieties are overblown, in some cases parents have quite legitimate fears about dangerous neighborhoods (and hence concerns about "someone physically harming" a child). And the generalized analysis fails to distinguish between anxieties about safety (Is my child at risk of being harmed by her- or himself or by someone else?), anxieties about psychological well-being (Is my child happy?), and anxieties about status reproduction (Will my child fulfill my social class expectations?).

Finally, I would suggest that starting from this standpoint of viewing parental anxiety as produced by a "culture of fear" or by the "erosion of adult solidarity" might lead to inaccurate predictions. That is, if we assume anxieties about safety are the same across all social classes, we have little reason to believe that parents will make different choices about, for example, whether to place filters on their computers to protect their children from online predators or whether to purchase a tracking device for a teen driver. However, social class differences do exist in attitudes toward implementing these new technologies, and they are not necessarily what might be expected.

Intensive Mothering and the Impact of Social Class

Those who write about the concerns parents have about the physical well-being of their children often also talk about the concerns parents have about their children's psychological well-being, daily activities, and future development. The recent shift toward more involvement in children's lives has been well described by two contemporary scholars, Sharon Hays in *The Cultural Contradictions of Motherhood* and Annette Lareau in *Unequal Childhoods: Class, Race, and Family Life.* Both books have helped shape the notion that parenting has become more intensive over the years, especially for those from a higher socioeconomic milieu.

Sharon Hays argues that parents from all social classes have recently developed a model of what she calls "intensive mothering," which, as she puts it, involves the focus on children to the exclusion of a focus on one's own concerns as an adult. Moreover, Hays argues that "intensive mothering" has its own internal logic:

> The willingness to . . . expend a great deal of physical, emotional, cognitive, and financial resources on the child . . . follows directly from the requirement of placing the child at the center of one's life and putting the child's needs above one's own. Centering one's time and energy on the child . . . [follows from] the fact that the child is understood as innocent, loving, and pure, and therefore deserving of protection from the corrupt and cruel outside world . . . [and from] the emotional intensity of mothers' feelings for their children that flows from the love they experience as they nurture that innocent (and dependent) child.[12]

In Hays's analysis of the "why" of intensive mothering, she argues that the relationship between mothers and children "comes to stand as a central symbol of the sustainable human ties, free of competition and selfish individualism, that are meant to preserve us . . . from an unbearable moral solitude."[13] This is a fascinating analysis of the moral roots of the new way of enacting maternal devotion. Hays, however, does not tell us what happens to the parent-child relationship as children move out of infancy and toddlerhood; nor does she tell us how the new form of maternal devotion translates into a particular parenting style when children begin the inevitable pull and tug of teenage years. And while she acknowledges that what she calls "middle-class" parents (which would include those I define as "professional middle class" and "middle class") are most likely to engage in the most extreme forms of "intensive mothering," Hays finds the same approach throughout the social spectrum.[14]

Annette Lareau picks up where Hays leaves off—with children aged nine and ten—and shifts the focus to explore social class differences in child rearing. She argues that while all parents might share the ideology of intensive mothering, the practice takes different forms within different social groupings. Like Hays, Lareau defines the "middle class" to include those I define as "professional middle class" and "middle class," and she contrasts that class with parents who are either from the "working class" or "poor."[15] Among the middle class she identifies a style she calls "concerted cultivation," and she locates its key element as residing in the fact that the parent "actively fosters and assesses [the] child's talents, opinions, and skill."[16] By way of contrast, Lareau characterizes the child-rearing style of the working class and the poor as being fashioned around providing basic care for the child and allowing the child to mature.

Lareau's research is a superb contemporary example within a long tradition of scholarship that demonstrates that child-rearing styles differ by social class.[17] These differences include the degree to which the parents are "child centered," meaning that adults are encouraged to shape their parenting around responding to the child's wants and needs.[18] These differences also include the style of discipline used in the home. In general, studies show that the higher the socioeconomic status, the more likely parents are to give children choices, negotiate with them about proper behavior, encourage them to share their own views, and give reasons for disciplinary practices. Those who are less privileged are more likely to expect children to acknowledge parental authority and do what is asked of them; less privileged parents are also more likely to use directives without offering reasoned explanations.[19] In addition, scholars have recorded differences in the patterns of language use encouraged within the home, differences in the kind and range of cultural capital with which parents supply children, and differences in the degree to which parents equip children to intervene in institutions on their own behalf.[20]

All these ideas have resonance in the responses of parents interviewed for this study, and I both build on this tradition of investigations into class-based child-rearing strategies and diverge from it in several ways. First, I focus on parental attitudes toward teenage children rather than on children who are considerably younger, as is the case for Hays, Lareau, and many other scholars. Second, whereas Lareau, for example, is describing differences in parental behavior, and I too am interested in these, I am also describing differences in parental belief systems—the ideas about parenting and the parent-child relationship that underlie the behavior. Moreover, I link the roots of these differences in belief system to the generational histories and ongoing concerns about the present and the future among contemporary parents as much as to efforts to reproduce social class. Finally, and perhaps most distinctively, I demonstrate (in part II) how these attitudes intersect with and are enacted through new technologies.

Because parents' ideas about their children's futures frame their notions of appropriate child-rearing styles, I begin with these in chapter 1. I then turn in chapter 2 to parents' understandings of the past and how those understandings are incorporated into a parenting style. In chapter 3, I consider the problems that parents believe they face on a daily basis as they strive to keep their children secure. In chapter 4, I demonstrate how emerging strategies intersect with and produce both satisfactions and ongoing tensions.

1 LOOKING TOWARD AN UNCERTAIN FUTURE

Francesca Guarino is a married working-class woman, the daughter of immigrants from Italy.[1] She lives on Staten Island in New York City with her husband, who is employed as a technician for a telephone company, and her three children. Their two daughters are aged seventeen and fifteen; they also have an eight-year-old boy, whom, without any false modesty, Francesca describes as "adorable" and "very attached" to his mom. She is a stay-at-home mother who believes that hers is the proper role for a married woman with children: "My parents are from the other side, and so we were raised with the old beliefs, and we believed that the mom should be home with the children raising children. In today's times it's just not possible for most parents, but I've been fortunate and I'm home with my children." Fortunate as she believes herself to be, with just the one income the Guarinos struggle to meet their children's needs in an era of rising costs. Francesca does not know whether they will be able to offer sufficient help to enable their children to achieve economic stability, much less upward mobility. She wants to see them go "at least" to college and possibly further. She worries that the task of securing the future of the next generation has become more difficult in recent times:

> I think everyone worries about the future. I believe [my parents] worried about the future, but I don't think they had the same worries that we do today. It changed. This world is just falling apart. You need more, and just nothing's enough. There's no set amount of money that's going to be enough for someone to live in today's times. I don't know how the kids are going to make it. I just don't know. As parents we just have to try to help them as much as we can with certain things—if we can.

From another economic and social niche, and all the way across the country, in sunny Berkeley, California, Susan Chase expresses similar concerns. Susan is an attorney married to an architect; their household income approaches two hundred thousand dollars, and they have only two children to support. Yet Susan also believes that in her generation the challenge of simple class reproduction has become more difficult: "[Our parents] just kind of took for granted that we would grow up and be able to take care of ourselves, whereas I don't necessarily think that about my kids—that they'll be able to buy a house or support a family."

Other parents throughout the economic spectrum worry that their children might even be downwardly mobile, rather than able simply to maintain, much less surpass, the achievements of their parents. A white, middle-class, and upwardly mobile mother was explicit about what she understood to be changing economic dynamics as she addressed the interviewer, a young woman just out of college: "I think yours is the first generation that is not expected to do as well as your parents. For the rest of us it was like a pyramid scheme: if you just muddled through, you would do better—and I don't mean just [financially]."

To be sure, some parents quite simply assume that economic success will be reliably there for their children—as it had been for them. Indeed, as my research assistants and I talked with professional middle-class respondents, some were almost cavalier as they imagined secure educational and occupational futures for their children. For example, one white, professional middle-class father of one child contrasted his parents' insecurity with his confidence in his ability to secure his child's well-being:

> [My parents] were of a generation that came out of the Depression and World War II, so [they] were mostly focused on are [their children] going to meet someone who's nice, are they going to have opportunities for college, are [they] going to have opportunities for good jobs. And to an extent those are no longer our concerns, because those opportunities are there.

These optimists notwithstanding, most parents expressed concern about their children's futures, and some intuited, even if they didn't fully understand the dynamics of the contemporary period, that economic uncertainty might demand a different, and more flexible, approach to child rearing than had been their parents' approach with them.

Realistic Concerns

By many measures, parents do, indeed, have good grounds to be concerned. Those who came of age in the 1980s could not have been unaware of a major stock market crash in the middle of that decade and then some significant bumps along the way to the first decade of the twenty-first century.[2] The boom time of the 1990s might have left some households awash in disposable income, but well before the recession that began in 2008, there were signs of an impending economic crisis, with periodic slowdowns in the economy. Even if families believe themselves to be unaffected by the rise and fall of the Dow Jones, they might be aware of studies that show increasing levels of inequality between the top income earners in the country and those at the bottom.[3] What has been called the squeezing out of the middle class—or even the disappearance of the middle class—has struck fear into the hearts of professional middle-class and middle-class parents who worry that should their children fail to make it, they will tumble farther down the social class ladder than was the case in the past.

Another set of statistics strikes a special fear in the hearts of the professional middle-class parents. Children born during the post–World War II baby boom (which began in 1946 and extended to 1964) are now themselves parents with children poised to enter college. That second baby boom produced a high school graduating class that was expected to peak in 2009 at about 2.9 million after a fifteen-year climb.[4] As a result, throughout most of the first decade of the twenty-first century the competition for entrance into elite colleges was claimed to be a lot tougher than it used to be. And the media avidly reports all the details about this new competition and stirs up anxieties about status reproduction. Stories appeared regularly with titles such as "Applications to Colleges Are Breaking Records"; "High Anxiety of Getting into College"; "Young, Gifted, and Not Getting into Harvard"; "A Great Year for Ivy League Colleges, but Not So Good for Applicants to Them."[5] They told the sad tales of students with perfect SAT scores, valedictorians of their high school class boasting résumés sparkling with extracurricular activities, who were still denied entrance to the college of their choice. Meanwhile *U.S. News & World Report* continues to tell parents just which colleges their children should choose—and which are lower down on the pecking order. Small wonder that parents and children alike feel under pressure.

Class Matters in Planning for Success

And small wonder that all the interviewed parents were making efforts to ensure that their children would have a competitive chance in these turbulent times, often starting very early in childhood. Before turning to the ways in which the goals and aspirations—and actions—of the professional middle class differed from those of the middle- and working-class parents, I want to stress this point: every single parent with whom my research assistants and I spoke expressed concern about her or his child's educational future, and every single parent expressed the hope that her or his child would go on to some form of education after high school (as more than two-thirds of all high school graduates do today).[6] In these aspirations parents made no distinction between their daughters and their sons: in this day and age, girls are expected along with boys to receive higher education and to strive for a career.

Of course, this is not to deny what decades of substantial research has demonstrated: social class matters in educational experience and educational performance, and this is true not least because wealthy parents have the social, cultural, and economic capital to ensure their children's success.[7] Several patterns are especially significant, albeit not necessarily new. For example, it is not only in contemporary times that privileged parents enroll their children in excellent private and public schools.[8] Testing for learning disabilities is a more recent development; so too is the nurturing of talents through extensive involvement in extracurricular activities. Even if these patterns have continuities with actions taken by privileged parents in the past, they have a heightened urgency today as they are linked to new anxieties about the future. Moreover, as enacted, these patterns become manifestations of a belief in a child's boundless potential and of the necessity for control over the details of a child's daily life to ensure that children do, indeed, reach their potential while beating out the competition. Because these actions make clear that parents hold high expectations for the future (and leave no room for failure), they may well create a pressure cooker out of children's lives.

Testing for Disabilities

Professional middle-class parents spoke knowledgeably about learning disabilities. When their children did not perform at a satisfactory level, they had their children tested to find out whether there might be some psychological or physiological cause. If tests confirmed one of the new class of learning disabilities (e.g., ADD, ADHD), parents requested that schools make special accommodations for their children. For example, Jeff Wright is a white (recent) widower and the father of one fourteen-year-old daughter. Because he is employed as the chief public relations officer for a private school, he has insider knowledge of the field of education. He explained that he had used this knowledge to good effect and that he and his wife had worked with the school staff at his daughter's school to ensure that she would have both a special place to do her homework and extra time for studying: "We were aware that [because of her learning disabilities] Katie worked slowly and can get distracted. We tried to set up time with one of the staff people who is assigned to help the students with study skills. . . . So Katie was in that office and had a cubby set up in that area." If such accommodations were not forthcoming, professional middle-class parents found a school that would serve their interests more fully. As one white mother of three children said of her youngest son, "Stephen is smart as a whip, but because of his disabilities he did badly in [public] school. . . . He now does well in a private school."[9]

Going to Better Schools

Even without disabilities, a parent's understanding of a specific child's personality, or a parent's desire to secure a "better" education, might lead to the conclusion that a private school education would be the best option to help that child maximize achievement.[10] A number of professional middle-class parents spontaneously explained that they had sent their children to private schools for at least some, if not all, of their educational careers: "We've been fortunate that he does go to a private school." And some were relieved that this option created an appropriately achievement-oriented milieu: "Most of her friends are private school kids; they're all top college bound, good students; [they] want to do well."

Parents whose children attended private schools also believed that they had the right to ask for special privileges to secure a competitive advantage for their children. One white mother of two children explained how she had become involved in her older son's educational career and requested that the school increase the pressure on him:

> I actually called the school and asked why they aren't pushing him as hard as I think he could be when you're paying for a private education. . . . I'm wondering why it's so easy to get 99s on your report card all the time. He's bright, but I just felt like I'm paying for private education, he should be challenged more.

Even if they didn't opt for private schools, the professional middle-class parents knew how to get the best out of the schools their children attended.[11] They also generally lived in neighborhoods with higher median incomes, more expensive homes, and a more highly educated population than did middle-class and working-class families. In all likelihood, these factors translate into better schools as well.[12] Indeed, many of the parents said that they had chosen a particular community because they knew it offered superior public schools.[13] As Jane Ferrara said of her Boston suburb, "It's a really great school system, and that's why we moved here."

Extracurricular Activities and Nurturing Talents

Most distinctly, the professional middle-class parents seek out extracurricular activities for their children to nurture the talents that will help them get into good schools down the road. They enroll children in music lessons if they show the slightest ability (and sometimes even if they don't); they sign them up for soccer leagues; they encourage particular interests in areas such as rock climbing and dance. When they describe their children, they enumerate the many activities in which their children are engaged on a weekly—and often daily—basis.[14]

Several parents carefully explained that discovering and nurturing a child's unique talents were significant aspects of a new style of parenting and part of what differentiated them from their own parents. Eve Todd is a white mother living in an essentially rural area in northern Vermont; with a master's degree in counseling in hand, she holds a professional position in a local public school system. Eve suggests that her parents had high goals for their children but that those goals were considerably narrower than what she wants for her two daughters now. Seeing her parents as being without the "tools" to opt for more than the "basics," Eve wants to be more fully supportive of her children's full range of ambitions and interests than her parents were with her, even if, as she herself notes, it might be "silly" to think that her younger, fourteen-year-old daughter will someday be a rock star.

EVE: And I think what we've done so far and what we do now is really important about how she perceives herself.

INTERVIEWER: Do you think your parents were concerned about those things?

EVE: Not at all, no. I don't think they were. I think that they were worried about much more basic things. I think they wanted us to have an education. They wanted us to have food, they wanted us to have a house, they wanted us to have enough stuff, and they wanted to have us be good so that people could see that they were good parents. . . . I think it's because they didn't have the tools to do more than that. And I know it's different. . . . I always make sure to stop and think, "What would it have been nice to have my mother do in that circumstance?" Some silly things like . . . Kara said recently, "Oh, I think I'll be in a band and be a rock star." And do I think it's likely? No. Do I think that [it's right] for me to say, "Well, that's stupid." No. So I say [instead], "Well, you know, if that's what you want to do."

Sarah Johnson is an Asian American with a master's degree in special education; she and her husband and two daughters live in Charlotte, North Carolina. Like Eve, Sarah described the way in which she differed from her parents. Her parents held specific expectations for their children; Sarah holds broad ones. And like Eve, Sarah contrasted her parents' narrow view with a positive appraisal of the ways in which she encourages the development of her daughter's interests, whatever they may be:

> It was my parents' dream that their children all be doctors, [and] not a single one of us is. That's pointless to hope for your children. They have to find that on their own, whatever that is. And I know for my daughter it's, like, painting all day. I know last week she spent all week solid on [this mural], and to her that's very affirming, that we've just let it sit. . . . To her, this is her territory and her space, and she will paint. If you sit still long enough, you will be painted on.

Eve's and Sarah's demurrals about a concern with basic success need to be taken with a grain of salt: both women, like the vast majority of their professional middle-class peers, report that they have oriented their lives to ensure their children's "basic" educational achievements. At the same time, the close attention to a flight of fancy is perceived as being a new form of parenting, as is the nurturance and encouragement of budding talents.

The Need for Flexibility

In turn, that nurturance and encouragement reflect an awareness not just of a diminished space for the professional middle class but of the demands of turbulent times. Contemporary social theorists such as Manuel Castells predict that in the future work will be increasingly transformed to require greater flexibility and will be less stable.[15] Others note that some of the traditional professions (e.g., doctor or lawyer) are less certain routes to prestige and security than they were in the past.[16] Contemporary parents with professional training are well aware of these shifts. As one parent, a college professor, said to a college-age woman who was interviewing him for a study of preschool educational choices among professional middle-class parents,

> Mobility is going to be less predictable. . . . Our ability to plan an educational track to get people to become a certain kind of person with certain kinds of prospects is going to be a lot less predictable as we shift away from the model of you grow up, you learn how to do something, and then you get the job that you're going to do for the rest of your life. For your generation the average is like ten or twelve jobs for your lifetime, or different occupations even. And so I think that the model of education being a unilinear process, or tracking to one thing, is not going to fit anymore with the reality. . . . You're going to have to have multiple skill sets and multiple occupation niches. All that means less predictability.[17]

Instead of planning one "educational track" to get his son ready for a particular career, this man is already planning for flexibility. Like Eve and Sarah, this father said that you never really know which skills will be relevant in the future, and, therefore, the wise parent encourages them all: "There isn't an explicit discussion that we do about this sort of thing. It's this implicit practice of, if a kid shows an interest in something, you follow it. Because who knows, maybe that will be a skill that they'll develop."

In the absence of a clear understanding of what the future might bring, elite parents seek to create adaptable children with multifaceted skills and abilities. They must remain alert for evidence of particular talents even as they discourage settling too early on a narrow route to achievement in a single sphere.

Hard Choices among the Nonelite

Some of the advantages of testing, private schools, neighborhoods with good public schools, extracurricular engagement, and encouragement of distinctive talents are not unique to the children in the more elite families. But less privileged parents indicate that they have to be more cautious about the accompanying financial burdens, and they talk about how they make hard choices among the competing ways of securing success for their children.[18] For example, one white, middle-class woman said that she wondered about the choice she had made to get a job selling real estate so that she and her husband could afford a home in an upscale Los Angeles suburb with a good school system rather than having stayed home to be more available to her child, who would then have attended what she thought was an inferior school. "Is it better to live in the right school district and be working to pay for it, [or] is it better to be home?" she asked.

And from Louisville, Kentucky, Peter Chaplin, a divorced, middle-class father with shared custody of his thirteen-year-old son, worried about a range of such accommodations—from specialized sports programs through summer camps to the possibility of private school—as he considered how to secure the appropriate advantages for his child in competition with the children of what he dubbed "hyperactive" parents, who (he believes) can ensure the best at every turn. Because he lives on an income of less than fifty thousand dollars a year from his landscaping business, it is not surprising that he worries about the financial implications of making the same kinds of choices for his son. He also doubts whether he has sufficient social and cultural capital to recognize which are the necessary—and right—possibilities:

> One of the questions [I have is], what are the activities, peer groups, surroundings that one should place Sam in where he can learn [the skills he needs to be successful]? I agonize over that a lot. I agonize over it in relation to public and private school. . . . We chose not to put him in the most competitive [soccer] programs early, and then we found last year that he sort of got boxed out of getting access. And one just sort of looks at the hyperactive parents that were so driven to get their children in just the right soccer programs and so on, and you sometimes wonder, am I doing Sam a disservice by not putting him into those environments all the time and [by not taking] the time and energy to identify those? . . . We try to make a decision as to whether these things are essential or not essential. . . . I think about that a lot, particularly in relation to putting Sam on a track where he can be successful and get into a good college. . . . We're going to invest eleven hundred dollars next year in soccer, . . . and it's not even the most competitive soccer echelon. . . . Summer camps and those kinds of things—that you really don't know how beneficial they are and which ones are the good ones to do and given our financial situation, consideration of all those is always problematic. We just haven't had the money, the readily available funds, to do that.

In the short run, Peter Chaplin, like parents both more and less privileged than himself, wants to secure educational and extracurricular opportunities for his son. In the long run, he wants his son to be able to compete with the children from the professional middle class and wend his way into a "good" college. His worries about costs, his questions about the necessity for high-powered environments, and his doubts about his own capacity to judge what matters are all echoed in the comments of other middle- and working-class parents who, as they weigh costs against an ongoing economic pinch, are aware that more privileged parents can do more for *their* children than they can. As is discussed in chapter 2, well-educated parents worry about these programs as well, but for them the worry centers on whether they have overscheduled, and placed too much pressure on, their children. Participation, however, often seems an inevitable accompaniment to, and basis for, ensuring that their children receive class privileges. And the capacity to afford such advantages is not the only difference between professional middle-class parents and their less privileged peers as they look toward the future.

Aspirations for the Future

More and More Education

Regardless of the demographic characteristics of the interviewed parents—their social class location, racial/ethnic identification, region of the country, marital status, age of children—they look toward higher education for their own children as a significant basis for securing an advantaged future. This is not an extraordinary group of parents. The National Center for Education Statistics provides testimony of just how widespread these ambitions are: "About 9 in 10 students (91 percent) in grades 6 through 12 had parents who expected them to continue their education beyond high school. Of these, 65 percent had parents who expected them to earn a bachelor's degree or higher, and 26 percent had parents who expected them to complete some postsecondary education."[19]

Indeed, most parents believe that a college education now constitutes a bare minimum requirement to get a "good" job. They also believe that this requirement represents a significant shift from the expectations their parents held for them. As one woman said, "I think that . . . parents had different expectations back then [when I was a child]. Not all kids were expected to go to college; now . . . a four-year degree [may not be] enough." And while some parents reluctantly—or disingenuously—acknowledge that how much education their children ultimately acquire will be their children's choice, most parents hope that that decision will include at least a bachelor's degree.

But there were notable differences among the interviewed parents.[20] Those who themselves had not completed an undergraduate degree (the working-class parents) simply want a college education for their children, and they expressed these aspirations with reference to their own more limited educational accomplishments: "[I want my daughter to go to] college because I did not, and I see the difference." Only a fifth of those who had themselves received a bachelor's degree (the middle-class parents) want "merely" a college education for their children; the rest hinted that they would prefer more than that. These parents also often referred to their own limitations as they embrace more substantial educational aspirations for their children: "Definitely through college . . . Neither [my husband] nor I have our master's or PhD, but if either of them would continue beyond four years of college, that would be great, but . . . as long as they will ever remember, it's been a given:

of course they will go to college." Among the parents who have postgraduate degrees themselves, every single respondent expects something more than a college education, and these parents were both more adamant and more specific about a higher standard than were the parents with less education: "As much as they want, but I would like them at least to go to graduate school."

All parents, then, want their children to do at least as well as they have done; most also want something better for their children. The professional middle-class parents were the most insistent about their children's continuing beyond college. Not surprisingly, they also talked with more knowledge about the college-admissions process and intimated that they won't be satisfied unless their children find their way into not just any but what they define as being *good* colleges, which will ensure their children's competitive position.[21] Indeed, they casually named specific colleges—Berkeley, Middlebury, Harvard, and Yale—as examples of places their children might consider. These casual references, which one assumes are as frequent in daily life as they are when an interviewer is present, represent ongoing pressure on children. And those children might on occasion feel that the pressure has gotten out of control.

Delayed Launching among the Professional Middle Class

Parents from different socioeconomic classes had different visions of what a college education should offer their children. Professional middle-class parents who make efforts to ensure that their children are headed for high-status educational institutions do not expect those institutions to be vocational training grounds.[22] To the contrary: in lieu of job preparation, elite parents talk about the important opportunities colleges might provide for self-discovery and for gaining self-confidence. Rather than viewing college as a launching pad to independent adulthood, parents see it as a time for their children to acquire the necessary cultural and social capital to be able to seize any opportunities for status that might arise.

Susan Chase, the white mother of two who works as an attorney in Berkeley, assumes that her children will "at least" attend a liberal arts college. She also assumes that career planning will wait until her children have explored the full range of their potential and discovered their innermost desires:

> [By the end of college they should] feel intellectually engaged with the world, through whatever path interests them, whether it's literature or music or economics or politics, I don't care what, but [they should find] some way of engaging with the world and have a certain sense of possibilities in dealing with the world. And hopefully [they would find] some kind of sense of direction and something that interests them and draws them that they care about.

Susan's neighbor, Ron Giddings, a city planner whose household income exceeds $125,000 a year, also thinks that the purpose of college is to create self-awareness rather than to provide concrete job training. Eventually, of course, Ron wants his children (both of whom are still very young) to settle down, but he also anticipates that it may take time for each child to find the "right" path to a satisfying life: "I don't have any particular career plans for [my kids]. If they don't have a lot of direction coming out of [college], I don't find that that concerning. I want them to eventually have direction—find what they want to do that makes them happy. My biggest concern is that they're on track for some sort of happiness."

The talk of these highly educated parents reflects the understanding that a college education can provide opportunities for student leadership, team participation, experience working with other people, internships, or simply, as one woman said, the possibility of "making good memories." One professional middle-class mother expressed a common sentiment when she spoke about her willingness to wait a long time before her children settled on their career choices: "I would like them to have enough education to do what they want to do in life, and it's looking now like undergraduate isn't enough. . . . That's where you muck around. . . . In grad school you finally decide what you want to do." This view that college should provide opportunities for self-discovery rests on the assumption that childhood can be lengthened.

Delayed Maturity among Professional Middle-Class Children

Professional middle-class parents are also aware that they are extending their own engagement in their children and that doing so represents a significant break from the practices of the past. Maria Ascoli is a stay-at-home mother of two; her husband has a degree in engineering, which he has parlayed into a position with a major construction firm. Maria is sometimes torn between professional middle-class aspirations (stemming from the milieu in which her husband's position has landed her) and the more middle-class commitments and concerns that emerge from her own education, which ended with a bachelor's degree from a state college. However, with respect to the issue of slow maturity on the part of her children, necessitating an extended period of parental oversight, Maria is firmly in tune with other elite parents. She is dismissive of her own parents, who she now believes failed to apply themselves seriously to the task of raising children; she anticipates carrying her own more intensive approach to parenting into the foreseeable future:

> I don't know if [my parents] gave [parenting] a whole lot of thought actually, to tell the truth. I just think that they were from that generation [where] you had your kids and you raised them, and they went out and did whatever they did and they didn't really—beyond the age of eighteen they weren't really all that worried about you. I think parents [today] are way more involved longer with their kids.

Like Maria, Lisa Thomas, the white mother of two teenage daughters, implicitly anticipates a longer period of parenting than what she herself received: "When we turned twenty-one . . . [our parents felt], finally our jobs are done." And Elizabeth Blake, who is also a member of the professional middle class, thinks it won't be until several years after college—when the older of her two children, her daughter, is twenty-five—that she might anticipate that child's being even partially settled: "Right now I'm thinking about colleges [for my daughter], . . . and you want to say to her, 'Between now and twenty-five your life will click.'"

Parents such as Maria, Lisa, and Elizabeth do not appear to view a prolonged adolescence as a problem. However, the personnel of some colleges and universities today link troublesome behaviors (e.g., binge drinking and reliance on parents for help with academic work) and troublesome signs of distress on the part of students (e.g., rising rates of depression) directly to delayed maturity engendered by intensive parental involvement and to the pressures on youngsters.[23] These concerns were not often mentioned by the interviewed parents. But when they were raised, parents then found reason to hold on tighter, rather than to loosen the reins of control. Susan Chase, the

Berkeley attorney, learned from a friend that she should not become lax even if her children should achieve that much desired admission to elite colleges:

> [I worry], Will [my sixteen-year-old son] get into college? Will he get into a good college? Will he be happy at college? I mean, one thing, you've got this big focus on, you know, getting them into college, and then it's like, "you're done," right? That's 'cause I think if they get into a good college, it's an affirmation of you as a parent. But a friend of mine, her daughter went to a good college, and she came home at Christmas and she weighed like eighty pounds.

Even without the threat of having an anorexic child, professional middle-class parents embrace a conviction that their children will need them for many years to come; they also relish the prospect that they will remain actively engaged in those children's lives.

Letting Go Earlier among the Working Class and Middle Class

Working-class and middle-class parents view a college education quite differently than do their more privileged peers, and they anticipate that their job as parents will be completed earlier. Not surprisingly, given that college represents a more significant financial sacrifice for these less privileged parents, they insist that by the end of a comparatively short educational career a child should be ready to pick a career, find a job, and begin the next stage of life as a fully formed young adult. For them, active parenting has time limits.

Some parents were quite explicit on this point. One white, middle-class mother of three children was adamant: "We prolong [adolescence] too much. . . . By the time [they graduate from college], [they should] be able to support themselves, know what they want to do in life." Another white mother, who also had a BA but no higher degree, was even more determined to be free from responsibilities once her child had reached what she viewed as adulthood: "I hope he's able to get a full-time job and live on his own [after college]. . . . If he can get a job and support himself and be clean and healthy, that's fine because I don't want him living here anymore. I'm done with that."

Sometimes much the same sentiment was expressed less as a push or shove out the door and more as an understanding of what would be acceptable for someone who had graduated from college. For example, Amy Price, a white, working-class mother from Charlotte, North Carolina, would like her three children to attend college and then "to have all the necessary tools to make it in life." Similarly, Virginia Williams, an African American, working-class mother of five from San Antonio, hopes that by the time her children are done with college they will "start trying to pursue their careers [and] become what they want to become."

Although there are some similarities across the social classes in the notion that children might have made career decisions by the time they finish their education, that time is different for the elite than for the nonelite. Professional middle-class parents extend that time to include the years spent in graduate school, while their middle- and working-class peers limit it to the years spent in college. A difference in material resources underwrites this distinction and determines whether parents work within a set of finite limits: most parents who hold down professional jobs can afford to delay their child's launching; most parents with less remunerative employment cannot do so. But the professional middle-class parents also appear to *want* to do so. The pleasures of parenting (as opposed to simply having your kids and raising them) mesh well with a realization that flexibility is significant. As a result, the professional middle-class parents delight in the thought that they will be parents—having dependent children who have not yet made up their minds about what it is they want to do; having children who might need coaching and advice about the best choices—far longer. These elite parents actively encourage their children to remain open to a wide range of possibilities; from both joy and duty, they remain willing to extend the time during which they will be called on for guidance and material support. The less privileged parents also find pleasures in raising children; however, they are readier at an earlier moment to move on to the next stage of their lives.

A Passionate Future for Professional Middle-Class Children

As might be expected from professional middle-class parents' statements about extracurricular activities, the goals of a higher education, and delayed launching, they view the future toward which they are guiding their children quite differently than do less privileged parents. Three examples can illustrate the distinctive goals of the elite parents.

I begin with Carol Clark, a white mother of four children ranging in age from two to fifteen. The older two children are from an earlier marriage and live with Carol and her current husband only half the time. The younger two are full-time residents in the Clark household in Louisville, Kentucky, where Carol works full-time as a high-level program administrator in a hospital and her husband, Carl, is a high school biology teacher. During the interview, Carol talked about how firm she is with respect to her children's homework: "Big rules, get it done, not necessarily right after school but before you're too tired." And when asked about how much education she wants for her daughters, she answered without hesitation, "In a perfect world they would all get a minimum of a college degree, preferably a master's on top of that." She then backed off and added, pro forma, "But it really depends on what they want to do." When asked what she hopes her children will have accomplished by the time they finish their long educational trajectories, she hedged. Carol feigned casualness about substantial achievement even as she acknowledged an intense desire to see her children be successful. She outlined a future that has those children changing careers multiple times in order to find what fits them best. She wants them to do well; she also wants them to find not just happiness but outright passion:

> I guess we don't expect them to be CEOs of a company. I don't expect them to kill themselves to go to Yale. If they were prone to that, to have that natural ambition, I would encourage it. I want them to be the best of whatever they're going to be, and if they change that five times in their twenties into their fifties, so be it. I want them to be happy. I want them to be passionate about what they do. I have, of course, very specific ideas on what I want them to be and see them being. I want them to tap into their natural abilities, their natural talents, and then take that somewhere wonderful.

Like Carol, Jeff Wright, the recently widowed father of one daughter, spoke about the intensity with which he monitors his child's homework: "I used to be a tyrant, I used to be really, really concerned. Katie would probably say I still am a tyrant." But in spite of his obvious concern about his daughter's academic performance, when he compared his ambitions for his daughter with the ambitions he felt his parents had for him, he focused less on educational accomplishments and more on goals that extend the meaning of happiness.

Jeff wants his child to go beyond mere happiness to become a more perfect being who approaches the world with zest and self-awareness:

> I think [my parents] valued educational accomplishment, and I think they valued jobs and those opportunities, and I think that's how their measurement of success was. I think we both say we want our kids to be happy and content and self-fulfilled, but I think . . . how we measure that is different. I think [for me] it's less on making a huge amount of money. . . . My parents were poor working-class people. They looked at college as an opportunity to be much more successful financially. . . . For me, I think it would be great if Katie were to find a position where she would be financially secure, but I realize that's not going to bring her security—it's having a sense of self-worth and self-respect and self-confidence. So I would love it if she were to get married and have a family and have a successful career, but first and foremost what I would want is for her to achieve all that with a sense of self-satisfaction.

Jeff believes that what he wants for his daughter is substantially different from what his parents wanted for him. Security remains a concern, but he wants security to come from inside, from an awareness of her own capabilities and interests, rather than from external achievements alone.

Finally, on this set of issues, consider Beth O'Brien, a white mother of four. Beth is a PhD psychologist married to a lawyer who works as a vice president of a major camping-equipment business. Beth is proud of her success. Indeed, she defines herself and her husband as "overachievers" who rose from considerably less privileged backgrounds to have professional degrees, prestigious jobs, and proud ownership of a glorious home in a wealthy Boston suburb and a vacation house on the very elite Martha's Vineyard.[24] Beth was cavalier and perhaps even disingenuous about her children's future. Of course, she wants success for them: it is no accident that she lives in a town with excellent schools. And she described her oldest three children (the youngest is considerably younger than these) in ways that show that she has interests in their day-to-day achievements as unique individuals:

> Let me start with Mark: he is very, very outgoing, charming, and intelligent. . . . He's also athletic. . . . Melissa is a very goal-oriented, athletic

> child. She decided she wanted to go to private school . . . to pursue her dream in hockey. . . . I'm very proud of her because she has worked very, very hard the past couple of years to make this boys' team, and she's [the only girl] on this elite boys team. . . . And what I love about Heather is that she's so well rounded—she loves drama, she love sports, she loves school.

Beth almost sounded as if she was filling out college applications for her children as she boasted of how accomplished they are. When asked about the future, she acknowledged that she wants her children to achieve at a very high level. But she also insisted that she does not want "achievement" to be the only focus of their lives:

> I guess because [my husband, Rick,] and I have both been overachievers in a lot of ways . . . we know that that's not where happiness really resides. It's good to have achievements, but you need to have balance. . . . Rick is a superstar. . . . He feels like, "Oh my god, I need more fun." And we turn around at forty-five saying we missed out, and I have that orientation too. I got my doctorate, I run marathons. We're trying to have our children be not so focused on achievement. Our parents didn't go to college, so it was important that we achieved, so they were giving us their dreams. And our dream for our kids is that they achieve, *but they achieve in the context of being able to have a really happy, fun life.* (Emphasis added)

When Beth talked about her ongoing concerns as a parent, her attention shifted to learning how to have fun. When asked about what she wants her children to have accomplished by the time they complete their formal education, she reiterated this point. She's not "worried about them being a success" because she believes she knows how to ensure that; she's less certain, however, whether she knows how to ensure "fun":

> I worry about my kids not having enough fun in their childhood. I worry about them being so achievement-oriented and goal-oriented that they don't take time to reap the pleasures, smell the roses. I worry that they have too much homework. I'd like to see them have a hell of a lot less. That's what I worry about. That's what I try to monitor. I'm not worried about them being a success. I'm worried about them having fun.

Passion, a sense of satisfaction, a capacity for having fun—these are significant elements of the goals that professional middle-class parents hold out for their children. And in their minds these goals differ dramatically from the "basic things" they believe their parents held out as goals for them. They are also quite different from the goals that middle- and working-class parents hold out for *their* children. Let me be clear: I am not saying that the less privileged parents do not care about whether their children find careers that give them satisfaction or that they be happy in their lives. I am saying that these parents are considerably less likely than their more privileged peers to state this satisfaction and happiness as goals that *supersede* economic independence, self-sufficiency, and the acquisition of useful skills.[25]

From the perspective of a child, the latter set of ambitions might seem like sufficient pressure. Understanding that parents also want them to be having fun and to be not merely happy but passionate about what they are doing—these might feel like significant new burdens and responsibilities. They might also be perceived as more controlling desires because they leave no room for superficial interest but require evidence of deep engagement. And they add to the pressure of performance the pressure of effortlessness, so that the achievements themselves appear to be fun.

Counterculture Dreams Meet Contemporary Realities

If we can anticipate some of the effects that parenting out of control might have when it takes the form of pressure under a microscope, we still want to explore the roots of these new controlling designs. Where have they come from, and why have they become so central? I have argued that an interest in "flexibility" derives from current concerns about economic uncertainty, the declining fortunes of the middle class, and a desire to ensure that children have unique abilities that will smooth the way into elite colleges.

I now suggest that in addition to practical concerns about economic and educational success, the interest in this new complex set of goals of passion, satisfaction, and fun might have a source in more underlying approaches to life framed in the generational history of the professional middle-class parents. This latter interpretation does not replace the first one but, rather, builds on it. With a median age of forty-eight, many of these trend-setting adults were in formative years during the era known as "the sixties" (which extended well into the literal 1970s).[26] Even if they didn't participate directly in the protest activities of the time, they were surrounded by a counterculture that proclaimed nonmaterialist values and extolled a commitment to social justice. The counterculture also urged people to "do your own thing" and to "question authority." The legacies of that time are echoed in the urging of these parents to their children to go beyond "mere" success, to follow their passions into a life worth living. The feminist movement, which overlapped with and continued after the antiwar movement, was also clearly a shaping force: all the professional middle-class women made investments in their own educations, and many leveraged their degrees to significant professional careers. This personal history probably helps to explain why neither the mothers nor their husbands make distinctions between the goals they hold out for their sons and those they hold out for their daughters.

Eve Todd, the mother of the budding rock star, explicitly linked her perception that she was trying to accomplish something different from what her parents had with her, not just to new "tools" for parenting, but to a new sense of what was possible. In turn, she located the source of this new sense of possibilities in the radical shifts during the historical era of her adolescence:

> I think . . . awareness, knowledge, education, what's out in the world is so different than 1950, and I think that what happened through the 1960s gave people a wider range of how to be, rather than "this is what you do, and then you stay home, and then you take care of your parents." And the world got bigger, and then with the technology and everything it just keeps expanding. So I think that the model [of adulthood] isn't the same, whereas it was very much the same for my parents as it was for their parents before them. I just think that the awareness of how we are as people and what we want is more readily available for people to find out about if they want to—almost to an extreme about kids and everything—but even though there was some stuff [in the generation before], it was very limited.

Eve locates "a wider range of how to be" in the ideas of the sixties. At the same time, like others, she must see that many of the social transformations promised during that time period have not been secured. And like her peers, she knows well that the vision of gender equity promised by the feminist movement has a long way yet to become a reality. Parents such as Eve hold tight to their dreams even as they experience disappointment with the pattern of their own lives.

Of course, these lives are not entirely disappointing. Eve enjoys her job as a guidance counselor. Beth takes pride in, even as she downplays, both her own and her husband's successes. But these women are aware of the costs of these achievements. And these costs are considerable. Not only are more of these women part of dual-earner couples than was true for their own parents, but as the sociologists Jerry Jacobs and Kathleen Gerson report in *The Time Divide: Work, Family, and Gender Inequality*, the substantial "growth in working time has been concentrated among couples with the most education."[27] However, this same group of adults has not necessarily reaped the economic rewards of this hard work. Since the 1970s, income inequality has increased; the truly rich have gotten considerably richer, and, relatively speaking, other groups have lost ground. Indeed, disillusionment with hard work alone might be especially the case among women who have found themselves staring up at glass ceilings and who have found that their efforts were not sufficiently rewarded.

Finding a Path

Concerns about the future are reflected in the somewhat contradictory language with which the professional middle-class parents discussed the aspirations they hold out for their children. They spoke about their kids "finding a path that interests them." Theoretically, the parents suggest, this path can go in a number of different directions. Eve Todd's daughter might decide, for example, to explore her love for music and her dream of becoming a rock star, and Sarah Johnson's daughter might become a painter. But no professional middle-class parent implied that she or he would joyfully accept a child's abandonment of higher education even while speaking about the delight of seeing a child's interest in rock music or painting. Moreover, professional middle-class parents imply that they will know when their children abandon an *acceptable* path. That is, professional middle-class parents accept twists and turns and a range of different directions. They do not, however, accept deviations from the broad outline of the life plan they have imagined for their children. College is imperative; postgraduate education is strongly, and routinely, encouraged. And if parents focus on the enjoyment of the journey, on the pleasures of "mucking around" in college, or on exploring one's passions, they make it clear that not all types of enjoyment, mucking around, or exploration are equally acceptable. Hence, they talked with concern about their children's not staying on track—likening it not just to wandering off but to something far more dire—even when the indications of wandering were quite mild. As one white, professional middle-class mother of two children said, "The long view is that you want your kid to be happy. You worry about whether they're going to be happy, whether something terrible is going to befall them, and day to day you worry that they stay on track, that they don't go over the cliff, where all of a sudden they say, 'I'm not doing my homework. I'm not going to soccer.'" For this mother, the "terrible" was the danger that her children would fail to excel in the schoolhouse and on the athletic field.

Less privileged parents, by way of comparison, spoke less about the journey and more about the achievements and accomplishments that are the signposts of successful progress (as many professional middle-class parents imply *their* parents did). They want their children to finish high school, then graduate from college, and perhaps go farther. By then they want their children to have achieved self-sufficiency through the commitment to, and engagement in, a career. Individual development, excitement, and adventure may be part of the picture, but the end product—and not the journey itself—is what is important. Moreover, the goals set out by the middle-class and working-class parents are considerably clearer than those set out by the professional middle-class parents who have as an ambition for their children not just economic success but also the existential goals of passion and self-confidence.

Professional middle-class parents introduce new variables into the child-rearing project. First, they lengthen the period during which they might be concerned about the direction their children take. Professional middle-class parents anticipate a long period of having dependent children, and they are reluctant to "launch" their children once they enter college (or even once they graduate from college); instead they are prepared to stand by, ready with advice, encouragement, and consolation.[28] The engaged, professional middle-class parent views a child in her or his late teens or early "adult" years as unformed and, quite possibly, as lacking an internal compass pointing in a clear direction.

By way of contrast, most of their less privileged peers see that their job as parents will be completed when their children have graduated from college, if not before then. At that point a child should have "realistic goals" and the "necessary tools" to support oneself and to live on one's own. To be sure, like all parents, those in the middle and working class want decent—even excellent—jobs for their children. Like all parents, they want their children to be happy. But they also want their young adult children to be financially self-sufficient and not to have to struggle making ends meet (as many of them did and many of them still are doing). Knowing that they will not be able to continue to support children forever, they hope and anticipate that college will bring about the necessary transformation to prepare their children for independent adult life. Less privileged parents raise their children with more constraining limits on their own time and money. Children of the same age, then, are viewed quite differently depending on the class position of their families. Professional middle-class adolescents have barely taken a first step on the road to maturity; their less privileged peers are much closer to the finish line.

In addition to lengthening the age of dependence for their children, the more privileged parents position their children to explore their own potential; they simultaneously have higher and more amorphous expectations for those children. All parents want their children to be decent human beings and to be happy in their life choices. The professional middle-class parents also want their children to be passionate, confident, and prepared to take advantage of opportunities that might shift and change with the times. The task of creating such children might feel like a particularly unknown and unknowable one. That is, if the professional middle-class parents know from the activities of *their* parents what it takes to produce successful children en route to being a doctor or a corporate executive, and if they do intervene in their children's daily and educational activities to ensure that success, they may not know what they need to do to ensure these complex, existential goals of self-confidence, passion, and flexibility. The close attention they pay to their children, as is discussed further in subsequent chapters, may reflect precisely this uncertainty: as their children veer—or are perceived as veering—too far in one direction or another off the route to self-fulfillment and self confidence, the parents might actively respond with what they believe to be appropriate midcourse corrections.

Moreover, these privileged parents may well be sending some mixed messages emerging out of their own ambivalence about the sacrifices they have made to ensure their own economic and professional success. That is, we need not take them at face value—that they don't care about economic success—but accept these protestations as the expression of some yearning (for themselves as much as for their children) and of a hope for something more fulfilling in a very uncertain world. As a result, control might be confusing—both for those at the helm and for those subject to a constantly changing course.

2 LOOKING BACK

Are the Good Times Gone?

As Sarah Johnson and I sat in her sunny North Carolina kitchen on an unseasonably warm April day, Sarah jokingly warned me that if I continued to occupy my seat, her daughter might include me in the mural she was painting. All joking aside, Sarah, an Asian American, professional middle-class mother of two, is quite proud of the contrast between her encouragement of her daughter's artistic talents and what she believes to have been her parents' narrow interest in seeing their children become doctors. Yet, at the same time as she celebrates her own attitude, Sarah regrets changes between her parents' generation and her own. Most notably she mourns the disappearance of a community that she believes supported individual families and the simultaneous emergence of a new form of busyness that she believes makes it almost impossible to reach beyond the nuclear family. Even though she is married, she thinks she faces the task of raising her children from a position of greater isolation than did her parents. She described for me what factors she thinks have been responsible for the change between the present and the past:

> There was an extended family [before], and now you don't have that extended family. So when you have two parents working outside the home, you don't have any support. And in order to raise a child effectively, that old proverb about a community raising a child, it's so true. . . . It could be anything—a neighborhood coffee klatch, the local Democratic or Republican Party, the bridge group—but you've got to have these connections in your community. You've got to have a support network of friends, both the wife and the husband, and I think that's harder now, because we have these really extravagant lifestyles that require two people to work outside the home.

Sarah illustrates a set of attitudes toward the past found among many professional middle-class parents. On the one hand, Sarah holds dear a nostalgic memory of a time when parenting was perceived to have been easier than it is today because parents were more supported, only one adult worked outside the home, and life was lived at a slower pace. On the other hand, she retains a critical sense that even in those earlier times parents muffed the challenge of raising teens. In response to these perceived changes, Sarah both feels a greater sense of individual responsibility for raising her children than she believes her parents did and wants to approach the task differently.

Sarah's conviction about the shift in responsibility and the increasing challenge of child rearing is shared by many parents less privileged than herself. They too believe that the task of raising adolescents today has become far more difficult than it was in the past, and they too attribute that change, at least in part, to greater degrees of busyness and isolation experienced by individual families. The less privileged parents, however, diverge from their more privileged peers on attitudes toward the generation before them: they have less uniform views about whether *their* parents made mistakes.[1] When asked about their parenting style, some of these less privileged parents explicitly stated that they modeled themselves on the parenting of those who raised them. For example, one working-class, Hispanic father said, in reference to the manner in which he was raising his fifteen-year-old son, "We're continuing what our parents have instilled in us, and we're trying to do the same thing with him." As a group, these parents speak less of forging a new path and more of adapting older ways to more difficult contemporary challenges. Theirs is often a voice of continuity that contrasts with the discontinuity in child-rearing styles that the professional middle-class parents proclaim.

Of course, we have no reason to believe that recollections of the past—whether affirmative or critical—accurately reflect lived experiences. Nor should we assume that even the most nostalgic recollections represent a desire to return to the conditions of an earlier time. Even so, respondents' recollections are revealing about how the past enters into rationales for child-rearing strategies.

And, of course, we can't answer a question about whether parenting was actually easier in the past. Even so, what is clear, as we listen to parents—across the social spectrum—is that they *perceive* it to be more difficult today. What is clear as well is that the parents' responses to that perception vary with socioeconomic standing. Elite parents respond with hovering and the intensive practice of parenting out of control. The less elite respond with an intensification of more traditional disciplinary practices of imposing limits in order to be aware of where their children are and what they are doing, whether or not those were the techniques used by their own parents.

Goodbye to the Golden Age

Let's begin with the shared perception of the increased difficulty of parenting today. Paula Brown, a white, professional middle-class mother to two teenagers, lives in the suburb of a southern city, where she holds an administrative position at the local university and her husband is employed as an executive in an insurance company. As she reminisced about her childhood, Paula recalled the comfort that was part and parcel of having an extended family. Even though she currently lives in a place where the resident population is almost exclusively white and the crime rate is well below the national average, Paula draws on the emergence of a new variety of family forms (including more single parents and more stepparents) as evidence that communities have changed since she was a young girl. Paula is convinced that in the absence of commonality, each individual now has to do the hard work of finding and sustaining her or his own approach to raising children:

> I was raised where brothers, sisters, aunts, uncles, cousins—you know, there was this intergenerational [family], this small community. So as you have more families that—maybe it is single parenting, there's stepparents. And I just think that brings in all different styles and values, and they get more challenging. It's not that they're any better or worse, but I just think that is a challenge. And I just think that's a huge [difference].

When pressed to discuss the difficulties she believes her own parents faced during the years they were raising her and her siblings, Paula is stumped. Because her parents had broad support and were able to meet basic needs, she "can't imagine" what problems they experienced. In her memory, a large family provided both a challenge—and a solution—to the task of child rearing:

> I would have no idea [what was difficult for them] because financially it was okay. I don't think we were extremely well off, but living on a farm, I do think they provided what we needed. And anybody went to college that

wanted to without even having to take out loans. And I can't imagine what they thought was challenging—maybe too many [children]. But I think that was even a solution more than a challenge—you know, that older person can take care of that younger person.

Martha Mackenzie is a white college professor and the married mother of two young children. Like Paula, she lives in a community that is predominantly white and has an extremely low crime rate.[2] Even so, Martha also is convinced that parents like herself can no longer rely on others in the community to share her values or to fill in for her. In spite of a strong network of colleagues and friends, and even though her home is located in a very cohesive neighborhood in a small town, she feels very alone in the task of raising her children:

> The neighborhood I grew up in all the parents had shared values. . . . That meant as a child you got the same messages reinforced. But it takes more effort [to sustain your values when] there are very different messages. I think the world is more dangerous. As we live more with strangers, you don't have the people to look after the kids. My parents knew more people. One [issue] is knowing and being around strangers; another is parents being afraid to talk to children they don't know. And I think it makes it more dangerous.

From suburban Pennsylvania, Wanda Jackson is a working-class, married mother of four. This thirty-three-year-old African American woman also bemoaned what she sees as increased dangers and the loss of a supportive community. She said that although her parents faced issues of "violence," it wasn't as "bad as it is now," and she listed the reasons: "You have younger parents being parents, you don't have people being older being parents, you have kids raising themselves, [and] you have a lot of teenage parents. . . . When I was growing up, [if she saw] misbehavior, my mom would always yell; now they just turn their heads. It's not the same any more; nobody wants to be held accountable."

Gail Albert was born and raised in Philadelphia; she still lives there today. At thirty-seven, this highly educated, single, African American mother of three struggles to support her children on disability payments of less than twenty-five thousand dollars a year. But rather than focusing on her economic difficulties, Gail responded quite similarly to Paula, Martha, and Wanda when asked what she thinks are the biggest problems facing parents today. Like her peers living in suburbs, small towns, and rural areas, she focused on the rising number of single parents and on the loss of a community in which other adults took care of one's children and kept an eye out for the neighborhood as a whole.[3]

> There are so many—there's just so many [problems]. The *greatest* problem [*she hesitates*] is the downfall of marriage, the separation of family, that you don't have families growing up in the same house any more. And then the next thing would be the downfall of community, you know. . . . [The father of my sons] lives in West Philly, and he lives in the house that he grew up in. And all the neighbors are the neighbors that grew him up, and now they're growing my sons up. This block [where I live]—not a soul. The communities are just so different. It's amazing how different they are. And I'm glad that they're having that experience [of spending time in West Philly]. . . . You know, personally, I try to keep an ear out. . . . I keep an ear out. That's what communities are all about, looking out for the kids when they are coming home from school. I mean, I just really believe that that is something that helps people raise kids up.

While Gail insists that she is able to provide her children and her neighborhood with some of the experiences she remembers from the past, her bottom line is that child rearing has become more difficult.

Going It Alone

Parents such as Sarah, Paula, Martha, Wanda, and Gail represent a range of locations and life circumstances. Despite these differences, they share similar views of the past. In describing their childhoods, not only do parents across the board speak about a sense that families in the past were more deeply embedded in extended families and caring communities, but they also speak about families having been more deeply embedded in supportive institutions. Peter Chaplin, the middle-class father from Louisville who was so concerned about whether to enroll his son in a competitive soccer program, compared his confusion about what he thinks is best for his child with the social reinforcement he believes his parents had for their decisions: "I don't think my parents worried about my education, my spiritual and emotional health. I think they sort of trusted the institutions to provide most of that guidance."

In a similar vein, other parents referred to specific forms of institutional and cultural support that they believe were more forthcoming in the past. Erica Harper is a white, forty-five-year-old, married mother of three who lives in a small Vermont city renowned both for its excellent schools and for being home to a major high-tech industry. Erica, who has parlayed her master's degree in psychology into a professional position in one of the local schools, mentioned both that her parents worried less about their children's futures than she does and that they had more community support for enforcing values. She feels she alone carries the burden of ensuring her children's development in a far broader range of areas: "I think that when I was growing up and my parents were parenting, they were less concerned about how we would make it in the world and contribute to the world; their whole focus was [education]. . . . [Now we] need to develop values and a moral base through the guidance of your parents. It doesn't just happen in communities [as it used to]."

One Hispanic, working-class mother of three children (all under the age of thirteen) who is employed as an office manager in Simi Valley, California, argued that during her childhood teachers could count on a more united front from parents: "I don't know, these days [children] get away with a lot more than they used to. Nowadays parents really believe what the kids say [and that] the teachers are always wrong. Kids nowadays are really spoiled. Back then the parents always stood behind the disciplinarian." From suburban Connecticut, Marian English, a white woman with a master's degree in business administration who is now a stay-at-home mother of three teenagers, was insistent that mass popular culture has undermined adult authority. She bemoaned the fact that at present parents are often derided in television programs. She recalled (although this memory may or may not be accurate) that in the television of her childhood, parents were upheld as a source of moral authority: "The shows were more . . . family oriented. . . . They didn't work against the parents. They were much more positive and much more working together. . . . The parents were seen more as helping to [solve problems]."

These comments about supportive institutions and a supportive culture in the past are also interesting for what is *not* mentioned. Many social commentators are quick to demonstrate that the government only minimally supports families in the United States (especially in comparison with other industrialized countries in Western Europe), and some are quick to claim that the state has actually retreated in recent years.[4] However, only one interviewed parent linked her sense of being very much alone in the job of raising children to the government's failure to offer more support. Annemarie Fernandez, a Hispanic, working-class, married mother of three children ranging in age from two to fifteen, lives in a small town in Texas and works as an administrative assistant in a hospital. She made reference to the absence of social services: "[There are] a lot of single-parent households out there. [There is a] lack of support, which can lead to stressed-out mothers, which can lead to bad parenting and things like that. [The biggest problem is a] lack of support from society, for day care and things like that." With Annemarie as the exception, all other parents assume entirely private responsibility for raising their children, even as they wax nostalgic about a time when they imagine kin, neighbors, friends, and the culture at large shared the burdens.[5]

This heightened sense of individual responsibility finds resonance in more general cultural trends. As commentators such as the sociologists Anthony Giddens and Ulrich Beck note, even if the world around us today were no more hazardous than it had been in the past, in a "risk society" individuals would perceive themselves to have more control over the fate of those dependent on them and would respond with greater vigilance and heightened surveillance.[6] In addition, the commonplace belief that the world *has* become more dangerous for children and teens lends fuel to this significant shift in perception.

A Nostalgic View of Safety and Security

Some of the parents—and these were often those who had grown up in comfortable surroundings—described their childhoods in the language of a magic idyll replete with steadfast stability, safety, and security. These parents did not exclusively characterize the *contemporary* problems they face in terms of the array of external dangers—predators, child abusers, kidnappers—that are now part of what has been labeled a "culture of fear."[7] Even so, as they recalled their youth, they added the bliss of childhood freedom to the nostalgic image of extended families and institutional support. Consider Marcia Caldwell, a white, middle-class mother of one eighteen-year-old daughter. She is a resident of rural Pennsylvania and works as an admissions associate in a private high school. When recalling her own youth, Marcia spoke about days spent outside parental control and astonished herself as she thought about swimming in the river without any adult supervision:

> I mean my parents would say to me, "Okay go outside, don't come back till lunch, go outside," and we'd get together with all our friends, and we'd be outside all day, baseball, football. . . . [We'd] go down to the river, jump in, swim—seriously!—come back for lunch. . . . My mother worked, but she was right across the street from our house, [and] we would check in with her. We would be out until dark, and there was no worry—my god!—[that] a sexual predator is going to come by and abduct you. We didn't lock our doors.

Jeff Wright, a white educator who is raising his child on his own now that his wife has died, spoke about being home alone at age ten and feeling entirely safe: "When I was ten I was home alone often during the summer and could wander around the neighborhood and could wander around the back yard, and my parents didn't know specifically where I was. But my parents thought I was safe, and I felt safe." And Dave Townsend, a white lawyer and now the father of three teenagers, recalled as well that when he was a kid, he "ran around the neighborhood wherever [he] wanted to go, whenever [he] wanted to go."

To be sure, these adults recognized that the past held challenges and even dangers. Some of the older respondents had parents who had grown up during the Depression and who could recall serious hardships in their own childhoods. Some respondents remembered that the Cold War was an ongoing issue of concern during their own childhoods. But as Sarah Johnson, the Asian American mother of the mural painter, discussed those times, she used the words of a child—"big scary guy"—to diminish the fear she might have felt. She also insisted that life is a lot more fraught with anxiety today than it was in the past, even though it was quite conceivable then that the world could be utterly destroyed:

> I have the same concerns [my parents did], but there is a difference in setting. I think kind of the post-9/11 aspect of the project. I suppose these days there are additional worries because there are worries [about] taking your shoes off, the Anthrax, and, you know, the terrorism and the war. They had wars that they had to worry about too. . . . We had the bomb shelters because of the whole bomb threat from Russia. I grew up with all that. There was a big scary guy out there that could come blow us to smithereens. I think again the technology has impacted—again these are useful things, they're helpful things—but because they're there and people are using them it puts it more into your face that there's a lot of scary things.

Like Sarah, many parents believe that because dangers outside the home have become closer and more immediate, children can no longer be left free to roam as they did in the past.[8] In some cases it is hard to tell whether the anxiety parents feel is about local dangers (the neighbor who might be a sexual predator) or about something more amorphous (the fears of terrorism striking anywhere and at any time). Most often, the vague sense that the world is more threatening has no concrete location even as it is expressed as a desire to maintain a greater awareness of what their children are doing. This sense could be heard when parents talked about taking care not to allow their children to be exposed to what they perceived as being dangers (both real and imaginary). Parents spoke about walking with or driving their children to school (often until the children could drive themselves), about supervising their children's play, and about checking out their children's friends.[9] These are routine, taken-for-granted activities that adults view as part of the responsibility of good parenting, especially in a moment when the perception of risk has been heightened and when parents assume that they alone have responsibility for helping their children evade those risks.[10] Many of these routine activities were described similarly by working-class, middle-class, and professional middle-class parents: contemporary forms of parenting with limits and the more recent shift to parenting out of control have some common roots.

Taken as a whole, then, whether or not the characterizations of the past are accurate, today's parents believe that the good times are gone. Most notably they feel that they lack support for the difficult project of raising their children. And this sense of being on one's own, of having individual rather than communal responsibility for the care of children, extends across social groupings and is found among parents in a range of types of communities, from cities to suburbs to small towns. But if the heightened vigilance that results from these perceptions of how the present differs from the past is part and parcel of parenting within all social classes, the form, range, and extent of that vigilance is different within the professional middle class than it is among the working class and middle class.

Family Changes as Moms Go to Work

The new, compelling sense that the world is more dangerous and that parents are more alone combines with other attitudes that have their roots in a major social change. At a median age of forty-four, most of the interviewed parents have lived through the enormous increase of women's labor force participation in the last half of the last century. Those born in the early sixties, for example, would have experienced a world where the labor force participation rates of married women with children under age eighteen rose from less than 40 percent to over 70 percent (in the 1990s), before dropping down to somewhat below 70 percent in the early twenty-first century.[11] This increase in the labor force participation of mothers is more marked among the elite than it is among those who are less privileged (where women's work outside the home has longer been the norm), even as it is found among all social classes; this increase is also more marked among white women than it is among women of color, even as it is found among all racial/ethnic groups. Parents view this rise in the labor force involvement of women with children as yet another reason why parenting has become so much more difficult.[12]

Many respondents waxed sentimental about having had a stay-at-home mother. Kevin Hansen, a fifty-three-year-old, white doctor from Missouri and the now-widowed father of three children (seventeen-year-old twin girls and a twenty-three-year-old son), remembered that in his parents' generation "the mom was usually home during the day," and he insisted that this meant that a mother was "always available, and there was more contact between the mom and the kids." Indeed, so strong is the "memory" of a world where mothers stayed home and solved all daily problems that it is recalled even by respondents for whom this was not the case.[13] For example, a white, forty-nine-year-old, middle-class mother of two daughters remembered that in her childhood "parents were around more" and then, as an aside, added, "although actually my mother did work." Erica Harper, the school psychologist from a small Vermont city, similarly noted simultaneously that her mother "stayed home" and that although her mother worked outside the home, she was certain to leave work in time to be home with the children after school. And a thirty-three-year-old, single, white, middle-class mother of one eleven-year-old daughter, when asked what problems her parents faced, responded simply that her "mom was a stay-at-home mom." She spoke as if that fact were sufficient evidence that her parents did *not* have significant problems, even though, as is true of her today, she acknowledged that they had to "struggle . . . sometimes for money."

Shared Concerns

Some aspects of the consequences of the shift in women's labor force participation are viewed similarly by parents with professional degrees and by those with less education. All parents worry about how they can create sufficient family time when there is so little time to be had, hope that they can "be there" at critical moments in their children's lives, and make attempts to monitor their children's activities when they cannot be home.[14]

These shared concerns might provide at least some of the impetus for the surprising finding that even though in 2000 it was more likely to be the case that both parents in a household were employed than in the generation before, contemporary parents are spending *more* time with their children. This increased devotion to one's children is true of both mothers and fathers and among parents who are employed as well as among those who are not. It represents more hours spent in both primary child care ("activities where parents report directly engaging in caregiving or other activities thought to promote children's well-being and where the main focus is the child") and secondary child care ("child care activities mentioned when respondents were asked, 'Were you doing anything else?'").[15]

Different Concerns

Professional middle-class parents extend these concerns into an elusive and, perhaps, unattainable goal. These are the parents who emphasize the efforts that go not just into creating family time but into creating "quality time" for each and every one of their children in the midst of their busy lives. And this enhanced goal might stand behind the finding that education is directly correlated to how much time one reports spending with one's children: college-educated mothers and college-educated fathers spend more time than those with less education.[16] This distinctive goal might also stand behind the even more relevant finding that even though women with education beyond college are more likely to be working—and to be working longer hours—than those with less education, the more educated mothers *still* spend more time with their children than do those with less education.[17] Statistical comparison between those I would term "middle class" (i.e., those with a college degree) and those in the "professional middle class" (i.e., those with some graduate education) reveals differences in time spent with children in all four categories of care (basic child care, educational child care, recreational child care, and travel child care) among nonworking mothers and, in two of these categories (basic child care and recreational child care), among working mothers. The differences between professional middle-class mothers and mothers with less education than a college degree are more striking: the ratio of time spent with children among nonworking mothers with graduate training in comparison with those with less than a high school degree is 1.55 to 1; among working mothers the same ratio increases to 1.72 to 1. Among working fathers the ratio comparing fathers with graduate training to fathers with less than a high school education is even higher than it is for women, at 2.16 to 1.[18]

Nostalgia, Guilt, and the Search for Quality Time

Given the increasing devotion to one's children—at least as measured by time put into their care—we should not be surprised to find that many of the professional middle-class parents are dismissive of the efforts their own parents put into being close to their own children. Ironically, however, they see in their mothers having been home the *potential* for intimacy. Even though they often describe their mothers as having engaged in a parenting style that could be characterized as benign neglect—as when they were allowed to swim in the river or wander through the neighborhood—nostalgia for what might have been becomes the guide for what should be. Parenting out of control has roots in and gains urgency from this nostalgia.

For example, consider how Kevin Hansen, the doctor who assumes total maternal availability in the past, described the dynamics of his own household in the years before his wife died. He worries that the busyness of parents *and* children means less time spent together:

> I think the big problem is [that in] a lot of families, parents and kids have so many things going on that it's hard to spend significant amounts of time with each other. And I think it's probably important that we do that. I don't think we do as much as we should. . . . I think that's one problem. . . . When [my wife] was working and I was working, there were other people taking care of the kids, and we weren't around as much.

Similarly, Erica Harper, a white mother of three teens—who noted that even though her mother had worked outside the home, she was able to leave work in time to be home when the children got out of school—mentioned that when both parents work full-time outside the home, or confront stresses of their own, they are less able to be fully present for their children. She, too, contrasted what she sees today with what she recalls of the past:

> I think the biggest problem that faces parents today are probably many parents' inability to be available physically and emotionally for their children, whether it's due to working or stress in life. . . . [For my parents it was] very, very, very different, and I think our culture and our society is very, very different. And that's another bigger piece, [and I think] that [it is] very difficult . . . to parent within our society right now. . . . My parents were able to be physically available; [their children] did not have to be put in child care or have a babysitter. . . . We had access to the family unit; it was a strong family unit; my mom stayed home.

If parenting out of control relies on nostalgia for what might have been, it also appears to rely on the perception—mistaken as it may be—among the elite that for women, work outside the home represents a choice. Working-class and middle-class women know they have to work; in some cases, especially among women of color, work outside the home is part of a long tradition rather than a new option for "liberated" women. But many of the professional middle-class women—and their spouses—still assume that women's employment means putting oneself before family concerns; in these cases, nostalgia combines with a sense of guilt for not providing children with a stay-at-home mother.

Thus, it is no surprise that parents like Erica struggle to find ways to remain "physically and emotionally" available even as they continue to work outside the home, and Erica specifically holds out as an ideal not just "family time" but rather distinctive "parenting to each one of [her three] children." When asked to describe her approach to parenting, Paula Brown, the administrator at a southern university and mother of two teenage children, gave a response that suggests the supreme importance she also places on creating opportunities for what she thinks of as "quality time":

> There's a book called *Language of Love,* and it talks about how different people have different languages that they try expressing love in and how they want people to express it to them. And mine is "quality time." So I know that's how I try to demonstrate and communicate. So I think that's kind of a baseline for everything about parenting. If we can just be together, somehow there's going to be some really good things coming from that.

Different attitudes between those who are less well educated and those with professional training have concrete manifestations as different amounts of time spent with children. As noted, highly educated parents who are employed outside the home and who devote long hours to their careers *also* devote long hours to their children. As the sociologist Mary Blair-Loy says, these may indeed be "competing devotions."[19] Hence, those adults who don't opt out of the labor force altogether might well find themselves squeezed for time: how could they possibly find the hours (or energy) to spend on any interests they might have separate from their careers or their children? In this context, perhaps, we should not be surprised that children become the stated site of friendship and fun, as well as of work and worry. Parenting out of control is time consuming; there may not be enough hours left over in the day for "quality" time in any other aspect of one's life. And indeed, contemporary studies of how Americans spend their time indicate that they are less involved in organizational activities and visiting in other people's homes than were generations before them. These studies also indicate that those who are married spend less time with their spouses than did adults in the generation before.[20] Children, then, constitute a more prominent source of one's social interaction on a daily basis today than was the case in the past. When children take up more of one's ongoing thoughts and activities, parenting might well be conceived of as having gotten "out of control."

Because I Said So?

Parenting across the social classes is perceived as being more difficult today than it was in the past for yet another reason: many parents believe that children's deference has given way to what they view as a culture of disrespect. Patsy Doria, a white, working-class mother of three, noted that because her parents could count on an authoritarian approach, raising children went more easily for them:[21] "I don't think we [children] were as hard to parent [as are children today]." Similarly, Anna Benton, a PhD-educated economist in Berkeley, California, said that raising children went more smoothly when parents controlled the reins of authority: "I don't think [my parents] found anything particularly difficult. I mean, they were the authority figures, and we [children] weren't all that much trouble."

The response to this new difficulty, however, is entirely different among the Patsy Dorias of the world than it is among the Anna Bentons. Like Patsy, Charlene Black, a white, working-class mother of two teenaged children, shook her head with dismay when she said, "When we were growing up I would have thought twice of yelling at my parents, [but my] kids don't think twice about yelling at me." Clearly, Charlene is troubled by what she understands to be children's new attitudes toward their parents. In contrast, many professional middle-class parents, while they also view their parents as having been seen as sources of authority in the past, generally reject both authoritativeness and authoritarianism for themselves. Indeed, Anna's social class peer Marian English had a different response from Charlene's to this shift. Although she acknowledged that her parents had an easier time with authority, because in her family it was "my way or the highway," Marian added this proviso: "They've also produced a society of people that aren't necessarily the best balanced people either."

Class is key to parenting; class is also key to the interpretation of, and the lessons taken from, the past. As we have seen, professional middle-class parents understand their mission to be entirely different from that of their parents. Secure in the assumption that their children will have at least some essential modicum of achievement, these parents want to guide their children to be flexible, self-confident, and passionately engaged with the world. And they view their children as having boundless potential. Thus, we should not be surprised to find that they speak with disdain about the focused ambitions their parents held. Nor, perhaps, should we be surprised to find that they also believe that their parents approached children—and especially adolescents—in the wrong way. But among the middle- and working-class parents, a group whose children's achievements cannot be so easily secured and who focus on a narrower set of goals, we find more appreciation of their own parents' emphasis on similarly constricted achievements. And they more often believe that the approach taken by their parents was appropriate, even if it sometimes failed.

Do as I Say, Not as I Did

The working-class and middle-class parents do not speak with a common voice about their own adolescent experiences. And they do not all have the same perceptions of how engaged and aware their own parents were. This is a varied group of adults; the experiences that they bring to bear on perceptions of appropriate relations between parents and children are also diverse. However, variation gives way to more uniformity as they discuss the issue of how important it is in a child's adolescence that parents be especially alert to possible dangers and especially vigilant about watching over their children.

Some working-class and middle-class parents express appreciation for the efforts of their parents to rear their children in a religious faith, with good morals, and with personal ambition. In retrospect, they appreciate the limits their parents set. Those who recall that they actively tested those limits often admire their parents for the efforts they made to raise them in spite of that testing. One working-class, Hispanic mother of three children was explicit on this point: "I was a difficult kid. . . . [My mother] would agree definitely that her satisfying moments are seeing me turn out the way I am now. . . . She taught me how to mother even though I didn't allow her to mother. She taught me how to be a good mom." She is thus satisfied that she can rely on the model her mother put forth even if, in her youth, she thought it was too strict and too constraining.

Other working-class and middle-class adults believe their parents were insufficiently attentive to the behavior of their teenage children. A white, middle-class woman regrets the mistakes she now believes her parents' lack of attention *allowed* her to make: "My parents left us to our own devices much more than I am [leaving my child to her own devices] probably. And I made some really stupid mistakes because of it. I did some really stupid stuff."

Still others noted that their parents were not only inattentive but that they severely underestimated the trouble that children could get into as teens. Lisa Thomas, a white, middle-class mother of two teenage children, recalled that although her parents were *concerned* about their children's activities, they were not sufficiently *aware* of what they were actually doing:

> We grew up in the city, and there were a lot of dangers in the city. And I think they worried about being in the city. . . . We were always up to no good all the time. We were doing all kinds of stuff as teenagers. When I think about it, it's really quite wild. And I think whatever they worried about, we were doing way worse stuff.

Another white, middle-class mother of two thinks that because her parents were "naive," she "saw a lot and did a lot and got away with things that [her own] kids [don't] get away with." And yet another white, middle-class mother of two teenagers also used the word "naive" to describe her parents, and she suggested that this naiveté might have been deliberate:

> Our parents were naive in terms of what was out there. . . . My parents were brought up in the fifties and forties, and they didn't know what was out there in my high school days. So in some ways that was probably better. My mom always says, "If you stick your head in the sand for four years and then pull it out, they will be fine." That's what her attitude was.

Some of these adults now live with the consequences of youthful indiscretions: a few of the interviewed women dropped out of school before receiving a high school diploma, and a few of them had children when they were very young.[22] When they talked about the concerns their parents had about their not finishing their education or their getting pregnant, they were talking about concerns to which they often believe, in retrospect, both they and their parents should have been even more attentive. For example, consider Amy Price, a white, working-class mother of three who is now separated from the father of her children. Although Amy does not say that she regrets having children at a relatively young age (her daughter was born when she had just turned twenty), she acknowledges that she does not want the same thing for her own daughter: "I got married at nineteen; my sister got married at eighteen. That was just how it was back then. Everybody we knew back then got married as teenagers. I hope [my daughter] will wait."

Whether they felt the consequences of youthful indiscretions or got off scot free, the acute awareness of how much they concealed from their parents—or, even more often, how little their parents knew or even wanted to know about what they were doing—serves as a lesson for the present. Working-class and middle-class parents draw from their own memories of having been young once too to conclude that they should be attentive and firm, diligent and authoritative. These perceptions are conjoined with other beliefs about the significance of setting limits for their children: they know that the world outside is dangerous and that they can no longer rely on others in their communities to keep an eye or ear out for their adolescent children; those who are employed outside the home know that the hours after school can become an occasion for all sorts of unwelcome behavior. They want to know what their children are doing at all times, they want to keep them safe, and they want to protect them from making mistakes that will have significant consequences down the road.

Recalling the Sixties

The more elite parents who were interviewed are often more separated from their parents in two ways. More of these adults have moved away from the communities in which they were raised and thus cannot draw on their parents for daily assistance in rearing their children, even if in all likelihood they have drawn on them for important financial support.[23] And more of these adults shudder when they think about the parenting regime under which they were raised, even as they acknowledge their own misadventures.

For some parents—especially the older professional middle-class parents—risky behavior was part and parcel of the rebellious spirit of the sixties.[24] Perhaps because the working-class and middle-class parents are, on average, a few years younger than the professional middle-class parents, none of them mentioned that era. But looking back, the older professional middle-class adults not only mentioned the sixties, but they also suggested that their involvement in the activities of that time period (or its legacies) knocked the socks off their parents, who were totally unprepared for the ways in which the world appeared to be turning upside down.[25] Susan Chase, the white attorney from Berkeley, said that her parents were in such "denial" and had such anger that they really didn't know how to handle their children's rebellion:

> My parents had their kids in the fifties, which means that we were all in high school in the seventies. And I think the whole counterculture, drug culture hit them like a ton of bricks. And they were really not ready for it. And they were in denial, and they were angry, and they were just so horrified that they didn't know what to do. Drug culture and the sexual permissiveness culture—my parents are Catholic, and you know, they were really surprised by the whole thing and didn't handle it particularly well.

One white professional middle-class woman, who is now in her fifties and is the mother of two children in their twenties and one teenager, suggested that her parents felt that their children were rejecting their successes as well as their values:

> I think that they were shocked by the sixties. . . . That probably shocked them tremendously, and I think they felt like, "how have we failed?" That just was devastating that we would throw away all the things that they had valued so highly. Some of that was just us being obnoxious. . . . There was a reason to be different, but I think it was heartbreaking for them.

The professional middle-class parents also take different lessons from what they see as being the gap between themselves and their own parents (whether caused by their involvement in counterculture activities or not) than do their less privileged peers. Professional middle-class parents do not just view their parents as having been ignorant (or shocked), but they view them as having been insufficient in their engagement and understanding. And these professional middle-class parents believe that these insufficiencies meant that their parents were unable to reap the immense pleasures and joys that parenting can hold. Blithely they dismiss their parents as not having had anything like the satisfactions they believe are available if one approaches parenting through connection and communication rather than hierarchical authority.

Susan Chase, who noted that she participated in the counterculture of the sixties, suggested that her own parents "missed out" because, she astonishingly suggested, they did not love their children as much as she loves hers. And whereas she saw herself as being quite distant from her parents, she takes pride in her belief that her own son (at age sixteen) does not regard her as being so very different from himself:

> Their generation and my parents in particular, because of who they were, I think they really missed out on a lot of stuff. *We really love our kids, way more than they did,* and again that may be a certain kind of involvement or parents trying to be their kid's best friend, whatever happens now, but I certainly thought of my parents as very alien and very "other" and people—my parents and their friends and my teachers—as kind of the enemy. I just don't think that kids [now] feel that way so much about adults. And yes, I know that Miles doesn't want to hang around with me all the time, and there are certain things that he doesn't want me to know, but I think at the same time I don't think that he sees me as alien or that he needs to kind of protect himself from me. (Emphasis added)

Like Susan, Anna Benton, who acknowledged that parenting is easier if parents remain in charge, wants to change the model from the one in which she was raised. She too insisted that she and her parents found entirely different satisfactions in child rearing. Her parents valued good behavior; she values intimacy. Moreover, Anna explicitly admitted that she is reacting to the absence of intimacy with her own parents by creating intimacy with her children:

> [My parents] were just not that involved. [They were satisfied] that they had kids that were good kids, and . . . I'm not sure [how to account for the change]. I think for me I was kind of more marginal and not really treated as that much of an equal, so I guess I'm retrying with my kids. That's not to say that retrying results in better kids—they're still brats—*but I'm sure it's more for my own need to be intimate and close because I wasn't that close with my parents.* (Emphasis added)

Contemporary parenting styles emerge from an effort to make up for, and even to reverse, the lessons of the past. The less well educated parents choose parenting with limits because they want to create relationships based on authority to ensure that their children follow the rules they set forth and because they do not accept the decline in deference. Moreover, because they perceive the world today as being more dangerous and themselves as having more responsibility to help their children avoid risks, they also want to be more aware of what their children are doing. The more highly educated parents also want greater vigilance, but they want to diminish the gap between parents and children by filling it with love, trust, and respect; parenting out of control rests on the assumption that a relationship based on authority alone is unsafe, unhealthy, and unsatisfying for all concerned.

Across the social spectrum, most parents feel that they are parenting on their own desert island, and they think that this isolation represents a significant change from the past. They hark back to a time when communities were supportive and when moms stayed at home. They view contemporary parenting as fraught with difficulty. Within this acute sense of isolation, each household believes itself to be an island of sanity and believes, as well, that it needs to be attentive to the threat outside its doors. Stranger danger extends among these parents to the man and woman living in the next house or apartment.[26] In response, parents feel the need to be more vigilant than their parents were with them.

All the interviewed parents also believe that there had been a sharp generational divide in the past. This generational divide meant not only that lines of authority were clear—children did what they were told and didn't question their parents—but for some of the interviewees, across the social classes, that generational divide meant that their own parents didn't know what their children were doing. But not all interviewees look back at this divide with the same sentiments. Some working-class and middle-class adults believe that the generational divide served them well and that they were thus guided to appropriate behavior; some believe that they were mistaken to have ignored the authority of their parents and to have indulged in risky behavior. And there are some who believe that the generational divide resulted in insufficient attention from their parents. No matter what their current assessments of the past, the middle-class and working-class parents now want to find better ways of ensuring that their children are attentive to lurking dangers, and they welcome any assistance they can get in monitoring their children more closely; this is especially true for those who view dangers as being very present and who view the world, in general, as having become less benign. They are unlikely to be particularly trusting about the specific answers their children give when questioned about their actions; they don't want to make the mistakes they attribute to their parents of naiveté or blind ignorance. They opt for tighter limits and greater surveillance.

The professional middle-class parents are in a trickier spot. Many professional middle-class parents now believe that the sixties impulses were excessive, but many of them link their own contemporary values—their rejection of pure materialism; their interest in the existential goals of passion, self-confidence, remaining flexible, and having "fun"—to the very same set of ideals that they embodied during those years of rebellion. In addition, their break with their parents was not just about authority; it was a fundamental rift about politics, values, lifestyle, and ideology. The scars of that rift might be more difficult to heal than those resting on "benign neglect" or on not having listened to sound advice.

Not only did many of the professional middle-class parents actively reject their own parents as being out of step with the changing times, but they also, as a group, are very mobile.[27] They might bemoan the fact that they have no family around now to help ease the daily burdens (and share the pleasures) of raising children, but they have actively sought careers and followed opportunities that have taken them far away from the communities in which they were raised. As a result of their own actions, they *are* more adrift in the world as they look for guidance on how to parent and as they look for bonds of connection.[28]

And ironically, given professional middle-class parents' own stance with respect to *their* parents, many of them seek these bonds in their relationships with their own children. These trends clearly have multiple sources: maternal guilt because of employment and the compensatory effort to create "quality time"; changing gender patterns and the greater involvement in parenting by fathers; and "nostalgia for a mythical family past."[29] I would add as well that among the professional middle-class parents especially, the new mode of parenting is at least in part driven by a drive for connection across generations, especially when upward ties have been frayed (by the events of the sixties) and when horizontal ties (e.g., with friends, in voluntary associations) are diminished among those whose employment combined with child rearing keeps them too busy to find much time for either sociability or civic engagement.[30]

3 CLEAR AND PRESENT DANGERS

On November 3, 2008, as voters in the United States held their breath for the outcome of the Obama-McCain election, an entirely unrelated story made headlines in the evening news. A study conducted by staff of the RAND Corporation and published in *Pediatrics* reported that a rise in teenage pregnancy could be attributed to the amount of sex teens viewed on television.[1] Parents were urged both to restrict the frequency and type of programs their children watched alone and, as much as possible, to watch television with their children. Had they been listening to Katie Couric's review of these findings on the television in my living room, the parents with whom I had spoken the year before would have nudged me with perverse satisfaction: "See, we were right: there is reason to be concerned."

Indeed, many of the interviewed parents, across the socioeconomic spectrum, expressed an intense anxiety about highly sexualized media images and ready access to pornography on the Internet. Among many parents, such concerns are conjoined almost reflexively with worries about images of violence, as if the parents perceived no difference in the impact of the two. Many parents also make little distinction between the violent images of fiction and those that depict current events. Nor do they distinguish between sensationalism about a contemporary figure such as Paris Hilton and equally "sensational" stories about global warming. All of this is combined in the minds of parents who worry that the world is too much with their children and that their children are being compelled to grow up too fast. These concerns are most prominent among the professional middle-class parents, even if, in one form or another, they extend throughout the range of the interviewed parents (as was the case with the sense of isolation). In this sentiment, the respondents in this study are in line with the vast majority of American parents, two-thirds of whom are "*very* concerned about the amount of inappropriate media content children in this country are exposed to."[2]

Childhood under Threat

Starting with the influential and admittedly highly contested research of historians such as Philippe Ariès, scholars have come to the conclusion that if childhood itself is not an invention of the relatively recent past, the particular stages of demarcation—infant, toddler, preschooler, preteen, adolescent—are themselves arbitrary and subject to ongoing change.[3] Several quite contemporary examples illustrate this point well. Currently the U.S. Census Bureau reports on the child care arrangements for children under the age of fifteen, thereby implicitly viewing that as an appropriate age for children to begin to be left on their own.[4] But as recently as in the 1950s (during which at least some of those interviewed were children themselves), the Census Bureau reported only on the child care arrangements of those under twelve.[5] Presumably anyone older than that could safely be left untended. Or consider this: teen parenting, which is identified as being a significant problem today, was the norm just a few generations ago.[6] Indeed, the notion of adolescence itself is but a hundred years old.[7] And recently psychologists have begun to extend the teen years out to a new stage—emerging adulthood—in recognition that even in their early twenties, "children" are not yet either autonomous in action or independent of parental guidance and support.[8]

Even outside these broad delineations we can find substantial regional and class differences. I vividly recall interviewing a farmer in Vermont, who told me that she had no trouble allowing her seven-year-old son to drive a tractor even though he had not yet learned the difference between left and right; she easily resolved this difficulty by giving him directions in terms of objects in the landscape (turn toward the barn; turn away from the apple tree). Read any contemporary account or memoir of growing up poor—as in Mary Childer's *Welfare Brat*—and we find very young children, who would be pampered in many environments, holding down jobs and caring for still younger siblings.[9]

In short, the periods of demarcation for different stages of childhood, and the degree of autonomy (or, when looked at from the flip side, the degree of coddling) deemed suitable for those stages, continue to shift and change. And, as is part of the broader argument of this book, distinctive and class-based parenting practices, along with the long projected period of immaturity for one's children discussed in chapter 1, are part of what is producing these changes today.

Controlling Stages

In spite of these realities, when professional middle-class parents talk, they sometimes imply that the stages of childhood are written in stone. Even more often they evince concern that the world is imposing itself too quickly on their children and that their children are being exposed to specific images at "way too young an age" or "at an earlier age than they should be." In response, the parents indicate that they want very much to monitor, and remain in control of, the timing of these influences. Hence, they say, their four-year-old should not have a Barbie doll because it has "too much curvature" (although an American Girl doll is "appropriate" for that age), their first-grader should not have "too much homework," their children of eight or ten should not have to "specialize in sports," their thirteen-year-old should not be watching *America's Next Top Model,* and their fifteen-year-old should not "know more about sex than his parents did when they were eighteen." A professional middle-class mother of two teenagers believes that she knows what little girls innately "want." Although she suggests that young girls have entirely "innocent" desires, she also believes that they are easily seduced into materialistic and sexualized pleasures: "I think that the kids grow up so fast. Little girls just want to be little girls, but what catches their eye is the movement, the fancy car commercials, very sexy girls. . . . It breaks my heart."

Here, too, nostalgia rears its head: quite frequently the specific prescriptions stem from what the parents themselves imagine were the activities and pleasures of their own childhoods. Hence, parents say their child of six shouldn't be "experimenting with makeup" but rather should be "reading books, playing outside with other children," or enjoying the simple delight of a board game.

The vision of a discrete stage of childhood thus rests on a notion of childhood innocence, a notion that contains within it implications of vulnerability, ignorance, and moral purity. It is also a notion that is intimately tied to social class and race/ethnicity, as it quietly ignores centuries of childhood slavery, children's labor, and children's exposure to, and involvement in, the everyday activities of the adult world.[10] And it ignores both children's own active engagement in sexual activities at an early age and the multiple ways in which our society eroticizes and makes a fetish of young children.[11] Parents simply declare that their children are, or should be, "innocent" (at least until they deem otherwise).[12]

The Impact of Media and Technology

Across the board—and especially among the professional middle class—parents view television, movies, and, more recently, the Internet as the primary, uncontrollable sources of threat to innocence. These parents thus sound much like the cultural critic Neil Postman in tying the "disappearance of childhood" to the introduction of these forms of mass media.[13]

Consider the answer that Dave Townsend gave when asked what he believes to be his biggest problem raising children today. A white attorney from Louisville, Kentucky, and the father of three teenage daughters, Dave focused on what he perceives to be images of sex in the media; he also tacked on the issue of violence:[14]

> I keep saying, oh, because I have girls, I think one of the big issues these days is the increasing emphasis on sex at earlier and earlier ages. These girls get exposed to things that I never got exposed to when I was a kid—probably would have been happier as a kid if I had—but they see things on TV that I couldn't have imagined or in the movies. You know, the PG-13 movies are like the R's or maybe the X's, assuming we had R's and X's when I was a kid—I don't think we did. They just get exposed to a lot more in the way of sexual references than I ever did. I don't know. I guess that there are a lot more violence kind of things that they get exposed to.

Note that Dave believes that he is particularly concerned about this issue because he has girls, suggesting that the moral purity of his daughters is of special significance to him. Indeed, Dave indicates that as a boy, he might have been "happier" if he had seen some of those sexy scenes on television. Even so, he wants to protect his daughters from them.

The recently widowed father of a fourteen-year-old girl, Jeff Wright, an educator in Connecticut, expressed similar concerns. On the one hand, like Dave, Jeff recognizes that there might be individuals for whom the shift to greater openness is a positive influence; on the other hand, he has a conservative, moral anxiety about whether this openness has gone too far. And this anxiety is directed at the purity and innocence of his daughter. Like Dave as well, Jeff referred to what he believes are the changing standards of regulations concerning the content of PG-13- and R-rated movies. Jeff also worries about his capacity to maintain his own values—and to pass them on to his daughter—in the face of a culture that he believes undermines what he holds dear:

> So she's part of a society now that's benefitting from the openness, that's benefitting from the more open dialogue that goes on. But at the same time, because of the coarsening of our lifestyle, the movies that she can see today that are PG-13 would have been R when I was growing up, in terms of violence, in terms of sexual content, and attitude. . . . There had to be a loosening of a lot of the restrictions and judgments that were made in our society, and I'm glad that has happened to a degree, and there's more that needs to be done. But at the same time, there's been a loosening of our expectations about how people behave and treat one another and even treat themselves. You know, a Paris Hilton is a perfect example: the woman became a celebrity because of a sex tape and is now some sort of cultural icon that we have her on the cover of the *New York Times,* for no other reason than for the fact that she is a celebrity and not even—you can't even call her a role model. How do parents create a value system that can stand up against that kind of coarseness and obnoxiousness and cheapening, especially in terms of self-worth and self-respect?

Mothers share these concerns. Marcia Caldwell, who lives in rural Pennsylvania, also spoke about Paris Hilton as an example of the kind of influence from which she would have liked to protect her daughter. While she acknowledges that her children might need to learn about other ongoing events—the war in Iraq, the space shuttle, ethnic violence in Africa—she wants to shield her child from the immediacy of threats and from "sensationalism":

> I think kids are living in a much more immediate kind of world, where there are scary things out there and we have more things we have to be vigilant about and help our kids understand. We don't understand them—the Internet, the constant media pressure. Please, Paris Hilton! Is this really the most important news in the world? The space shuttle is taking off, and people are being killed in Iraq every day, and what's happening in Africa. I just think it's harder to raise kids today because of all that. I just think there's too much sensationalism.

While parents are especially concerned with images of sex and violence, which they believe hasten "maturity," they are also concerned, more generally, that there is no escape for children into what the parents deem to be a more "normal" innocence. One mother talked about 9/11 and how the events of that day were shown on television even though, she believes, it was not appropriate for young children to see those images. In her rendition, networks showed those images specifically to children: "It shows stuff the kids don't even need to know at certain ages, like when 9/11 happened. . . . Just that they immediately showed it to the kids at way too young an age, and I thought it was inappropriate."[15] And another woman, Susan Chase, the white mother of two who works as an attorney in northern California, more generally worries about the cultural influences impinging on adolescents: "I do think that our culture really is pretty toxic, and I think that's really too bad, that they live in a culture—that part of our job as parents now, along with all of the other jobs, is to protect our children from their own culture. And so that's certainly a problem."

As these comments suggest, parents are particularly anxious because they believe they are losing control over the environments in which their children are raised; they believe that environments constructed by the media and technology are beyond their sphere of influence. And they view this as a significant social change: as one middle-class mother of three children said, her parents "had more control" because they "didn't have twenty-four-hour TV."

For some parents, not fully understanding the technology that so seduces their children—the instant messaging, the texting—constitutes an additional source of anxiety. Parents believe that they cannot control what they haven't mastered themselves. Tom Audet is a college professor in northern California. Even though the demands of his job require him to remain technologically adept, he believes his two teenage children are far more sophisticated than he is with respect to recent developments. When asked what he sees as the greatest problem, he spoke about the technology gap:

> We finally raised a generation of children that are ahead of us in terms of the technology that's available. . . . Children [are] the cutting edge, and the parents [are] scrambling to catch up and maybe never catch up. That's certainly true for me. There's younger parents who also mastered this technology, but kids are way ahead of their parents most of the time.

The concern with the media and technology, most extreme among the elite parents, generated different responses among parents in different social classes. As is discussed in chapter 6, middle-class and working-class parents are more interested in devices that constrain children: these parents want to ensure that their offspring do not wander onto websites of which they do not approve, and they are interested in putting blocks on programs and channels on their television. However, these concerns do not lead the more privileged parents to impose similar limits. Nor do these concerns lead these parents to ban televisions from their homes or prohibit their children from having cell phones and laptop computers. To the contrary: the elite parents actively purchase these material goods (even though they worry about a materialistic culture). But they also act in ways to assess their children's readiness for different influences and to ensure that their values are inculcated along with the values that they believe the media is projecting. Hence, parents talk about the necessity for discussion with their children and for remaining attentive to the influences that come from outside the home. Through this discussion and attentiveness they aim to intervene in, to mediate, and occasionally to counteract the effects of influences that would make their children "mature too fast." Ironically, these discussions themselves often assume considerable intellectual maturity on the part of children. Indeed, professional middle-class parents express great pride in how sophisticated these discussions turn out to be.

Pressures to Preserve Class Privilege

Equally ironic, a set of concerns found exclusively among the professional middle-class parents has to do with precisely what it is that parents are doing to ensure their children's success. In their efforts to secure status reproduction by preparing their children to seize advantage, parents move to neighborhoods with demanding public schools, pressure their children to do homework, nurture budding talents, and load knapsacks down with the latest consumer goods. They also then worry that have caused childhood to disappear. More specifically, they fear their children are "overscheduled," are under too much pressure, and are overindulged. "Concerted cultivation," as described by Annette Lareau in *Unequal Childhoods: Class, Race, and Family Life,* may, indeed, be the desired strategy of parents; it is not one, however, that the parents themselves see as being without problems for their children.[16] Let's take these concerns one by one.

Material Overindulgence

Professional middle-class parents find it necessary to indulge their children's material desires as a means of supporting their children's enthusiasms and interests, as well as a way of enabling them to keep up with and, as the sociologist Allison Pugh suggests, join in conversation with their peers.[18] At the same time, they worry about the effects of doing so.

As they discussed the issue of material indulgence, the parents once again made reference to a kind of innocence—a less materialistic childhood—that they imagine could be available to their children, even as they find themselves making moves that undermine that vision.[19] Some parents acknowledge that material indulgence is part of a competitive practice, an effort to ensure that their children do not get left behind. On these grounds, they believe it is impossible to stop what they are doing. Anna Benton, for example, is critical of the interest in consumer goods that she finds prevalent among her children and her children's friends. Yet, she acknowledges, the lifestyle she and her husband have chosen—which includes living in Berkeley, California, in a lovely house overlooking the Bay—is a source of those values:

> [The greatest problem is] just the world of glamour and glitz. You know, when I was a kid the TV shows weren't these reality shows, and there wasn't just instant feedback and get online and talk to seven of your friends about "what's the best shoes to wear," that kind of thing, the materialism. Also, [my children are] being raised more affluent than I was.

Kevin Hansen, a white physician from University City, Missouri, and the widowed father of three children, even more explicitly noted that the affluence of his lifestyle creates its own separate pressures to indulge children. At the same time, however, he believes that indulgence undermines other values he holds dear:

> I think for my kids in some ways our relative affluence is an issue because it makes things easy for them when they want to get money. I say no sometimes, but a lot of times I say yes to things. That probably makes it a little bit too easy [for them] to get hold of things—clothes, electronic things,

> you know, going out to eat lunch on the weekend. They don't have to think about those things, the cost of those things as I did when I was growing up, and I think . . . for [my own peers] that's a problem.

And Susan Chase, having already noted her concerns about a "toxic culture," added a thought about how a materialist culture might inhibit the development of alternative ways of viewing the world: "I think, well, for middle-class parents, I think there's a pretty material overabundance, which I actually think is kind of stifling and, you know, very materialistic."

Psychological Overindulgence

Some of the elite parents focused less on material overindulgence than what we might think of as psychological overindulgence. Professional middle-class parents spoke about being responsive to their children, about respecting individual needs, and creating "quality time" to make up for their daily absence at work. But these actions create concerns as well. In Berkeley, Jenna Hall, a white mother of two teenagers, worries that she is producing children who are overly concerned with the "here and now"; she also worries about the ways in which schools and parents alike celebrate children's accomplishments whether or not they are worthy of that celebration. Ultimately Jenna believes that a world that has been made gentle and supportive might inadequately prepare children for the tough challenges of daily life.

> [The biggest problem today is] raising bratty, unhelpful kids. I feel like my kids are so self-centered. Kids . . . feel so entitled and impatient. . . . Like with cell phones, everything is so "now," and everything kids do is somehow rewarded. I get really frustrated. Like the school, they celebrate every little thing, like it's the last day of school, we need to have a party. And I'm thinking, "The last day of school, it's the last day of school. It's great by itself. Why do we have to have a party?" End of soccer season everyone gets a medal even though they were on the losing team. So it's almost, like, not real. All the celebration for these things that aren't that great that I worry that later on these kids are going to be really disappointed. Things aren't going to be fun enough. No one gives me a medal for making dinner every

> day. You know, these are kind of mundane things that are being, I believe, overly celebrated. And I know my kids get—if they ever heard a busy signal, they might just fall apart. Like I don't think you hear busy signals anymore, just like that instant [*snaps her fingers*] "I need to have everything done immediately." I guess that is my biggest fear for these guys.

Also from Berkeley, Susan Chase acknowledges that the amount of encouragement she provides her children might sometimes have the negative effect of making life appear too easy. She is glad that she has a husband who is better than she is at creating opportunities for her children to face challenges:

> I think I am quite typical of my generation. I think I'm very kid centered. I think I'm probably quite indulgent by traditional standards. I adore my kids. . . . I don't have any doubts about how much I love them, and I think that is the first thing that has to be there. But I have to keep on reminding myself that it is necessary but not sufficient, that there may be things like [actions that encourage] character building. And . . . I'm glad that I have a husband who is better about those things than I am. I try to give them a lot of encouragement, but I also am aware of the fact that there really is a downside to these kids who are encouraged and given positive reinforcement at every possible step, and they have never really been challenged or had to deal with adversity. And the strange paradox of you don't want your kids to experience any adversity, but at the same time it is kind of adversity that makes us the people we are and gives us character. So I try to balance those out.

The indulgent stance that emerges from parents' being "kid centered" gives rise to anxieties about not imposing sufficient limits and about not letting their children experience "real" life.

Taken as a whole, then, the professional middle-class parents who were interviewed are concerned about raising the overscheduled child, the highly pressured child, and the overindulged child. But they see no way out since these actions are taken in response to their own and other parents' anxieties about the reproduction of class privilege. Susan Chase was explicit about this:

> A friend of mine, I was talking with about this, she called it "hoarding advantage." You know, parents are so anxious about the world that we think every little thing that will give them some sort of a little edge in this competitive and uncertain world, we're gonna cling to, and we're not going to say, "whatever, he'll work it out." It's like we can't afford to let our kids screw around like we did when most of us were kids, and I think that's really too bad.[20]

Professional middle-class parents thus find themselves in a bind that is, at least in part, of their own making. They may not want their children to grow up too fast, but they cannot and will not simply allow their children to be children: they treat them like adults when they tell them to make choices and when they discuss media images with them. They are also busy "hoarding advantages" and ensuring that their children can compete successfully in the academic realm, in the sports arena, and eventually as adults themselves. These practices draw these parents into ever closer vigilance—not just with respect to issues of physical safety but also with respect to assessing whether their children are ready for the next movie rating, an Advanced Placement class, or a higher level of competitive sports and with respect to keeping a close eye on the effects of the lifestyles they have adopted.

Dangers in the World

Rather than worrying only about the media images and their own actions as parents, less privileged parents often view the real world directly outside their homes as being a very concrete threat to the safety and well-being of their children. The concerns they identify are thus neither imaginary nor distant. They are more central to the lives of the working-class (and some middle-class) parents because, in contrast to the vast majority of professional middle-class parents, these less privileged adults cannot always move their children to environments with adequate police protection and lower crime rates.[21] Indeed, the differences in crime rates in communities in which different social classes reside are striking.[22]

Wanda Jackson, a married, African American, working-class mother of four children who has moved her family from Philadelphia to a nearby suburb, is one of the lucky ones. She explained that even though her children prefer the city ("it's a little closer to get to the corner store"), she is relieved to be away from the "violence, the drugs, the shootings, and the killings" that had characterized their previous neighborhood and into a place that is "a little bit safer." Another parent, this one a white, working-class, married mother of two, also recently moved from an unsafe neighborhood to a safer one in Charlotte, North Carolina:

> The neighborhood we're living in now is better; the one we were living in before, you could hear gunshots. . . . I let them do very little when they came home. I am very protective of my kids. I almost got picked up as a child myself by a stranger, so I was very aware of stranger danger. . . . I'm pretty comfortable [now] with the neighbors we have. I don't hear gunfire every month or so, you know. I'm more comfortable in this neighborhood.

Other parents have not been so lucky. As Virginia Williams, the African American mother of five children, said of living in San Antonio, the dangers threatening her children seem very immediate:

> I worry the most because the violence is so bad now. You're leaving your kids to just have a good time, and then someone may steal your kids, or they're killed just because of jealousy or envy or whatever. Someone [might] just kill them, and that's scary. When we were coming up, it was more or less kids just had fights. You didn't have weapons and all that stuff. Now, you don't know. Your kids have to watch their backs. They can't just be children and enjoy their life. They have to look over their shoulder. I tell them that you can't be a total—I don't want to say—free spirit, that not everybody's going to have the same reaction towards you because maybe someone's just mean for no reason, you know, and it's scary.

Martin Sanchez is a divorced, Hispanic, middle-class father of a seventeen-year-old daughter and a thirteen-year-old son. His job as a police officer (in the city where Virginia lives) exposes him to crime on a daily basis. Like Virginia, Martin suggested that the dangers facing children today are more intense than those of a generation before. And like Virginia, Martin is less concerned about protecting childhood innocence than in making certain that his children understand, and are prepared to deal with, life-threatening dangers:

> Being the profession that I am—a police officer—you see society has changed greatly. So yes, I think that there are many great concerns and problems that are facing our children today, . . . and these problems are concerns for our parents also if they care about their kids. We have gangs, drugs, things that are much more prevalent than they were when I was growing up. So in answer to your question, yes, there are a great many more problems in my opinion. . . . I think society's changing. I can't tell you why. . . . I try to expose them and let them know what's out there, what's in the real world. I try to shelter them from it but at the same time let them know what's going on rather than completely blind them from it, so that they're aware when they get out there in the real world these are the issues you're going to face and things you need to prepare yourself for.

Although a white, working-class mother with one teenage daughter might not have the professional expertise of Martin, Linda Casey also believes that she has to guard against dangers that did not concern her parents:

> I think the uprise of drug use, gangs—I think these are all problems. . . . I think a lot of it didn't exist [when I was a child]. Times were different, bottom line—just times have changed. I think we're in a society that crime's on the uprise, sexual predators are on the uprise, gang violence is on the uprise, things that didn't exist back [when I was a child].

Even when middle- and working-class parents talked about issues that overlap with those discussed by the professional middle-class parents, that talk had a different resonance. For example, although professional middle-class parents are concerned about sexualized images disrupting childhood innocence, they often implied that their young teenage children are not themselves actively involved in sexual activity. However, working-class and middle-class parents worry about sexualized images *and* about what they see as the likelihood that their children could become involved in the sexual activity that they believe occurs regularly in their children's schools. For example, Charlene Black, the white mother of two who lives in West Chester, Pennsylvania, spoke about her fourteen-year-old daughter. Charlene openly acknowledges that her children's peer group is involved in sexual activities and that her daughter is interested in presenting a sexy image and in competing with her peers for the most daring dress:

> They just seem so much more mature than we were at their age. When I was her age I could have cared less what I looked like, and she's into makeup, trying this, trying that. I think the peer pressure on the kids is very great. . . . We didn't seem to have all that stuff, as far as even sex and what you hear is going on in these kids' schools, I didn't even think of when I was in eighth grade. And that's the biggest thing because these eighth graders are doing it, right in my kids' schools. . . . I think it's just they seem to be so much more mature now than they were before, and there's so much out there. You've got the computers and you've got the TVs, and it all dramatizes it. And that's a big part of it. And with the girls especially, the shortest skirt that you can wear—they try to compete with each other in how you look.

Similarly, an African American mother of four children, ranging in age from seven to fifteen, worries about these influences on her oldest daughter:

> [I worry about] what happens next. I say "what happens next" because you never know what's coming through that door. I don't know if Tessa's going to become a teenage mother. I don't know if she's going to want to drop out of school. I say "what happens next" 'cause I don't know what's coming. Not knowing what's coming is the biggest challenge. . . . I'm really afraid for my kids. I'm afraid that they may get swept up in the wrong stuff. There's always that possibility. I mean, you can't step outside without seeing someone getting high. I'm afraid that—my daughter [who is fifteen] has a friend who's already had an abortion. She doesn't know that. I would never tell her that—they're the same age—but I can't control what goes on outside.

When an African American mother of two biological children and three foster children talks about teaching them about sex, weapons, and drugs, it is because she knows that these are present in her children's daily lives:

> [The biggest problem is] society. There's so much crap out there. Like, if you have a kid, you're not ready to teach him about sex, but you better 'cause somebody outside's gonna tell 'em. Or you don't want them exposed to knives and guns—you better, because somebody outside's gonna tell 'em. You don't

> want 'em exposed to drugs—no matter what it is, it's out there in society, in the classroom, sitting on the steps, wherever. You've gotta tell 'em so much. [My oldest daughter], Candy was very sheltered. Candy's world, she was very spoiled. She wasn't allowed to do anything. I would ask Candy when she was like fifteen, sixteen, "What happens when a girl gets pregnant?" "Oh, she gets married!" Yeah . . . so I was like, "Okay, gotta take you outside." . . . You had to let her know, yeah, maybe it should be like that, but that's not how it is.

Among those who are less privileged, too much protection can carry as many risks as too little.[23]

Significant social class differences emerged when parents were asked what challenges they face in the new configuration of daily life and what they do in response to those challenges. The elite parents hold to a vision of an essential childhood (similar to the one they nostalgically recall), which they believe is under threat from both outside and inside forces. From the outside they identify sexualized and violent images as disrupting and undermining childhood innocence.[24] In the face of this perceived threat, one of their jobs, as they conceive of it, is to protect their children—or, more accurately, the *childhoods* of their children. These elite parents also believe that the very lives that they have chosen—the pressures to achieve, the material wealth, the psychological indulgence, and the overscheduling—threaten their children's happiness. Ironically, then, they worry precisely about what it is they are doing to ensure economic, educational, and occupational successes—phenomena that they disparage even as they make serious efforts to (re-)create them. These contradictory and complex concerns require a new form of parental vigilance.

Middle-class and working-class parents share some of these concerns about media influences. They also worry about some very concrete dangers in a violent world. In the face of these dangers, they are not particularly interested in ensuring that their children have a prolonged and "pure" childhood; in fact, they recognize that they have to assist their children in maturing sufficiently so that they understand and can resist the dangers that are a significant part of the environments in which they live. Hence, they focus on concrete, physical, and imminent dangers that threaten not just some notion of an essentialized childhood but real children whose lives occur in neighborhoods where guns, violence, drug use, gangs, and sex may well be present.

4 HOW THEY PARENT

Styles, Satisfactions, and Tensions

The Elite Approach

Paula Brown works full-time as a high-level administrator at a university near the southern suburb in which she lives with her two teenage children. When asked to describe her approach to parenting, she indicated that she aims for honesty and flexibility even if doing so sometimes leaves her in an awkward position vis-à-vis her teenage daughter: "I'm really honest with Emily [who is fifteen]. You know, 'I've never done this before. I'm not an expert.' You know, not to feel like I'm jeopardizing my authority but at the same time I guess I'm just humanly presenting it and saying, 'We're gonna try this, . . . and we can always come back and reexamine.'"

In chapter 1 we met Eve Todd, another white, professional middle-class mother of two teens, both daughters, who lives in cold northern New England. She insists that she and her husband each make an effort to maintain authority without inculcating fear. And she identified the effort involved in this approach as being constituted not of love—which she believed comes easily—but of finding the right balance between encouragement and discipline. As Eve described her approach, she, like Paula, acknowledged that she does not have hard and fast rules that are applied in all situations but, rather, that she adapts her rules to fit events as they arise. She was also explicit about reversing her parents' model as she enacts parenting with her children:

> Well, I think that [my husband and I] both have tried to not have the kids be afraid of us, because I think that, you know, we both came from situations where the parents were "you do it because we said so," and there was retribution if you didn't. There was fear. There was hitting. . . . With our kids . . . we wanted to be encouraging and supportive in what their views were . . . and still maintain that we're the parents and they're the kids and sometimes it isn't fair and you have to do it. . . . But generally speaking we

> have tried to be encouraging. . . . We don't "ground" the kids. And it's basically taking it incident by incident or time by time and trying to deal with it that way.

Paula and Eve represent the parenting approach taken by the professional middle-class parents who were interviewed. Like these two women, most privileged adults emphasize the importance of honest communication, minimizing the generational gap, and responding with flexibility. These are all aspects of parenting that they feel had been neglected in their own upbringing. Although many of these parents—like Eve—were quick to point out that they know the difference between being a parent and being a friend, and insisted that they do not abdicate the parental role, they also acknowledged that they occasionally come very close to undermining their own authority. In upholding a nonauthoritarian approach to raising children, these parents line up well with what decades of research and much casual observation suggest: the higher one's class status, the more likely one is to rely on discussion and negotiation rather than clear rules and physical punishment.[1]

The flexibility that Paula and Eve describe is associated with three additional and distinctive components of parenting out of control among the professional middle class: belief in their children's boundless potential, a reliance on what they call "trust," and a strategy of ongoing availability.

Developing Potential

The link between flexibility and belief in a child's potential is made clear as college professor Tom Audet described his approach to parenting his eighteen-year-old son and fourteen-year-old daughter:

> I'm a believer that you should allow the child as much latitude as you possibly can to develop to their own potential. So far that has worked out all right. [There have been] a couple of issues where we wish they hadn't done [something], but it hasn't been serious, and so that's my attitude. I tend to [give] them the leeway to manage their own issues, manage their own problems, find their own solutions, and try to grow up with experience that doesn't harm them but they learn by.

In Tom's understanding, a flexible approach to child rearing—what he calls "latitude"—is key to helping his children "develop to their own potential." Occasionally, this strategy might result in his children's venturing into territory beyond that which he finds acceptable; for the most part, however, latitude helps them attain a breadth of experience.

An Asian father of two, a research scientist living in St. Louis, Missouri, spoke very similarly about the connection he sees between latitude and potential: "I think . . . the main role for parents is to help guide your kids to get to the best possible potential that they have. So it's giving them independence to do things with concerns for keeping security and safety and keeping your family values. . . . So within that framework kids are allowed to explore what they want to." Erica Harper reiterated this same theme: "I am there to be a safety net for my kids, a guide, perhaps to be the voice of experience. I just think the most important thing I do as a parent is to help them discover who is the best person they can be, acknowledging their passions, their strengths."

All these parents spoke simultaneously about a framework of loose rather than narrow constraints and about their children as having boundless potential that could be fulfilled if parents are appropriate guides. For them, children are *in process,* and neither their character nor their accomplishments are foreordained. Of course, parents must apply some rules as they raise these precious beings: as one father said, he feels free "to point out the path that's a good one and to say when [he doesn't] think that's a good path to go down," adding, "I think that's part of my job to say that's not a good direction." But professional middle-class parents assume that latitude creates opportunities for character to develop and for potential to reveal itself. They also assume that their children will become "the best."

Trusting Children

Latitude itself depends on trusting children, and many professional middle-class parents insisted that they take this stance most of the time: they believe that their children will generally remain within the framework of what their parents view as acceptable behavior and that those children will strive to become the "best" as their parents understand that "best" to be. In chapter 7, I pursue more precisely how the professional middle-class parents enact trust—and how contradictory that enactment may be. For now it is important to note that trust is closely aligned with both flexibility and continual guidance. As one father, a physician, said, "I think it's the sort of 'try to trust your kids' [approach]. You give them advice when you think they need advice even if they don't ask for it." The same alignment could be heard as Dave Townsend talked about his approach to dealing with his three teenage daughters:

> I like to come from a place where I trust my children. I believe in them, and I try to give them positive reinforcement. I try to be a positive influence. I have them contribute to whatever the decision might be, unless it's jut one of those things where I feel it's one hundred percent my responsibility and I feel I should make the decision. . . . I discuss things with them.

Dave's trust relies on nudging his children—giving them "positive reinforcement"—and engaging in ongoing discussion with them.

Availability

These professional middle-class parents ensure that this nudging and discussion will occur by being constantly available. The physician quoted earlier, after talking about trust and giving advice, continued, "And I think [good parenting is] being available for them and letting them know that you're always available." In claiming the necessity for constant availability, parents indicate that their children's needs and concerns are significant and should have a central place in family life. Being available also ensures that children can receive appropriate redirection, should trust fail.

Annette Lareau's phrase "concerted cultivation" has become commonplace in discussions of middle-class approaches to child care.[2] The elite parents who were interviewed might not use the same gardening imagery, and they talk less about pruning and shaping than they do about providing the right environment to help children become the best, about trusting their children to do the right thing, and about hovering. But like the parents Lareau described, in action, rather than as an abstract position on the chosen way to parent, the ever-present guidance parents provide can reach deep into their children's hearts and minds. A reliance on discussion rather than external constraint and on negotiation rather than clear punishment have as a shared aim the eventual internalization of parental norms and values. This is why these strategies are aligned with "trust." A constant presence is the safety net to ensure that parental values can be inserted into each decision ("they need advice even if they don't ask for it") and to pick up where trust leaves off—or fails.

These are practices that demand much of both parents and children. Parents have to provide the context in which children can learn what it is their parents expect of them, and parents have to make case-by-case decisions about the nature of that context as well as about whether a specific child has transgressed their expectations. This is yet another way that parenting out of control becomes time-consuming parenting. And children have to discern just what it is their parents expect within the "latitude" provided and which of their actions violate those unstated rules and venture into untrustworthy territory.[3] In this context, children may learn that parental trust turns out to be less a practice than a hope.

Ongoing Rewards

Demanding as it might be, this approach to parenting clearly has its own, very significant rewards. Professional middle-class parents take immense delight in the close bonds they believe they have established with each and every one of their children. Indeed, when asked specifically about the source of the deepest satisfaction they experience as parents, rather than pointing to their own or their children's achievements and accomplishments or to morals and manners, they talk about their relationship with their children and about the pleasures they find in an intense, abiding connection. And it is here especially—in close bonds—that the professional middle-parents see themselves as carving out a new mode of parenting.

Recall how Susan Chase, an attorney from California, who noted that she participated in the counterculture of the sixties and that as a parent she chose to be very "kid centered," casually suggested that her own parents "missed out" because they did not love their children as much as she loves hers. As evidence that she has created a different relationship with her children than her parents had with theirs, she proudly proclaimed that her son does not see her "as alien." Moreover, Susan insisted that her involvement with her children is less self-centered (even if it is motivated by her own needs) than she believes her parents' involvement was with her: "I have no idea [what my parents found satisfying]. . . . I can certainly imagine [my mother] taking pleasure in things [I did], but I can only think of it as a sort of reflection of herself kind of thing. 'My child is being so clever'—or something like that." Susan's then, is the deeper satisfaction, contrasted with her mother's concern with her own self-reflection.

Jeff Wright, the widowed father of a teenage daughter, similarly claimed that the interest he has in his daughter is deeper, more personal, and less focused on achievements than was the case for his parents.[4] He positions himself as maintaining sufficient distance to observe and find pleasure in Katie's independent development and simultaneously as being very close:

> I think for me being a parent [what is most satisfying is] just watching this young woman grow and develop and discover things about herself and reveal things about herself that are just marvelous. It's watching. It's not quite a caterpillar turning into a butterfly—she's always been a butterfly. It's new colors, new things, . . . watching her develop into a young, responsible poised adult. . . . She and I have been able to talk about things that are so difficult in terms of her mother's illness and death, in terms of just being who she is. So it's having those conversations and realizing how far—how many talents and abilities she has. And seeing them come to fruition is very satisfying. . . . *I think families are much more child centered than they used to be.* My mother never knew I was doing as well in school as I was. My father somehow was more aware of it. And they were not as focused on who our friends were and what we were up to. So I think they valued educational accomplishment, and I think they valued jobs and those opportunities. And I think that's how their measurement of success was. (Emphasis added)

As Jeff watches his "butterfly" daughter, he is certain that he has satisfactions more profound than any his parents might have imagined.

Ongoing Tensions

Availability, intimacy, trust, flexibility, and belief in potential are the hallmarks of the style that I call parenting out of control; these produce great satisfaction and provide a way for professional middle-class parents to distinguish themselves from their own parents. Yet, as has been implied, elite parents often acknowledge that the attributes of parenting out of control are the source of enduring dilemmas and tensions. Indeed, when asked to describe what is most difficult about being a parent, many of the interviewees gave some answer that could fall within the general set of concerns of fearing that they often got *too* involved in their children's lives, of having difficulty in drawing appropriate limits with respect to disciplinary issues, and of not knowing how to enact trust when the stakes were so very high.

Consider again Jeff Wright, who takes immense pride in the deep conversations he has with his daughter. When asked to dwell on problems, he talked about how very hard it is to maintain boundaries and to know when it would be best to step back from an intense engagement in Katie's life. As he reflected on this issue, he recognized that because he is forging a new mode of parenting, he can not simply rely on the practice and approach of the generation before him:

> [The greatest difficulty is] knowing when to step in and when to let her be on her own. . . . I think my parents were parents that didn't ask questions that much, so I don't know if they ever really knew what I was thinking about. I didn't find myself confiding in them and sharing, but I think [my daughter and I] have a different form of communication where she can share if she needs to. And I'm not sure my parents would have been ready to share.

To be sure, Jeff faces particularly difficult challenges: he has to guide his daughter through her adolescence while helping her cope with the recent death of her mother. But, as we have seen, he is not unique in describing this closeness (though it may more commonly be found between mothers and children than between fathers and children). Nor is he unique in his sense of concern about not knowing just when to get involved—and when to back off.

When asked whether the new approach is more difficult than that adopted by her parents, Eve Todd gave an answer that explicitly links respect for children's feelings and ideas to endless negotiation. Eve's interview took place over two sessions, and in the first conversation Eve had prided herself on her support of her daughter Kara's ambition to be a rock star. She had explicitly noted, as well, that her parents had been more concerned with "basic things." In contrast, Eve said she and her husband wanted to be "encouraging and supportive in what their [children's] views were." During our second meeting I asked Eve whether she thinks this new, supportive approach makes parenting more difficult. She responded thoughtfully. She denied that having envisioned more options for a child's development is the source of the dilemmas she faces as a parent. Instead she struggles with the consequences of having loosened the reins of authority and of having become more attentive to her daughter's feelings:

> Yeah [it is more difficult], and I think that the options [expanded]. It created its own set of problems as not having the options, but I don't think that it's the kind of problem that I have with my daughter, where she's confronting me and asking me to explain myself a lot. Or "Well, gee, Mom, you get to do that" or "Gee, can't a person be tired?" You know, that kind of conversation would never have happened with my parents because the rules were much tighter, rather than looking at the individuals and thinking, "Let's do it this way. Let's consider how they feel." There wasn't as much consideration about how the kids felt. It was more taking care of food and everything.

Early in my conversation with Anna Benton, she had mentioned that she thought parenting was easier for her parents than it is for her because her parents had been more authoritarian. Anna had also insisted that she and her parents found entirely different satisfactions in child rearing. Her parents valued good behavior; she values intimacy. In fact, Anna explicitly acknowledged that the intimacy she has with her children fills in for the intimacy she feels she did not have with her own parents. When asked to discuss more fully her particular parenting style, she referred to Thomas Phelan's book *1-2-3 Magic: Effective Discipline for Children 2–12* as she quipped about how her own approach differs from that one:[5]

> There are some parenting books that you have to be so regulated to follow their approach. There was one that was called "1-2-3 stop" or something; it's some sort of behavior modification program. So many of those aren't helpful to me because that's just not my personal way of doing things. Mine is "1-2-3 maybe."

Anna also spoke of how her "1-2-3 maybe" approach is the source of intense personal frustration. She wants to remain close to her children, and she values responding in a flexible manner. Yet she is sometimes irritated because she views her children as insufficiently attentive to the demands of family life, and she does not know how to inculcate different attitudes:

> ANNA: [I'm] probably not strict enough. We are a very close family. We do a lot of things together. I think that we don't have enough fixed rules, so there tends to be more arguing and negotiating that goes on.
>
> INTERVIEWER: What are some of the areas where you have conflicts?
>
> ANNA: You know, about how much TV, and I don't think that they contribute enough in terms of chores and kitchen, and things like that. . . . Like I was saying, there's something about the seventies and the, you know, we should all be close and talking on pillows and everybody's in therapy and talking about their feelings and somehow feeling like more should be resolved in a consensual way with your kids. There isn't any of this, you know, "that's the rule," and I think a little more of that is a good thing. I'm trying to do that more with my kids. Sadie's more obedient, but Leah pushes the limits—not like risky behavior but a little too much of a prima donna.

Anna thus both boasts and worries about her relationship with her children. She also both embraces and mocks her new approach to being a parent.

Donna Gibson, Anna's friend in Berkeley, raised a related set of concerns. Donna believes that she and her husband are both permissive *and* protective, but she too worries that she leans too much toward permissiveness. Interestingly, Donna sees permissiveness as standing in opposition to being protective, rather than as the converse of being authoritative (or even authoritarian), which suggests that she conflates the two issues of permissiveness and protectiveness. That opposition also suggests, perhaps, that Donna cannot even imagine being authoritative (or authoritarian) about routine matters that do not involve safety, even though she thinks that might be a more appropriate stance some of the time: "On the spectrum of things we're relatively—I was going to say permissive, but sometimes people say we're not; they characterize us as being more on the protective end. . . . But in terms of like rules, operating in this house, we're very permissive and probably too permissive, particularly for Jordan. He could probably use more rules, truthfully." When asked what her greatest difficulty as a parent is, Donna answered that she sometimes becomes a "bit hysterical" around issues of safety and around issues having to do with her children's academic performance, demonstrating once again her conflation of two quite different issues:

> [My greatest difficulty is] keeping fear under, you know, not letting your fear drive your reaction to your kid. . . . The thing that happened with Sophie [who at age fifteen wanted to go to an underage club] is in my mind. [I had] a lot of fears around her doing this, and I think that my fear drove some of my decision making around it, and I became a little bit hysterical with her about it. . . . And the same with Jordan [who is twelve]. I worry if he says, "I don't want to do any more homework, and I don't care." I worry that that means he will be an unemployed bum.

Donna laughed as she talked about her son being a "bum," but the laughter was nervous. Donna makes no distinction between fears about safety (Will Sophie be all right as she travels to an underage club across the San Francisco Bay?) and fears about status reproduction (Will Jordan do his homework?). Both sets of fears prompt Donna to become more vigilant—thus violating her commitment to trust—even as she values her own "permissive" stance. She then is left not knowing what to do should her son refuse to do his homework and refuse to remain engaged in the family practice of high achievement. The same kind of status anxiety is also lurking in the comment of Kristen Garner, a white, widowed mother of two living in suburban Connecticut, as she wrestles with the issue of whether to intervene when one of her two children is experiencing academic difficulties: "I think one of the hardest things is to get involved to the right extent and not to too much of an extent."

Ongoing Negotiation

The professional middle-class parents have differentiated themselves from their parents—even rejected their parents—as they make decisions about how to approach the care of their own children. Not only do they believe that the world holds greater dangers than was the case when they were children, but they feel more alone in the task of warding off those dangers. At the same time, they want more flexibility and more communication. Hence, they opt for both greater protectiveness and greater intimacy. And if these stances are sometimes burdensome, the latter especially is also the source of immense satisfaction and a way in which elite parents feel superior to their own parents. At the same time, the location of the balance point between being too involved and not being sufficiently attentive eludes them. So too does finding the balance between being close to their children and having enough distance to discipline them. They know they should be parents rather than friends and can repeat that litany, although their repetitions are sometimes pro forma. They find themselves torn.

It is, of course, entirely possible that these professional middle-class parents are unable to draw clear lines of authority because at least some of what they want is so very amorphous. How does one know when a child is sufficiently "happy," deeply engaged in finding her or his true passions, and living up to her or his boundless potential? Given this essential uncertainty, the parents who worry that they are too involved in their children's lives have no choice but to remain precisely that involved: the goals they hold out require that they check in with their children and examine both their psychological state and their daily activities.

But it is also entirely possible that the troublesome negotiation in which these parents engage with their children is precisely what they want because it keeps them close to their children, even as that negotiation means that their children do not always meet their expectations about appropriate behavior or appropriate activities. Moreover, their desires are not just ambiguous; they are also fundamentally contradictory. These parents want their children to succeed, but they worry about the stress those children experience as they strive to live up to their parents' expectations of success. They want to provide their children with what they need to fit in with the crowd—a laptop computer, a cell phone—but they worry about being too indulgent.[6] They want to protect their children from growing up too fast, but by their own admission, they talk to them as if they are adults and encourage them to make choices from a very young age.[7]

Denying Privilege

When the professional middle-class parents are asked about their approach to raising children, they definitely do not respond with reference to the multiple advantages they can afford. Some of the less privileged parents, on the other hand, do speak about what is beyond their reach, about the limits that frame their consumption patterns. On this issue, recall Peter Chaplin and his struggles over whether he could enroll his child in a competitive soccer program or send him to private school. But the professional middle-class parents do *not* talk in terms of the range of resources available to their children—the testing for disabilities, the private school education, and the opportunities to nurture individual skills. As we have seen, sometimes parents do worry that they are *too* indulgent with respect to material goods. But the provision of these extraordinary resources is so taken for granted that it is not considered a part of how they approach the task of raising their children.

A Less Privileged, and Firmer, Approach

In contrast to Anna Benton's "1-2-3 maybe," Margaret Davies, a white, self-employed craftsperson married to an African American building contractor, characterized her parenting approach as "tell, tell, tell, yell." Margaret's approach represents well the parenting style of the working-class and middle-class parents, who seem more confident in their ability to say no, who talk more explicitly about being a parent and not a friend, and who more often define themselves as being "strict."

Among these less privileged adults, the pro forma response often appears to be about respecting children's input, rather than about knowing that they as parents should remain figures of authority. Charlene Black, for example, put it this way: "I think I try to be close to them, and we do have an open relationship. At the same time, you have to have a line between being a parent and a friend." Similarly, Amy Price said,

> I consider myself a friend to my children, but I'm a parent foremost. . . . I'm kind of middle-of-the-road. I think it's important to be somewhat of a friend with them, so you do have that open communication like we did, but I do think that you also have to be a parent foremost to set the bound-

> aries. . . . I've always been one of those [parents who believes] you're not here to be their friend; you're here to be their parent.

Some of these parents present their own strictness as a contrast to what it is that they believe *other* parents do. For example, Francesca Guarino made reference to her immigrant roots to explain her approach to raising her children while noting that her daughter believes that other parents are far more lenient:

> I think we're both—like I said earlier—we come from parents from the other side, and it's not like the parents in today's times, in today's America. I should say, I noticed that they raise their children a little more "free"—I don't know the proper word. We are a little more strict. My daughter tells me all the time, "You know, you guys are so different from everyone else. You should see the other parents. [Their kids] can do this, and they can do that."

Similarly, Christopher Rodriguez, a Hispanic father who, like Francesca, lives on Staten Island, explained his approach as a "two-way" street, even as he differentiated himself from what he believes to be the indulgent parents around him:

> In a way [my approach is] a two-way street. I'll make it very simple: it's a give and take. We live in a time that is very different than times past, okay. Children used to respect their parents, not only their parents, their elders; the [current] generation became the "X generation," the "Me generation." It's a shame. . . . Before the kids respect the parents; now the kids expect the parents to respect them. And everything shifted, and . . . children became very rebellious. And I don't blame them. I don't blame them because they felt like they became an object, and then parents tried to compensate by buying everything. Things will never replace parents, that's my philosophy.

Other working-class and middle-class parents quite simply commented that they are strict: "I'm pretty much 85 percent 'do what I say'"; "The way I look at it is it is my responsibility to prepare these children to go out and function in today's world, today's society, and to prepare them for it the best way I can by, I guess, sharing the knowledge and experience I have in my life and preparing them, guiding them, on the path I think will be best for them to function and survive in today's society. I'm more strict than lax." In short, unlike the professional middle-class parents, these less privileged adults are certain about boundaries and ready to be firm. And although few of these parents spoke about relying on physical punishment, they emphasized their commitment to having their children know that rule violations would have significant consequences.

Acceptance and Mistrust

Anita Mayer, a middle-class resident of rural Texas and mother to four children, used a garden image to explain her view of parenting: "I think children are like plants, that they're predestined flowers to whatever they're supposed to be, and you're just the good gardener who provides a decent environment, . . . and they become who they are meant to be. So I don't have to make them be who they are." Anita might be a more engaged cultivator than might be suggested by Annette Lareau's phrase "accomplishment of natural growth" (used with working-class and poor parents): she wants to be a "good gardener" of her children.[8] But Anita also believes that her children are "predestined" to be who they will be: their characters are fixed, and her role is relatively minimal, as summed up in the notion of a "decent environment." Another white, middle-class mother explained that she believes that "kids come as their own entities" and that it is the obligation of parents to accept those entities while teaching children "'yes' and 'no' in order for them to develop that moral compass." She continued, "I never appreciated [and] I did not gravitate to the parents who let their kids do whatever they wanted. I felt it was okay to say no and move on." Christopher Rodriguez also spoke about the necessity for "correcting [his son] in the manner he needed to be corrected" and listed as his concerns that his son be "respectful to his uncles and aunts and elders and that type of thing." Like others, Christopher tacked on a view about the proper relationship between parents and children: "We're his parents, we're not his friends, and that's just the way it is. We're the ultimate decision makers and that's it."

These less privileged parents want to encourage their children to grow; they want to garden well. But their role involves acceptance of the particularities of their children and does not rest on a view of *unlimited* potential, of children who can become "the best." These parents do not wait for transgressions but instead establish concrete rules and discrete expectations early on. Nor do they blend love with unmitigated trust. Even if they sometimes give a pro forma nod to trust, they almost immediately qualify it. As one mother said, "I do like to give them freedom in decision making and trust *when I can.*"

In action, this approach might be less demanding of parents and children than that enacted by the professional middle class—not because it involves ignoring children (as Lareau sometimes implies), but because of its clarity about rules and about children's developing personalities.[9] Like the clearly painted line on a road, narrow limits make visible transgressions. Without fear that they are stunting their children's potential, parents can accept them as they are while seeking to improve their *behavior* through correction.

Satisfactions

Like the more elite parents who were interviewed, middle-class and working-class parents find great satisfaction in raising their children. But these satisfactions less often hinge on their relationship with their children than do those described by the professional middle-class parents. Rather, middle-class and working-class parents cherish distinct achievements and personal successes, much as the professional middle-class parents said their own parents did with them. In some cases these are vague, amorphous accomplishments such as "growing up to be a good person." In other cases they are concrete accomplishments along the way to very possible educational success and upward mobility: "[Most satisfying is] watching your child grow up and seeing their accomplishments"; "[Most satisfying] is watching my child succeed in school"; "I'm very proud of their accomplishments, seeing them grow and take the steps to being a productive adult that they're working on right now at this point."

Different Difficulties

When asked about problems they faced, middle- and working-class parents discussed a very different set of issues than did their professional middle-class counterparts. Of course, not all middle-class and working-class parents find that the same issues cause problems. Some focus on the absence of sufficient resources. As one parent responded, "most difficult is not having enough time or money." And this issue of insufficient time and money is especially significant among single working- and middle-class parents. In addition, some among the small group of single parents who were interviewed mentioned that it is difficult to raise a child of a different gender. A white, middle-class mother of two was explicit about this issue: "Most difficult thing for me has been parenting by myself, especially raising a son without a father. . . . [My son] would be a better athlete if someone went out to play with him." Similarly, a working-class, Hispanic, single father of two worried about what his daughters might be missing:

> Being a single parent right now is very tough. It's a lot of extra work, which I don't mind doing, but I still think what bothers me is that I think that my children are being short-changed. They don't get the mother side of it. I'm not a woman. I never have been. I try to nurture my children as much as I can, but I'm still a guy, and these are two girls. And I feel like sometimes they get short-changed, and I feel bad for that. But there's nothing I can do to help that at this point.

If this father accepts the "extra work" of parenting on his own, other working-class and middle-class parents, including those with spouses, openly acknowledged that they resented just how much effort they had to put into raising children (a sentiment that was less evident among the professional middle-class parents). A married, white, middle-class mother of one child bemoaned the fact that as a parent she finds it difficult "not having the freedom . . . to be able to get up and go" and having to be aware of what she called "a pretty large responsibility that has to be dealt with." Another married, white, middle-class mother was even more dissatisfied with her responsibilities as a parent: "I think the hardest thing about being a parent [is that] you have to be selfless. Your life seems to be put way in the back [for] kids' schedules. If you have a hundred dollars, and they need school clothes and they need shoes, you're more apt to worry about them than yourself. I think that's the hardest thing." This woman also clearly believes that these burdens fall more heavily on her than on her husband, and although her switch from the first person to the second person might represent an attempt to minimize the resentment she feels, the conflicted feelings come through quite clearly: "[I am] a cook and a cleaner and a day care giver and a bus driver, and I just feel that sometimes you feel like, 'What am I?' You sometimes forget about yourself and that can affect marriage."

It is not surprising to find that the middle- and working-class parents face significant challenges: how best to allocate scarce resources and how to find time for oneself while holding down a job and raising children loom large in their accounts. What is surprising is that these parents experience both challenges and satisfactions in a very different way than do their more privileged peers. The professional middle-class parents often find that their very style of parenting (intense closeness) leads them into difficulties (not being able to know how involved to be, not knowing when to say no, not knowing just how much they should trust their children). In contrast, the middle- and working-class parents do not find their satisfactions enmeshed with problems. They are able to find satisfaction in their children's accomplishments without having those satisfactions themselves turn into ongoing difficulties.

Not surprisingly, the professional middle-class parents describe themselves as more permissive than authoritarian: they speak about allowing and encouraging their children to make choices as they find their way to fulfilling their potential and becoming the best that they can possibly be. These parents see their role as intense nurturers of children in the process of development. Professional middle-class parents also describe a style of care that relies on communication, negotiation, flexibility, trust, and being endlessly (and immediately) available. Partly as a result of this style, they find great pleasures in their open and close relationships with their children. They speak of their children as people they enjoy knowing, as people they want to hang out with, and sometimes as the people who are their best friends. And they take both pleasure and pride in being able to enact trust. Admixed with these satisfactions, however, are their greatest difficulties as parents: they worry whether they are engaging in too much negotiation with their children; they also worry about not having enough authority to say no. But this negotiation may be what they want: negotiation maintains connection and keeps them from appearing too authoritarian. As they enact the new approach to interacting with their adolescent children—what I have called parenting out of control—they face the distinctive challenge of how to parent those who have been identified as "friends."

In contrast to the professional middle-class parents, both the working-class and middle-class parents are more likely to describe themselves as being strict: they talk about being role models for their children, about knowing the difference between being parents and being friends, and about having rules and imposing consequences for violations of these rules. They too want to nurture their children, but they are more likely to see their children's personalities as set, as constituting the material with which they must work. They find their satisfaction in their children's concrete accomplishments and achievements. And they find their difficulties in an array of different issues that include the material demands of trying to raise children on low incomes (and sometimes as single parents). In contrast to the professional middle class, neither the middle-class nor the working-class parents—who follow what I have called parenting with limits—encounter fundamental contradictions in the nature and content of their parenting: that is, they do not find that both their satisfactions and their difficulties as parents have the same source.

As we will see in part II, parenting out of control and parenting with limits become guiding principles for parental decisions concerning the implementation of new technologies of connection, constraint, and surveillance; in turn, these new technologies bring these principles to life and are a mechanism through which these principles are enacted.

PART II

Parenting and Technology

◈ INTRODUCTION TO PART II

Do You Know Where Your Children Are?

A vast new array of surveillance technologies has become a taken-for-granted feature of our daily lives. Cameras tape our behavior on the street, smart cards record our purchases at the grocery store, and our employers can, if they choose, keep track of the time we spend playing solitaire on the computer.[1] Not surprisingly, these new technologies have been subject to considerable analysis.[2] By and large, however, the family and its internal dynamics have been ignored in these studies.[3] When the surveillance literature *does* address the family, it generally assumes what I call "surveillance creep": that is, writers suggest that the new technologies of surveillance are insinuating themselves into our everyday lives and are used (willy-nilly) by individuals at home as well as by governments and organizations. William Staples provides an excellent example of this perspective in his book *Everyday Surveillance: Vigilance and Visibility in Postmodern Life.* Staples adopts a Foucauldian framework to describe what he calls "meticulous rituals of power":

> These are knowledge-gathering activities that involve surveillance, information and evidence collection, and analysis. I call them meticulous because they are "small" procedures and techniques that are precisely and thoroughly exercised. I see them as ritualistic because they are faithfully repeated. . . . And they are about power because they are intended to discipline people into acting in ways that others have deemed to be lawful or have defined as appropriate or simply "normal."[4]

In discussing further what he means, Staples argues that we *all* engage in these meticulous rituals of power; in fact, he suggests, "we should 'forget Big Brother'" because "surveillance power is bi-directional, and is more-often-than-not triggered by us."[5]

Staples moves freely among the practices of surveillance by the state (e.g., wiretapping), the market (e.g., customer cards), institutions (e.g., programs that enable parents to see what homework has been assigned), and the family (e.g., home drug testing). In mixing and matching in this way, Staples encourages us to believe that these various "meticulous rituals of power" are similar in their effects; he further encourages us to believe that all parents eagerly (and perhaps thoughtlessly) adopt the available technologies to protect *and* discipline (in the broadest sense) their children. Other writers, however, imply that more elite parents will be especially inclined to engage in some of these "meticulous rituals of power." This is true of the sociologists Dawn Moore and Kevin Haggerty, who argue that home drug testing is aimed particularly at the well-off parents who can afford to pull these items off the shelf of the drug store, and it is also true of the geographer Cindi Katz, who focuses on devices such as nanny cams.[6]

Both sets of assumptions are definitively challenged in this book. In the next several chapters I explore a number of new technologies for connecting with, constraining the actions of, and spying on children. I've divided these into three separate sets. The first set I call "connection" devices (chapter 5). This set is the least restrictive one (from the point of view of the child); it includes two relatively new devices, baby monitors and cell phones.[7] Each of these devices enables a parent to gather information about a child when the parent is not in that child's immediate presence, but neither makes a permanent record of that information and neither in and of itself constrains behavior. Rather, each provides a kind of connection across distance. To be sure, these two devices differ in significant ways: not only are they used with children at very different stages of development, but children are generally unaware of baby monitors and they do not need to participate in any way for them to be effective. On the other hand, and much to the regret of many of the interviewed parents, unless cell phones have a GPS attached to them and are turned on, they do not provide an accurate indicator of a child's location, and cell phones only work as a device for obtaining information if children choose to answer them.[8]

The second set, what I call devices of "constraint," can actually prevent behavior and, more specifically, the behavior of physical or virtual "wandering" (chapter 6). A device known as a "child locator" alerts parents to literal wandering. An advertisement perhaps describes this device best:

> The BrickHouse Child Locator by BrickHouse is a device that lets you keep a constant watch on your child in public areas. This device works by attaching a tag to your child's clothes or shoes to work as a homing device should your child leave the safety zone, the BrickHouse Child Locator will alert you when that happens. The portable tracking device will beep, vibrate, and visually lead you to your (tagged) child quickly and easily. This device also comes with a "panic button" on the homing tag for your child to use in the event of an emergency.[9]

A variety of these devices are available through Amazon.com. They are advertised as being appropriate for use with young children; they are also advertised for use with people with memory problems (such as elderly people with Alzheimer's disease) and for use with older children who might have difficulty learning appropriate rules (such as children with what are called "autism spectrum" disorders).[10]

Other devices are designed to deal with wandering in the media and in virtual space. Parents can rely on a V-chip to block specific channels or programs on a television.[11] Parents can also install software on the computer to deny access to specific Internet sites.[12] In contrast to the cell phones and baby monitors, devices of constraint directly stop behavior. And two of these—filters on the computer and blocks on the television—operate without ongoing parental intervention.

The last set of devices do not prevent behavior but rather gather information that can then be used to make disciplinary decisions (chapter 7). This set includes GPS tracking/speed devices installed in a car. Originally for fleet management, these devices sense movement and report where a car is and how fast it is going. These reports can be sent electronically to a distant computer.[13] Two sites explain these services; the second site offers concealment as a special feature:

> The Vehicle Tracker monitors vehicle location, speed and other parameters via global positioning satellites (GPS) and makes reports when pre-set limits are exceeded using an integrated cellular device to parents' phone and email. A secure, password-protected website allows you to view vehicle driving history in great detail. This history of driving behavior includes maps

> and reports showing where the vehicle has been at specific times, at what speed it has been driven and related information that helps parents monitor and enforce the agreements they have established with their youngsters.[14]

> SafeTrak is a real-time web based system utilizing GPS Technology and your web browser. The GPS System is reasonably priced with a low flat monthly fee and no term contract, is simple to install and will automatically update according to the service plan . . . that best suits your requirements. There are no additional charges for reports, web access, e-mail alerts, etc. One low monthly fee allows you unlimited use of everything the GPS Vehicle Tracking System provides. There is no cost for mapping and no software required. Mapping is updated every 6 months and software is constantly improved at no additional cost to you. SafeTrak GPS System provides fast, easy access to key information such as where you're [*sic*] teen is, where they're going, where they have been, and how fast they're driving. The Teen Driver Tracking Device is easy to install and maintain. The SafeTrak unit and antenna can both be easily concealed for covert operation.[15]

Recently, a father used the SafeTrak device successfully to challenge his teen's speeding ticket, claiming that his GPS system was more accurate than the police radar gun. This incident led to widespread publicity about this device. There has also been publicity as insurers have been offering this device to parents.[16]

I include within this last set of surveillance devices a mechanism for keeping a record of keystrokes on the computer and home drug tests, the latter of which checks for a range of legal and illegal substances. These also are relatively recent innovations with their own promotional material designed to attract parents eager to control their children's actions.[17] Home drug testing sites often appear to be "merely" an informed and concerned agency or individual who has the best interests of parents and teens at heart. For example, the website drugtestyourteen.com shows a picture of three young girls sitting on a bench in the classic monkey "see no evil, speak no evil, hear no evil" pose; they are giggling and happy. The text underneath reads,

> Parents—You really can prevent teen drug, alcohol, and tobacco use. Quick, accurate, inexpensive, and private in-home tests. Give your teen another reason to say NO.

> Linzy, Melissa, & Delaney want to remind parents to keep their eyes and ears open, and to communicate even when your kids act like they are not listening.

The site then seeks both to arouse fears about the possibility that *your* child could be using drugs and to offer a way to find out if that is the case. The promotional material suggests making teens complicit in the testing:

> The prospect that your child could be using drugs is one of the scariest things imaginable. None of us ever wants to believe that it could be "our child." I know because I have been there. My teen daughters and I have found one way for parents to take loving control. We offer several inexpensive, accurate, FDA-cleared drug, alcohol, and tobacco tests that are easy to use in the privacy of your own home. Whether you are trying to prevent drug use, discover possible drug use, stop current use, or just be reassured that a teen is on the right road, home testing will help.

Once surveillance devices have been implemented and information is gathered—about how fast and where a child has driven, about what messages a child has sent or has written in a file on the computer, or about what substances are in a child's body—the parent has to decide what to do with that information.

Two of these devices can be used without a child's awareness (and in fact these are advertised as offering "stealth" use); most drug tests require some cooperation from a teen (i.e., the provision of a urine sample), although some use hair samples, which, presumably, can be acquired without a child's cooperation or knowledge.

In what follows, I explore how existing notions of the appropriate relationship between parents and children shape perceptions of the desirability of these new technologies (and, in some cases, perceptions of their effects as well). As parents talk about their responses to these options, they reveal how the two different styles of parenting—parenting out of control and parenting with limits—are enacted. My argument steers clear of a strict technological determinist position that might view the technologies themselves as the *cause* of specific social relations; rather, I emphasize how social relations enter into evaluations and use of new technologies.[18] Of course, I also recognize that causality rarely runs only one way: some of these technologies have already helped to shape parental assessments of the best way to raise their children. As I investigate these new technologies, the mystery of my students' conversations with their parents, with the cell phones glued to their ears, begins to dissolve.

5 STAYING CONNECTED

The Baby Monitor: A Relatively Modern "Necessity"

Before I began conducting interviews for this book, I researched parental attitudes toward baby monitors on the consumer advice website Epinions.com. Although baby monitors have only appeared on the scene relatively recently, parental use of these devices is now assumed rather than explained in consumer reviews.[1] That is, reviewers do not appear to think that they need to account for why they want or need a baby monitor, indicating that they do not view their actions as being either "unanticipated or untoward."[2] Instead, they dive right in with a discussion of the benefits—and drawbacks—of the particular monitor they are evaluating. For example, a reviewer on Epinions.com said, "[This monitor] was a mother's dream. This is the monitor I wanted. . . . I researched them, spent hours in the baby stores, etc. I registered for this monitor, and received it." A casual reader of these reviews would thus learn that monitors are expected equipment: the central question is not whether to buy one but rather which one to buy. In fact, among the one hundred reviews I examined, only one parent said that on the advice of her pediatrician she had chosen to forgo this device; she suggested that parents might be better off if they remained somewhat less aware of what, precisely, a baby was doing:

> I registered and received the [monitor] for a shower gift when I was pregnant with my first child. I thought this would be something we couldn't do without but found out differently. . . . If your baby doesn't sleep very well, our pediatrician tells you to put the monitor away because you jump at every noise you hear or you get them up when perhaps they might comfort themselves back to sleep.[3]

When I interviewed parents in person for this book, I anticipated that I would find more of this type of questioning of the utility of having a baby monitor.[4] But again, among almost a hundred respondents across all socioeconomic classes, only one parent—the mother of triplets—indicated that she did not want to use a baby monitor because it would make her *too* aware of her infants' needs: "[I] didn't use [a baby monitor]. . . . They were loud criers, why would I? And once they were screaming [I could hear them]. I didn't want to know when they were awake." The remaining parents who chose not to use a monitor—and this was true of parents from the full range of socioeconomic positions—said it was because they lived in such small apartments or homes that a monitor was totally unnecessary.[5]

Safety and Vigilance

In the several decades since baby monitors first appeared on the scene, most parents have come to insist on their necessity. As noted earlier, theoretical accounts of the rise of a more generalized "anxiety" rest on the work of Anthony Giddens and Ulrich Beck regarding the emergence of a "risk society."[6] In the case of baby monitors, an intensified sense of individual responsibility combines with—and ultimately re-creates—a perception that babies are very fragile and can easily get into some form of distress. When the interviewed parents were pushed to explain why they purchase and use baby monitors, safety concerns were dominant, as they are in advertisements for this technology.[7] In turn, concerns about safety lead to a practice of vigilance. These concerns—and the necessity for a vigilant response—were expressed quite similarly by the working-class, middle-class, and professional middle-class parents.[8] A white, working-class mother of three, for example, commented that she wanted to have a baby monitor because she wanted "to hear everything," out of fear her child could be in danger: "What if they're choking or something? I guess that's why you use it." A considerably more privileged woman, a professional middle-class, white mother of two children, raised almost precisely the same issues: "The advantages are you can hear what's going on in another room. . . . Things can happen in an instant with a baby: they can strangle themselves, they can be coughing. . . . So I wanted to be able to respond right away."

Of course, this attentiveness to safety not only rests on an assumption about the intrinsic fragility of babies, but it also has its own repercussions. That is, hearing every sound a baby makes might make parents more, rather than less, anxious. Parents suggest that anxiety is one of the inevitable costs of having a baby, and if vigilance intensifies that cost, then they are more than willing to pay that price. For example, one professional middle-class mother, when asked about the advantage of having a monitor, acknowledged that even as it ensured "safety, making sure the kid's alive," it might very well have made her "more uptight." Similarly, a middle-class mother said that when she was a "new mother" she "didn't want to miss anything" and then added, "You can get really neurotic having something like that too; I was kind of neurotic with [my first child]." This mother further explained that she didn't use a baby monitor with her second child.

Parents, particularly new parents, thus normalize a child's fragility rather than a child's inherent ability to keep itself alive; in response to this perceived fragility, they want to be able to hear every sound the baby makes. Parents also normalize anxiety rather than calm self-assurance; they readily accept that as new parents they will be very concerned about—perhaps even "neurotic" with respect to—the well-being of their infants. And, ultimately, they normalize vigilance. None of these attitudes resides more often among one group of parents than another: that is, all parents agree that baby monitors are important for safety; all parents think it "normal" for a new parent to be anxious about a baby's well-being; and all parents respond with oversight. Baby monitors are thus the ground zero of good parenting in an era of individual responsibility for risk. But those who are parenting out of control relish baby monitors for yet another reason.

Responding to Every Need

Professional middle-class parents suggested that in addition to allowing them to know if a child was in some kind of danger, baby monitors were important devices because they allowed them to be deeply connected to their children, to know what was happening at every moment, and thus to be responsive in a very immediate and personal way. As was the case when elite parents talked more generally about their approach to parenting, they drew a contrast between their own level of engagement and the more casual attitude of previous generations. Their connection, they claim, not only provides them with immense satisfaction, but it helps to create a more secure bond between parent and child.

Marian English, a white mother of three teens, was explicit about her belief in the necessity of immediate responsiveness. She was also explicit about the ways in which she believes this style of care deviates from that adopted by other members of her extended family:

> I really didn't believe in letting them just sit there and cry; as soon as they woke up I went to get them. Same thing if they were crying; I went to get them, always. My family would criticize me for that. . . . I wanted to be able to get [the babies]. I just don't believe that babies cry for nothing—they needed a change or they were hungry or they needed to be held. I don't think babies need to have a reason to be held. I think they should be held whenever they felt like it. I think the big advantage [of a monitor was for the child]—it's not a quantifiable advantage. Part of the whole realm of invisible assumptions they have about life is if they cry someone will come, if they need help someone will help. . . . I don't think it had a major effect one way or another [on my relationship to my children] except for that invisible part—the unquantifiable part—about knowing that someone will always respond.

Marian's comments take seriously an infant's cries and incorporate the belief that ready responsiveness—what she calls the "unquantifiable" benefit—is good for a child; children learn that whatever they define as a need or want will be met with a supportive response. Marian also happily believes that her children have learned that "someone" will always respond.

Professional middle-class parents thus position children as not only in need of surveillance for the sake of protection (there are safety issues, children are fragile, and parents are anxious) but also in need of what one parent called "totally immediate service." Rather than assuming children should learn to soothe themselves or being concerned that children might become in any way "spoiled" by a parent's too-hasty responsiveness, professional middle-class parents believe it is their obligation to be always available and at the ready to meet the needs of their infants as soon as those needs are expressed. They assume that this responsiveness leads to secure bonds. As they do so, they legitimate children's needs. These assumptions and responses are compatible with (and may even provide the basis for) what we have seen to be the other components of parenting out of control: the respectful—even deferential—attitudes parents hold toward an infant's needs and desires pave the way for the subsequent negotiation that takes place between parents and teens, a negotiation that has as its premise the legitimacy of adolescents' stated needs and desires. Thus, the closeness created by hearing every peep an infant makes might be carried into more sophisticated verbal communication in later years. The patterns set in infancy may have lasting effects. It may also be the case, however, that these early patterns emerge *because* they are compatible with the style of parenting anticipated during a child's adolescence.[9]

Everybody Has a Cell Phone

Almost all the children of respondents in this study had access to a cell phone by age thirteen; some parents bought it earlier, and most parents with younger children said that they would buy a phone when their child hit middle school. There is only a very modest class difference in the frequency of cell phone ownership among children.[10] These findings are in line with those emerging from a study conducted by the Pew Internet & American Life Project, which found that among households composed of married couples with children, 89 percent own multiple cell phones and that 57 percent of the children (aged seven to seventeen) in these households have their own cell phone. A study by U.S. Cellular had a similar finding, that at least 60 percent of all teens have cell phones.[11]

Safety and Monitoring

As the interviewed parents discussed why they have purchased—or will purchase—a cell phone for their children, a key theme was that these devices, like baby monitors, help keep children safe.[12] Parents said that children with cell phones can let their parents know if they need help, or they can reach emergency resources if their parents are not available. This concern with safety is in keeping with an increased sense of individual responsibility for curtailing risk.

In general, parents in all socioeconomic classes do not make a distinction between safety issues and monitoring issues. That is, parents speak as if safety depends on monitoring—on knowing precisely what it is their children are doing and precisely where they are. And parents link the need to know these details at least in part to new conditions of parenting, to the fact that moms are at work and thus cannot be available in the same way it is imagined they were in earlier times, and to the perception that not only are others less available, but neighbors now have different values and may be less appropriate substitutes. Thus, parents who cannot be home to greet their children after school said that they find cell phones particularly useful for monitoring kids' activities to ensure that they remain safe. Danielle Jones, a single, African American, working-class mother of five children who hails from Philadelphia, explained that while she is at work (as an intake representative in a local social service agency), she calls home repeatedly once she knows the children are out of school:

> [The main advantage of having a cell phone is] being able to contact them immediately. . . . I get off of work at five. . . . I think I might call them about three or four times while I'm at work. And when I come home, if they're out, I call maybe three or four times, to find out where they are: "When [are] you coming home? What [are] you doing? Try to come in." You know, to remind them of curfew, stuff like that.

Another single, African American mother, Larissa Small, a professional middle-class woman with a master's degree in social work, said very much the same thing:

> Everyone has a cell phone. [I got the children one] when . . . I was working at the police department. . . . They would go out with their friends. I wanted to always be able to contact them. Sometimes calling the friends' homes, you can never contact the kids. And then if they walk out the door, I like to know where they are at all times. Just in case if something did occur, they could pick up the phone and if not call me, call 911.

Elite Emergencies

If monitoring (parents keeping track of their children's activities and whereabouts) is conflated with safety across the board, among the more elite parents the notion of safety is frequently expanded to cover a wide spectrum of situations that become *defined* as "emergencies" and therefore are thought to require parental responsiveness. Much as the sounds made audible through a baby monitor might enhance the perception of an infant's vulnerabilities, so might the connection made possible through a cell phone enhance the perception that an older child is in need.[13] Parents who stand at the ready to respond to infant whimpers choose also to stand at the ready to respond to adolescent angst. Technology and parenting styles go hand in hand and mutually reinforce each other. Hence, professional middle-class parents talk about how children can use cell phones to reach a parent if they need help with—or simply want to get out of—a broad range of what children and parents alike consider "difficult" situations.

One white, professional middle-class mother told a story about her daughter being "hit on" by a boy at a party and then sending a text message to her mother (who the daughter seemed to assume would be available at that very moment). When the mother called back, her daughter made it clear that she wanted to be picked up:

> Recently she could text and let me know she wanted me to pick her up because a boy was hitting on her in a way that made her feel very uncomfortable. She texted and said, "call me." So I called, and she [pretended that I was insisting that she come home]. She started to say, "What do you mean I have to leave right now?" And I said, "I get it. I will be right there." So she saved herself from a situation that was very uncomfortable, by first texting.

Another white mother, Beth O'Brien, a psychologist with four children (who described herself and her husband as "overachievers"), taught one of her daughters how to use a "code word" on the telephone to indicate if she needed to be rescued from a party:[14]

> Heather was going to a party the other night where there were going to be older boys there, and these boys had been known to [play the drinking game] beer pong. And it was, "Heather, if you're feeling uncomfortable in any way, here's the code word: use the code word 'mother.'" . . . So if she says, "mom," everything's okay, but if she says, "mother," I know that's code for [getting her]. I said, "You can blame it totally on me. Use those acting skills." She felt like she had a tool in her back pocket if she was in an uncomfortable situation.

Parents also appreciate knowing if a child is released from some event earlier or later than anticipated. Parents also enjoy being able to respond (with "totally immediate service") if a child has forgotten something needed at school. A white, professional middle-class woman living in Pennsylvania noted with enthusiasm that although phones aren't allowed to be on during school hours, if her daughter has forgotten something, she can find a way to contact her mother: "If she has an emergency, she can go to the bathroom [in school] and call me. There's certain things—something she had forgotten, a project or something at home—and she didn't want to go to class without it."

Although all parents perceive cell phones and baby monitors as sound investments to secure safety in the face of children's vulnerabilities, there are class differences in the breadth and immediacy of perceptions of danger: professional middle-class parents are more likely to expand the notion of danger to include imagined crises and routine problems. They may worry about psychological overindulgence, but they readily give way to their children's slightest anxieties. The working-class and middle-class parents, who often live with more present, concrete dangers in their daily environments, impose sharper limits on the definition of a crisis. Indeed, they believe it is necessary for their children to toughen up and deal with the world around them. These differences show up when parents explained why they initially purchased a cell phone: whereas a white, professional middle-class mother said that she got her son a cell phone because he ended up sitting outside a school and waiting for her for two hours when they had crossed signals about the pickup time that day, an African American, working-class mother said she got her daughter a cell phone because that child had been followed from the school into a store by a stranger who was harassing her.[15]

In short, parents from a wide variety of backgrounds mentioned that cell phones promise the advantage of enhanced safety. For professional middle-class parents, however, cell phones take on an additional meaning. Referring to times when their children might *need* a cell phone for reasons of safety, the professional middle-class parents rapidly shift into a language of responsiveness that sounds very much like the language of responsiveness used in conjunction with baby monitors. In turn, this responsiveness emerges from the desire to create close bonds with their children. Overall, the more privileged parents were far more likely than the other parents to speak about intimacy and about the significance of being on call for whatever they defined as "legitimate" needs.

Elite Connection

Parenting out of control comes alive through these practices of connection. One white, professional middle-class mother of three waxed sentimental as she explained, "[The cell phone is] a way for [my daughter] to connect when she needs to, or a way [for me] to connect with her." Another white, professional middle-class mother of three explained that frequent communication secured intimacy with her oldest daughter: "I think it's kept us closer because I can always reach her—not that she always wants to hear from me or I want to hear from her, but she'll call just to leave me a message." Indeed, Marian English, who spoke so articulately about responding to a baby's "needs," finds that cell phones enable a kind of private communication that she believes helps ensure occasions for open and intimate relationships with her teenage children:

> I will call one or the other of them [while in the car], and we will just talk. . . . Just a couple of times this year on the phone I could ask [my daughter] about [things that seemed to have upset her], and because we both have time and there's nobody else around [she will open up]. I think it was a very good move; it keeps us available to each other.

Marian then told a story about how she had sent a text message to her daughter wishing her luck on a final exam and how her daughter was impressed by her mother's ability to text.[16]

Which Comes First?

These examples inevitably raise broader, chicken-egg-style questions. Do the more privileged parents want cell phones for their children because along with their children they have defined so many situations as emergencies, including many that others might *not* define in that way (e.g., a child being hit on at a party, leaving a project at home, or getting out early after a sports practice)? Or does access to a cell phone create the definition of the situation itself as one requiring adult intervention? Do these parents cherish cell phones because they smooth the way to intimate communication? Or do they create intimacy by texting? The same kind of questions, of course, can be asked of baby monitors. Do parents want a baby monitor because they perceive infants as being especially vulnerable? Or does having a baby monitor create that perception itself? This is the standard form of questions about the impact of any new technology.

In response, a technological determinist would argue for the autonomous role of technology in producing and creating new sets of social relations: from that perspective, baby monitors and cell phones (with the help of advertising) *create* the perceptions of dependency that they then resolve. In contrast, a social determinist position essentially reduces technological developments themselves (and often their effects as well) to preexisting sets of social relationships: from that perspective, parents want baby monitors and cell phones because they have come to perceive their children as being in need of close contact and connection. When the questions and answers are phrased in such stark terms, it is apparent that a less definitive approach might be better than a more certain one. And indeed, most commentators (especially those commenting on the new technologies of surveillance) suggest the need for understanding the dynamic interplay of technology and social forces.[17] With respect to baby monitors, for example, we could recall how parents say they start out being "neurotic" and become more so because they can hear every whimper and cry; with respect to cell phones, we might note the complex interaction between a mother's being available to rescue her daughter from a party and her own (and her daughter's) perception that being hit on constitutes a crisis.

Breaking a Link

Although I have linked baby monitors and cell phones, it is time to break that link. After all, cell phones are not baby monitors (cell phones, for example, require the participation of two parties), and teens are not infants (and therefore can resist as well as participate in the use of a monitoring device). Moreover, cell phones appear to provide somewhat greater freedom to children, albeit with increased monitoring and connection through the "electronic tether," and this is true within all socioeconomic groupings.[18]

Anna Benton, a white, professional middle-class mother from northern California, talked without irony about how tethering allowed her children of sixteen and thirteen to have greater autonomy: "It made me slightly more comfortable and made them more independent, because I knew I could stay in touch with them." Similarly, Matty Borden, a white, working-class mother also from California, talked about how she both allows her seventeen-year-old son, Darren, to use public transportation to go to Hollywood *and* requires that he stay in very close touch with her:

> I know Darren feels too supervised. . . . The discussion [with him] is that if he doesn't want me calling him, then he needs to be proactive and call me and check in. . . . I think that it has allowed [my children] to be able to do more things than maybe I would normally allow them to do if I wasn't able to contact them and check in with them. So hopefully that would be a positive on the relationship—like Darren takes trips down to Hollywood: they get on the bus, the train. And I don't know how comfortable I would be letting him do that if he didn't have a phone.

Tethered Independence and Ongoing Negotiation within the Professional Middle Class

Parents from the range of social locations allow tethered independence. But the degree to which the prevailing rules remain firm is different in the accounts of parents such as Anna Benton, with their "1-2-3 maybe," than in the accounts of parents such as Matty Borden who rely on "tell, tell, tell, yell."

Anna Benton, who said that tethering allowed her children to be "more independent," continued her discussion of this issue by describing an occasion when she first encouraged her daughter to attend a party and then, at the last moment, urged her to come home. Using the excuse that she thought her daughter was probably ambivalent (after acknowledging that she was ambivalent herself), she explained how she claimed her own loneliness as a reason why her daughter should not go to the party after all, how "maybe" turned into "no":

> I trust Sadie [who is sixteen], and she's a goody two shoes, and I almost feel like it's good for her to experience different things. . . . Sadie was invited . . . to a party. And she's never really been to a party. And she told me that there would probably be kids smoking pot and drinking. And she wanted to go. . . . And I was really ambivalent about it. And I tried call-

> ing the home, but nobody answered. And she said she could get a ride with this girl. . . . But then she got scared and said, "Mom what if the girl drinks?" And I said, "I will pick you up." But then I sort of encouraged her. . . . I wanted her to go because I wanted her to be exposed, and I wanted her to be comfortable—everyone probably smokes pot and drinks at some point—and not to be freaked out. She was going to go, and then at the last minute—I'm probably a bad mother—I said, "I'm lonely, come home." And she came home. She was ambivalent.

Clearly this was a complex situation for both Anna and her daughter. Two aspects are especially interesting to me: first, in this incident the cell phone became the means whereby Anna could change the rules of the game for Sadie, and second, the intimate bond between parent and child became the basis on which those rules were changed. Having initially thought that she wanted her daughter to get the experience of being at a party where people were drinking and using drugs, Anna ultimately decided that she thought that kind of experience might be too much, too soon. Because of the close bond between them, Anna could use her *own* loneliness as a "legitimate" excuse for changing horses midstream.

Even more commonly, elite parents tell stories of *children* using cell phones to alter and expand the limits parents set. After having read a draft of this chapter, a colleague described having heard precisely this kind of negotiation. On a Sunday afternoon she was in a car with several peers campaigning for Obama, when one of the women received a phone call from her adolescent son. The mother reminded her son that she had planned for the whole family to get together for dinner and that he had agreed to be home no later than 6:00 p.m. so that he could be there for the family meal and still have time to complete the homework he had not yet done over the weekend. By the time the phone call had ended a very tedious ten minutes later, the mother had agreed that her son did not have to join the family for dinner and that he could stay out with his friends, until 8:30 p.m., long past her initial deadline; she also agreed to wake him early the next day so that he could finish his homework in the morning.

Of course, even when parents rely on cell phones for monitoring and negotiating about their children's whereabouts, they are not totally naive. Parents know that their children can be duplicitous.[19] One professional middle-class mother from northern Vermont told a story about some other children who had gone across the border into Canada while staying in touch with their parents. Their parents did not know where they were and assumed that they were where they said they were. This mother generalized that deceit to the possibility that at least one of her own children could, on occasion, have been dishonest with her:

> I think once we had computers and cell phones and things like that, gone was really the ease of knowing what sort of planning was going on between your children and their friends, who was calling, who were they talking to. They're on the cell phone or online, [and] you don't have a clue who they are talking to. And if our children did this, I don't know about it, but it could happen. I don't know. I did hear stories of kids who with their cell phones were able to travel farther from home and do things and keep it hidden from their parents. For example, I have a friend whose daughter went to Montreal. They were underage. Her parents would have told her, no, she couldn't, and what they did—I'm sure this happens a lot—they used cell phones [to say they were somewhere where they weren't]. Probably of the three, if anybody would have done it, it would have been [my middle child, who is now twenty-two]. I don't know that he ever did.

Other parents similarly acknowledge that the cell phone has the drawback of their not knowing to whom their children are talking as they would on a landline; and they say that there is more room for children to have relationships of which the parents are totally unaware.[20] In response, some parents monitor not just whereabouts but phone activity itself, checking over call lists and making sure that they know—and approve of—every name on the list. Paula Brown, a white college administrator and mother of two teens, for example, said this was her approach:

> Text messaging, I'm definitely reading them. She knows I am. Our phone is kind of a community family phone, and so we'll say, "So, Emily, you left this message, and somebody left this message back for you," or even saying, "I don't recognize the name" [or] "Who is Sean? How do you know him? Why would he be calling you?" and talking about text messaging, saying, "Why are they text messaging you at midnight?" I'm talking [to them] about the time, talking about the message.

For the most part parents do not see disadvantages to providing their children with cell phones, but when pressed and asked explicitly about this issue, they do acknowledge that cell phones might undermine their children's emerging autonomy—even as they say they grant somewhat more independence to their children than they might have done if they could not stay in touch. For the professional middle-class parents who already find it difficult to find the appropriate balance between being involved in a child's life and encouraging children to take responsibility for their own actions, the introduction of a technology that allows for ongoing and instantaneous connection becomes the instrument through which that difficulty is enacted, and even intensified. Having decided that rules should be flexible and open to negotiation, professional middle-class parents find their children more than willing to enter the fray. Working-class and middle-class parents talk less about negotiation. Although they too allow their children to use cell phones, they do so more often to check that their children are abiding by the limits they have set.

Working-class and middle-class parents eagerly seek out devices that help them maintain connection, such as baby monitors for infants and cell phones for older children. They view these devices as aids to help them keep their children safe. Working-class and middle-class parents also view the cell phone as a way to monitor teens. A cell phone creates opportunities for random checks: an adolescent might never know when she or he is going to be called and asked to account for her or his actions.

Professional middle-class parents value these devices of connection for many of the same reasons. In addition, the professional middle-class parents value these devices because they allow for close contact between parent and child and immediate responsiveness to a child. The intensely close relationship between professional middle-class parents and their children *underwrites* their attitude toward cell phones and baby monitors: parents want to know immediately if their children need (or simply want) them. The intensely close relationship between professional middle-class parents and their children is also *abetted by* cell phones and baby monitors: parents can stay attuned to infants and respond quickly to whimpers of discontent; parents can send and receive messages that keep them up-to-date with the minutiae of their children's lives. But it is hard to believe that this closeness *requires* either of those two devices: as the foregoing discussion suggests, the underlying motivations for the desire to be close have broader roots than technology alone. Nor does the negotiation about limits that so befuddles the professional middle-class parent depend on the constant contact through cell phone technology, even if cell phones make that negotiation ever more likely to occur.

6 CONSTRAINING PRACTICES

Child Locators

In a televised commercial for Duracell batteries, an attractive, white woman daydreaming in a park becomes aware that her young child is missing. As the advertisement says, this "beautiful day" suddenly "turned into every parent's nightmare." Frantically the mother looks around, only to catch a glimpse of an ominous white van driving away. She sees no sign of her son. Ever more distressed, she searches in her pocketbook to find her "child locator." Once she has pressed the appropriate button, she is guided toward her child, who, it turns out, is simply walking calmly with his red balloon, hidden from view for a moment by a small rise in the landscape. The joyful reunion between mother and child is secured through a new technology brought to her by a company called BrickHouse and made reliable by Duracell.[1]

The child locator, an electronic device that can be attached to a child's wrist, pinned to clothing, or tied to a shoelace is, on the face of it, an unobtrusive way to keep children from wandering. Interestingly, perhaps because my research assistants and I discussed these devices with parents before widespread distribution of the Duracell advertisement, those with whom we spoke had very strong, mostly negative reactions to this particular device. No parent had ever used such a device, and fewer than half of all parents said that they might or would have used one if it had been available when they had young children. Interestingly, as well, there were fairly sharp class differences in the responses. Over 80 percent of all professional middle-class parents said that they would not have used such a device had it been available when they had young children; many fewer working-class and middle-class parents gave this negative response.[2]

No Child Locator for the Elite

Opposition to a child locator among the professional middle class drew on two distinct themes, both of which are in some way linked to the commitment to parenting out of control. Elite parents are noticeably affronted by the notion that they would not always be aware of what their children are doing and what they need; because they make responsiveness and availability key components of their parenting style, they are sensitive to the slightest hint that they might not always be attentive. They are equally bothered by the notion that control itself should rest on external constraint rather than parental guidance toward appropriate behavior. Theirs is a style that requires that parents be always ready to make assessments about children's capabilities, wants, and needs.

BEING AFFRONTED

In discussions about a child locator, some of the professional middle-class parents were offended by the mere notion that they would ever use this device, seeing in it something that they feel undermines their own understanding of what it means to be a competent parent. For example, Carol Clark, a white woman from Louisville, Kentucky, who was not familiar with the device before we described it for her, said she would "probably not" use it with the youngest of her four children (aged two). When asked to explain why not, she said, "I feel that when we're out in public, we're all keeping an eye on her and her whereabouts." Asked to reflect on a situation with large crowds—such as the Kentucky Derby—and whether she might use it then, Carol insisted that she feels "comfortable enough" in her family's ability to keep track of their child and that she would thus have no need for a mechanical device. Elizabeth Blake, a mother of two from California, similarly seemed almost insulted by the implication that she might need technology to help her keep track of her children, and she proclaimed her conviction that she knows how to keep a close eye on them: "See, when they were that little I was there. . . . If they were out in the yard, I was out with them. . . . Kids are not supposed to be left unattended. That's the bottom line."

A closely related set of responses came from professional middle-class parents who insisted that a device of this sort not only appears to disparage their competence as parents but also is an entirely inappropriate substitute for doing what they defined as being their job. In turn, they defined their job as taking responsibility for, and paying close attention to, their children. One mother insisted, "It's my job as a parent to watch over my child." She sighed, and then continued, ironically using technological language to express how totally she discounts this new piece of technology: "It would just not be on my radar screen as a device." Like the woman just quoted, Paula Brown spoke about what she believes to be the nature of good parenting and contrasted that definition with the use of an electronic device: "It's just relying on technology when it's really your job to keep track of them. Obviously errors happen. Mishappens. 'What if . . . ?' But I just can't imagine ever thinking that was for us something we'd have to default to—a beep, versus knowing where my kid really is." And Ellen Barnes, another married, professional middle-class mother, used almost precisely the same language to explain that she thinks parents should look after their children themselves, rather than rely on a mechanical aid:

ELLEN: No, I wouldn't use it. I would hope you wouldn't be in a situation where you'd be that worried.

INTERVIEWER: Are there any circumstance you would?

ELLEN: No. I wouldn't want to be in that situation.

INTERVIEWER: Why wouldn't you even consider it?

ELLEN: I don't know, it just seems too . . . I mean if you're going to be a parent, be a parent. You don't need a device; you should be watching them anyway. I don't know, it just seems odd. That would be like, "Beep! Beep! Where the hell are you, Parent?" You know what I mean? If you need a crutch like that, you would wonder what the deal is.

PARENTAL CONTROL VERSUS EXTERNAL CONSTRAINT

Significantly, professional middle-class parents also located their opposition to child locator devices in their commitment to alternative methods of control. They thereby demonstrated that a commitment to psychological and moral training directed by the parents—even with all its ambiguities—is preferable to physical constraint and clear limits. Thus, in addition to holding hands with toddlers, elite parents suggested communicating directly with children so that they learn not to wander off. A mother of two teenagers was particularly appalled by the technological alternative: "Are they attached to the parent like a dog on a leash? I never heard of them. . . . I never would do that. I don't think it's inhumane: it doesn't hurt them. But I don't know why you couldn't communicate and hold their hand if you needed to keep them near you."

As professional middle-class parents discussed the alternative approach of what one father called "working with" his child, it was clear that they believe in starting control early; they also discount the notion that changing people might ultimately be more "controlling" than changing the situation itself. The same parents who worry about pushing their children too hard and too early also believe that children can act in an adult manner when they are very young. For example, consider the response given by Erica Harper, a white mother who wants her child to learn impulse control from an early age:

> I actually have heard of those [child locator devices], and I would never, ever consider using one of those, even for Nick, who tended to be very impulsive. . . . I just sort of feel like there are other ways to manage kids. [The locator] just seems like a nursing home. [It is] unnecessary, and *maybe [it] wouldn't help the child to be able to internalize what's been learned, safety behaviors, or listening.* It feels unnatural to me as a parent to do something like that. (Emphasis added)

Like other parents in her peer group, Erica commits herself to finding ways to "manage" her children while eschewing simple solutions. She also hopes that she can change her children and help them internalize lessons ("what's been learned") so that ultimately she will be able to trust them to do the right thing.

"It Seems Like That Might Be a Pretty Nice Thing": Child Locators and the Working and Middle Classes

To be sure, the working-class and middle-class parents are also not entirely accepting of child locators. Fewer than half the parents in these two groups thought that they would rely on this device were it available to them (and when they objected, they often used language similar to that of the professional middle-class parents). But there were several undercurrents in the discussions with these less privileged parents that are worth noting.

First, as working-class and middle-class parents talked about why they *might* use such a device, they indicated that they are sensible gardeners of children with predestined personalities. Yvonne Wood, a working-class, African American mother of two who is employed by UPS, said that she has one daughter, Samantha, whose "mind was like somewhere else all the time." Rather than advocating "working with" Samantha or insisting on internalization of safety behaviors, Yvonne suggested a locator would have been an appropriate—and useful—device. Similarly, Danielle Jones, another working-class, African American woman, spoke of one of her children, "who wanders." She reported, "If I knew where I could get [a child locator], yes, I could get one. Yes, I would get one and put it on his wrist, you know, when we go out shopping, and, you know, [then] he can't get lost." In this kind of talk, these parents suggest a greater willingness to accept their children—with all their foibles and difficulties—as they are and then to find solutions that work for both parent and child without pushing the child to engage in sophisticated conversation.

Second, the working-class and middle-class parents spoke about dangers as being closer at hand. Tom Audet, the white college professor in Berkeley, explained that he would not need a child locator because where he lives "it's not really very conducive for them to get out of the house and into places where they could get into trouble." In contrast, Christopher Rodriguez, a Hispanic, working-class father who lives on Staten Island, New York, thinks child snatching "could happen anywhere."

Finally, and perhaps most significantly, the working-class and middle-class parents do not view the child locator as something that undercuts their competence or takes away from the importance of the job of being a parent. Instead, they view it quite simply, as something that would make their lives easier. As one working-class father said, "It seems like that might be a pretty nice thing."

All the interviewed parents appear to have an interest in evaluating technological solutions to perceived problems, and none immediately accepts any and all technologies. Whatever a device's ultimate effects might have been (and parents might not know what those were when they purchased it), parents do not believe that devices such as a baby monitor or cell phone would fundamentally alter the parent-child relationship as they want it to exist. Indeed, they believe those devices could enhance that relationship by ensuring greater attentiveness to safety concerns. Especially among the professional middle class, some parents believe that these devices would enhance that relationship in a different way also, by enabling greater attentiveness to children's needs and desires while keeping them close to their children. The same is not true of child locators, as they are evaluated through the lens of the appropriate relationship between a parent and a child—even though they, too, might offer protection. For the professional middle-class parents, this "appropriate" relationship builds on ongoing parental attentiveness (which they resist making easier, as if that would make them appear negligent or unwilling to devote themselves wholeheartedly to their children) and a deep conviction that children can be "modified" to conform to parental expectations. For more of the working-class and middle-class parents, that appropriate relationship can be made less burdensome both by relying on technological assistance and by finding solutions that work with, rather than subvert or alter, a child's intrinsic nature.

V-Chips and Software Filters

The professional middle-class parents would have been the first to nudge me when Katie Couric reported on the RAND Corporation's finding that watching sexually explicit television programs is linked to teenage pregnancy.[3] But these same parents are less likely than their less privileged peers to activate the V-chip on the television.[4] They also differ in their use of filtering or blocking software on the computer. Nationwide, about a third of all parents do use this kind of software (with an additional 5 percent having done so previously but having discontinued its use within the past year).[5] But as the sociologists Rong Wang, Suzanne Bianchi, and Sara Raley report, parents with *lower* levels of education are more likely to rely on filters than are those who are more highly educated.[6] The same was true in the present study: whereas three-quarters of the working-class and middle-class parents were interested in a software filter on a computer in the home, only slightly more than half the professional middle-class parents expressed similar interest.[7] These findings do not mean that the professional middle-class parents are unwilling to impose controls on the use their children make of computers. Nor do they indicate that parents are uninterested in monitoring what their children watch on television. To the contrary: they eagerly embrace hovering over and directing their children as they surf the Internet or watch television. However, as with a child locator, these highly educated parents are far more willing than are those with fewer educational accomplishments to substitute their own control for the control created through technology.

"I'd Rather Do It Myself": The Perspective of the Professional Middle Class toward Controlling Media Exposure

The professional middle-class parents were less likely to be affronted by the mere notion that devices that constrain access to the media could substitute for parental control or undermine parental competence than they were when confronted with the idea of a child locator. However, as they talked about how they decide what their children may watch on television or what movies their kids may go to, it was clear that analogous concerns arise. Here, too, parents focus on internalized restraint rather than external control. Moreover, they are not just interested in the content of the programs available to their children; they also see it as their job to monitor and assess how their children interpret or comprehend what they see. And professional middle-class parents want to make decisions about what is appropriate by themselves rather than relying on a potentially unreliable source such as government ratings.

All these inclinations were apparent in the discussion with Erica Harper, the professional middle-class mother of three children who likened a child locator to the kind of restraint used in nursing homes. When she was asked how much her children watch television and whether she sets limits on hours and programs, Erica became defensive: "I'm really not a Nazi mom." She then went on to explain the elaborate arrangements she has put in place to supervise the media to which her children are exposed. Erica's three children range in age from nine to sixteen. Erica said that she tries to have different rules for each of her children depending on their level of maturity, illustrating well the efforts she makes to individualize the care she provides for her children. Moreover, she said that she does not simply restrict television viewing with a V-chip or rely on industry ratings to make those decisions for her. If she has concerns, she draws on the subtly coercive language of "make a different choice" to turn their attention elsewhere.[8] She might also stay with her children to watch programs with which she is unfamiliar:

> We have limits on TV and the shows they watch. I watch along with them if I have any questions about a show or a movie or a DVD that they've selected. And I definitely have criteria for the nine-year-old that's different for the thirteen-year-old, that's different for Nate [who is sixteen]. . . . For Nate . . . I'm watching [out for] sex and violence. . . . I always ask him to

> tell me what movie it is. Rose [at thirteen] is told to make a different choice [if it is an R-rated movie]. I think that any sort of adult content, sex, or violence or foul language is just . . . not appropriate for Caitlin [the nine-year-old]

Erica relies on a similar approach to the movies her children view in public settings; she also requires that they discuss the content of movies (and presumably television programs) to help them understand what it is they have seen:

> I also like going out to movies. I check to see what the content of those movies are, and we have conversations about is that appropriate. . . . I do remember sitting and watching a movie with Rose. [It was a] cheerleading movie, . . . and we had some conversation about behavior and some of the words and some of the characters that were in there. We try to do that. . . . I will comment [to Nate] if there's a particularly violent movie. . . . We'll have some conversation. I ask him to talk with me afterwards when he's seen R-rated movies.

Like Erica, Alice Osborne works in a nonteaching, professional position within a public school system. Also like Erica, Alice acknowledges that she has loosened the controls as her sons (aged twelve and fifteen) have gotten older. But she also suggested that, again like Erica, she opts to watch with her children when she can: this practice means that, on occasion, her older son has to forgo something he might have wanted to see, if he doesn't want to view it with his mother by his side. Alice unabashedly admitted that she knows that through watching with her children she is "projecting [her] values on them," a practice to which her children offer strenuous objections. Alice also indicated that the ensuing discussions are prompted as much by *her* being upset as by her children's reactions and that she holds dear what she believes are "normal" values about human relationships:

> Television [*she sighs*]. That's gotten harder as they've gotten older because I can't supervise the television. I don't have blocks, but they know. There were a couple of shows I found out they were watching I wasn't comfortable [with]—or it was okay for Jared [who is fifteen] but not David [who

> is twelve], and if they were watching TV together [the younger would see something inappropriate]. It's a big issue in my house. I'll watch it with them [to decide if it is appropriate]. I might tell Jared he can do it with his friends [but not with his brother]. For instance, Jared likes R movies. My kids think I'm ridiculous that I won't let them go to R movies—like if it's really violent or really graphic, women, drugs. Recently I took Jared to an R movie, and we saw it together. . . . And actually when we got into the theater Jared said [about the movie we originally intended to see], "This is a movie I don't think I could watch with you. I'll be really embarrassed" [because of the] sexual innuendo. . . . So we made the choice to go to a different movie, an R movie. And yeah, there were times [when he said], "I wish you weren't here," [when there is] sexual stuff. But we talked about it.

Even if making decisions is, as Alice said, harder than it was when her children were younger, Alice is unwilling to trust anyone but herself to determine what is—and what is not—appropriate content for her children. And even though making these determinations brings her into conflict with her children, Alice is unwilling to remove herself from the situation.

"Just Put It in a Public Place": The Professional Middle-Class Approach to Computer Use

As noted earlier, the professional middle-class parents are also unlikely to have software filtering devices on their computers. For the most part, as with the television, the absence of such a device does not mean the absence of parental control.[9] Parents described a variety of techniques for keeping tabs on their children's computer use: they put computers in open areas of the house where they can walk by at any moment; they make sure to stop into a child's room unannounced to observe what is going on; they check web browser histories on a regular basis; they make their way to a child's Facebook or MySpace page; and they require their children to give them their passwords.[10]

In short, the professional middle-class parents *are* vigilant, but the vigilance—as with television and movies—is *personal* and not technological. And, as with the control of television and movies, the practices in which they engage are time-consuming and require being constantly alert and ever aware of what is going on. They are also extremely intrusive practices because they do not allow a child freedom to roam within clearly stated and predetermined constraints. These practices rely on ongoing monitoring and periodic negotiation about just where to draw the lines.

These are also arbitrary practices. If one parent believes that it is acceptable for his son to "take a look at some [pornography] on occasion, in the realm of curiosity," as Tom Audet does, other parents might take a very different position. And even Tom, a white college professor who finds an occasional foray into pornography acceptable, is quite certain that he would feel differently if what he saw were what he defines as beyond the bounds of normal curiosity: "There's always some concern about pornography. I don't think either of the children is concerned about that, even the boy. I mean, probably everybody takes a look at some things on occasion, in the realm of curiosity, but there's no obsession." From the perspective of children, parental controls, like that mentioned by Tom, require subtle understanding of what their parents might find "reasonable."[11]

A white, professional middle-class mother explained why her family no longer relies on the preestablished parental controls that AOL provides:

> For a long time we had AOL, and we had some of the parental controls, different levels—the preteen or whatever—but we ultimately got rid of that. Part of the issue was . . . the kids couldn't do certain research. . . . You can't, for example, research breast disease because you couldn't use the word *breast*. . . . The kids [were constantly saying], "I can't do this." . . . At some point we said, "Forget this." Then it just became a matter of either being aware of what they were doing and *them knowing what our limits were. Just them knowing what we thought was acceptable and not acceptable and us being very reasonable*. . . . I guess it's on every computer: you can go in and [check the history]. I don't [make a conscious effort on a daily basis], but I do on occasion. . . . At this point I feel like we have set the limits, [and] we're certainly visible and around. (Emphasis added)

All the themes discussed by professional middle-class parents—the time-consuming nature of direct parental control, the hope of internalization, the safety net of oversight, the unpredictability, and the arbitrariness—are present in this woman's account.

A Distinction between Television and Computers

Among the professional middle-class parents, some of the reasons for not having a block on the television and not having a filter on the computer were the same. But there was one key difference. Television constitutes a big part of what these privileged parents don't like, and they see no reason to allow the programming they find offensive. On the other hand, although the professional middle-class parents are also anxious about what happens on the Internet, they spoke about the importance of having their children learn by themselves what computers have to offer and to indulge their own curiosity and imagination. They discussed the dangers and rules (i.e., don't correspond with people you don't know, and don't give out personal information), but within these rules (which can shift without notice) they encourage exploration. Kevin Hansen, a white doctor in St. Louis, in describing his seventeen-year-old twins and twenty-year-old college student said, "I guess I sort of feel that they need to learn for themselves what they should do with computers. I don't want to censor what they should and shouldn't look at." Mark Ortiz, a Hispanic college professor and the father of four, said the following about the possibility that his children would be exposed to pornography on the Internet:

> I think maybe it's part of how I see the education of my kids—in this kind of situation I wouldn't be so much proactive as reactive. . . . I'm curious to see the reaction of the kids if they stumbled on something. Would they talk about it? Rather than pretending it's not there, would they talk to me about it? And if they did, I think that's a better learning opportunity. . . . I'm willing to take that risk.

Pornography is a risk this parent is willing to take if it leads to insight into his children and encourages communication between parent and child.

Overt Constraint: The Working and Middle Classes

Working-class and middle-class parents choose a different style of supervision for both the television and the Internet. Technological solutions are more attractive to these parents. Many limit television in a straightforward manner by not subscribing to channels with programs they find distasteful. As one white, working-class mother of two said, "I've never forbidden certain programs [because] we don't get the channels that those programs will be on." Cost is clearly a factor here: cable is expensive. These parents also activate the V-chip on the television in order to prevent their children from watching specific programs. As a white, middle-class mother of two said, "[There's no] 'R.' We have the blocks on all those channels if there's an R movie. So they watch PG or PG-13, which they can get anywhere." In addition, working-class and middle-class parents purchase software to control computer use. And some parents frankly admitted that they *need* these varied technologies because they can't otherwise make certain that their children are staying within the limits they have drawn. Indeed, the working-class and middle-class parents acknowledged that their work schedules and other obligations prevent them from ensuring that their children are not watching programs or going places on the Internet of which they wouldn't approve. Danielle Jones, an African American mother of three, explained:

> I had to call in and put in a code to block out certain channels. . . . I had a problem with the kids watching things. . . . And I'm not home at all times. Even when I wasn't working, and I was home, if I ran to the store, they would cheat on the TV and watch that stuff. So I did do a code with [the cable company]. We're working on [a filter for the computer]. That's what I'm going to get when I get the other computers up and running.

But the approach of getting a block on the television or on the computer goes beyond practicality to the broader issues of parenting that are at stake here and that are the subject of this book as a whole. The working-class and middle-class parents trust the technology more than they trust their children (and perhaps more than they trust themselves), and they also want to contain curiosity and nip problematic behavior in the bud in order to keep their children safe. In addition, they see advantages in having their children negotiate the world without constant parental intervention even as they are protected by arbitrary limits. In their minds, freedom from parental intervention is as meaningful as other earned freedoms. It thus constitutes a real benefit to children as well as to parents. Danielle Jones, who said she is working on getting a filter for the computer, added that one of the reasons is because she wants her children "to be able to use the computers without . . . being over their shoulder all the time." Annemarie Fernandez, a Hispanic mother of three from Texas, similarly spoke about how the AOL filter could give her, as a parent, peace of mind while giving her daughter more freedom and autonomy:

> I'm hoping that [the AOL filter] will prevent her from getting curious and going to sites where she shouldn't be. . . . I started [using those] when I bought the computer, five years ago. [It gives me] peace of mind—as much as can be had with the computer. There's always some way around it, [but I like] just feeling at least there is that one wall up there. [And] *it gives her more freedom because I'm not constantly questioning her.* (Emphasis added)

From the working-class and middle-class point of view, devices such as filters are advantageous to parents who no longer have to make subtle distinctions about what is or is not too much of something or worry about what happens when they are not at home. A professional middle-class father such as Tom Audet deliberates about whether looking at pornography constitutes an "obsession" before he acts. In contrast, Maria Ascoli, a woman who sometimes acts more like the professional middle-class parents, was securely "middle class" in her response to pornography. She explained that, "like every other boy, we had caught Gary looking at pornography on the Internet [in] seventh grade." She laughed easily when she recalled the conversation with her son, indicating how comfortable she was with a straightforward resolution: "I just said, I had caught him. . . . I just told him as a parent I can't have him looking at all this stuff on the Internet. When he grows up if this is what he wants to do, [he can do it], but he can't do it here. I'd be remiss. So we have some software."

In contrast to the professional middle-class parents, then, the middle-class and working-class parents avoid unpredictability in their child-rearing style: certain things are *always* off-limits. The latter group of parents also save themselves from the burden of having to know precisely what it is their children are doing at all times: the blocks and filters free them to turn their attention elsewhere. The parents also free their children to wander within defined limits rather than controlling their every move.

When it comes to employing devices that prevent wandering through the creation of enclosures, significant class differences emerge. In general, middle- and working-class parents more readily adopt these modes of discipline.

They believe that a child locator could make life simpler and that filtering and blocking devices free both themselves and their children. They are comfortable with external constraints.

Professional middle-class parents reject such devices because they say it is *their job as parents* to maintain control over their children and because they believe that their children can learn at a relatively early age to internalize parental values. The rejection of filters on computers and televisions is especially interesting given that these professional middle-class parents, as shown in chapter 2, are vitally concerned about their children's exposure to images of both sex and violence. However, the parents suggest that they view mechanical devices as being insufficiently fine-tuned and insufficiently responsive to their ongoing assessments of what it is each of their children can and should be able to do. They not only see it as their responsibility to maintain control, but they much prefer to do so *in person*; "being there" gives them the opportunity to interact with their children about just what it is they are seeing and then to guide them to "appropriate" responses. They thus define the job of parenting in a particular way that demands engagement of themselves. No playpen for the professional middle-class parent. Rather, they opt for ongoing, intensive monitoring. As parents, they can never be off duty. Indeed, the "second shift" expands to fill ever more time and ever more of one's attention.[12]

7 WHAT THEY'RE HIDING

Spying and Surveillance

The winter before I spoke with her, Beth O'Brien, a PhD psychologist who runs marathons and worries about her children having fun, had become increasingly concerned about the behavior of one of her four children. She explained that fifteen-year-old Melissa's problems had gone from bad to worse. Not only was Melissa not sleeping, but "at one point she actually got out of her bed at two in the morning" and went out. Naturally Beth was consumed with worry. Believing that she simply had "to find out what [was] going on with this kid," Beth broke down and bought—and installed—a piece of software that would allow her to read everything her daughter wrote on the computer. After several days of "monitoring her text with her friends," Beth discovered that Melissa "was stressed about applying to private school." Armed with this knowledge, Beth was able to intensify the help she gave to her daughter as she navigated the application process; she was also better prepared to reassure her daughter that her parents were happy to see her remain in the local public school if that is what she would prefer. As we talked at the large oak table in her spacious kitchen and watched the leaves swirl around outside, Beth explained that she believes she made a wise choice when she decided to buy a spyware program. Learning about her daughter's concerns, she said, "made us aware of how to manage her differently, and I feel like for that purpose it was so helpful."[1] Beth also explained that her action of installing spyware on the computer had been an anomaly and that usually she has no need to resort to technology to find out about her children's concerns. As Beth told me (without any awareness of the intrinsic contradiction), her children usually show her "what they're hiding." But Beth was quick to add that she has not tossed the spyware into the garbage compactor even though it is no longer installed on any of the three computers in her house: "I would not hesitate to use it again if I were really worried and I couldn't figure it out [through] the regular route."

Beth's story represents well what the makers of similar spyware programs wish parents to do. Advertisements for programs with names like NetNanny, Cybersitter, SafeEyes, and IamBigBrother promise stealth access to everything a child has written on a computer. For example, an advertisement for IamBigBrother says,

> When using IamBigBrother, you'll know exactly who your kids chatted with last night and be able to read the full conversation! Our software runs in stealth mode where it is not detected by the user of the computer. It captures everything from chats and instant messages to email, web sites and much more. . . . Not only do you see what your child types online but what is said back as well. It monitors both incoming and outgoing activity—no other program offers this feature! . . . IamBigBrother runs in total secrecy, and is very hard to find. . . . Do your kids use Yahoo for email? We monitor it! . . . Additionally, the user cannot get around IamBigBrother by clearing cache or history—it gets everything as it happens . . . including passwords! See a complete list of all web sites visited with the web page URL, title and time visited. . . . Another useful feature is to let IamBigBrother capture the screen when certain keywords are typed. If any of the words you set up are typed, IamBigBrother will capture the whole screen and save it for later viewing by the parent.[2]

Beth's story also represents what I assumed would be the norm among professional middle-class women like herself: that concerns about the safety and well-being of their adolescent children would lead them to engage in practices of concealed surveillance and that these parents would welcome with open arms such new devices as the keystroke monitoring system that Beth used, home drug testing kits, and GPS tracking systems for adolescent drivers.

But Beth's story actually represents a relatively unique and isolated case among the parents I interviewed. Only six other parents had used a keystroke monitoring system (and no other professional middle-class parent had done so), four parents (one of them professional middle class) had relied on home drug testing, and none had installed a GPS tracking system in a car.[3] Moreover, most of the elite parents suggested that they were quite horrified by the notion that they would rely on any such mechanisms for engaging in the surveillance of their adolescent children. The middle- and working-class parents, however, showed genuine interest far more often. If they hadn't yet heard of these mechanisms, once informed, they wondered if they could afford to purchase them.

To understand these different responses, we need to explore the ways in which surveillance technology intersects with, and is imagined as being relevant to, different sets of relationships between parents and children. As we explore these issues, we can see quite vividly how parenting with limits and parenting out of control are enacted on a daily basis.

An Interest in Spying among Working-Class and Middle-Class Parents

By and large, working-class and middle-class parents do not reject out of hand the possibility of using technological devices to spy on their children. Many of these parents say something that sounds like this: "Yes, indeed, there might be conditions under which I would want to use something like that device, and if it were affordable, I would definitely buy it." At the same time, many of these parents say they would hesitate to rely on this kind of stealth surveillance because they respect the privacy of their children. In fact, one of the most adamant negative responses to the possibility of spying came from Anita Mayer, a middle-class, white mother of four children (ranging in age from fourteen to twenty-four) who lives in rural Texas. When asked about using a keystroke reading program, she blurted out,

> My God, I'm not the KGB. This is not communist China. You can have private conversations. If my child were a drug addict or an addict of some stripe that was unbearable, maybe I would. Desperate people will do desperate things. But in the ordinary course of events I cannot imagine using it. I believe in privacy. People have private lives. 'Cause people have private lives, unless people have problems, I as their mother shouldn't be prying into their private lives.

But even Anita, like so many others, put in qualifications that indicated a slippery slope easily traversed from protecting privacy to violating it. If her child were "a drug addict or an addict of some stripe that was unbearable," Anita would use a home drug test; she believes people who "have problems" need not be granted privacy.

Surveillance to Ensure Safety

As with issues concerning devices of connection and constraint, safety concerns are paramount when working- and middle-class parents consider adopting technological aids for surveillance. Parents say that if they have reason to believe that a child is in some kind of danger, they will turn to some piece of technology to obtain the information necessary to protect that child. Concerns about threats from outside are common; concerns about shifts in a child's behavior are even more common.

Parents appear to know well the signs and portents that might indicate drug use or drinking among their children.[4] They learn these by talking with other parents, venturing onto relevant websites, and reading handouts they receive from their children's schools. Parents readily acknowledge that if they were to see changes in their children's behavior, they would institute drug testing, in spite of what initially appears to be opposition to engaging in that practice. As one Hispanic, working-class mother of three children said of her daughter, "She's not given me any reason to believe she's doing drugs." "But," she continued, "if her behavior were to change, out of the ordinary, erratic, all the signs whatever, if things started adding up, I would definitely drug test." A middle-class, African American mother of four was similarly inclined to consider the possibility of testing with one of her sons: "I can't say no, never. . . . If [there were reason], I would definitely use [a home drug test]. If he comes in smelling like marijuana or his behavior's different, I would definitely use it."

The same kinds of indicators function as signals for parents to consider other surveillance technologies, especially if they believe the normal routes of communication have broken down. The Hispanic, working-class mother of three who would use a home drug testing kit if she saw "any reason to believe" one of her children was using drugs would also use a keystroke monitoring device "if the circumstances called for it." A perhaps overly cautious mother, she included among suspicious circumstances her daughter's going to the mall too often or always talking about a certain boy. A middle-class, white mother of two children said she thinks that keystroke monitoring would be "invasive" and that she "wouldn't want anyone doing that" with her children. At the same time, however, this mother said if she thought her daughter "was into drugs or something or she was real depressed or didn't talk to [her] or something," she wouldn't hesitate to snoop. A white, working-class mother of three said she thinks there might be occasions when she would want to reconsider her initial negative decision about a GPS tracking device:

> I think [the GPS tracking system is] probably a great tool. I haven't felt the need to use it. . . . At this point I'm going to give them the benefit of the doubt. [But I would use it] if they were showing some behavior that would lead me to believe that they were doing something harmful to themselves or going somewhere where they weren't supposed to be.

Some working-class and middle-class parents were actually enthusiastic about the possibility of using these surveillance devices even if they haven't yet seen signs indicating trouble. In Philadelphia, Danielle Jones, an African American, working-class mother of five, simply stated that she might be interested in looking over her child's writings on the computer to check for the possibility of problematic behavior:

> DANIELLE: You know, if like the theory behind that is to find out who's doing what, and you can address those issues with that particular thing, I would use [the keystroke reading device].
>
> INTERVIEWER: What kind of stuff would you be looking for?
>
> DANIELLE: The drugs, the chatting, porn, just anything that I would feel is inappropriate.

Darlene Walker, an African American, working-class mother of two children, said that she would "definitely" use a GPS tracking device when her daughter begins to drive. As was the case with Danielle Jones and Annemarie Fernandez, who was discussed in the previous chapter, Darlene expressed her belief that clear parental restrictions can actually free a child. And Darlene sees no more contradiction in the idea of tethered independence than do parents who talk about cell phones as providing for both autonomy and parental supervision:

> Oh yeah, I'm definitely going to use that [car tracker], just to keep track of where she's at, and so if something happens, I can track her. So I can give her a little independence, and while she's still in those teenage years let her

> go out there and see those things while I still have control. . . . I just want to keep track of her at all times.

Some parents remember that during their own teen years they concealed information from their parents or even lied outright to them; these memories motivate them to go beyond a respect for privacy to straightforward surveillance. A Hispanic, working-class mother of three children was explicit about her enthusiasm for the GPS tracking system: "That's great. . . . I'm all for [the GPS system]. . . . *I was a kid, I know what happens*. If I feel like they can't account for where they've been, [I'll use it]" (emphasis added). A white, working-class mother of three noted frankly that such a system would be appropriate because, as a general rule, teens are not to be trusted:

> I didn't know you could [install a system to track driving]. I'm going to have to look into this. I wasn't familiar with that. . . . I trust [my daughter]. She's not a stupid girl. I guess she knows right from wrong. *I trust her, but you know what kids are. Kids are kids. You can't just give the message that you're trusting them. You just have to watch them at all times*. . . . She lied to me once, and she was punished for it. and I don't believe she'd do it again, but you never know. I don't trust anybody one hundred percent. I don't think my daughter just yet [needs it], but who knows. (Emphasis added)

Parents like these do not want their children to engage in the risky behavior they did when they were young. Nor do they want to be as oblivious as they remember their own parents having been. A heightened sense of danger combines with a parental belief that responsibility for children's well-being falls on their shoulders alone. In response, parents want all the help they can get to keep their children safe.

And some of these parents have very good reason to worry. When Danielle Jones considers the possible conditions that might motivate her to track her children, she is acutely aware that her surveillance is preferable to that of the criminal justice system:

> They have their cell phones, [so] I don't think that I would have to track them like that. . . . If I felt that they were doing some really mischievous behavior, on the street, or involved with people who are doing the wrong

> things, you know, drug dealers, trying to run a scam, yeah, I probably would try to use [the GPS tracking system] then [to] see where they're going and who they're going with so I can try to put a stop to it and try to get them help before the law gets involved.

As the mother of African American children, Danielle knows she must be especially vigilant.[5]

"Why Would I Want to Do a Thing Like That?" A Professional Middle-Class Approach

In contrast to Beth O'Brien, whose story opened this chapter, most professional middle-class parents assert disinterest in the three devices that allow access to information that children do not make available themselves. A few of the more elite parents said that the reason for their reluctance lies in their commitment to a child's "right to privacy." As one white attorney said, "That type of device, to me, is a little bit invasive, going into their privacy." But even more commonly, these privileged parents offered three other reasons for opposition to engaging in forms of surveillance that rely on technology. First, the parents insisted that their children are good kids who do what is expected of them. Second, they insisted that mechanical surveillance is unnecessary; they backed up this assertion with evidence that their children communicate sufficiently and that they, as involved and invested parents, would know if there were a problem. And finally (and most significantly), they insisted that they would not engage in this kind of surveillance because they trust their children. Within this framework, spying has to be adamantly denied—even, and perhaps especially, to oneself.

Drugs and Privilege

Before looking more closely at these three responses, I want to make a particular note about how the distinctive issue of drug testing has a different resonance among professional middle-class parents than among those with less privilege.[6] Several points are relevant. First, by virtue of their cultural, social, and economic capital not only do professional middle-class parents have access to counselors and treatment centers when drug or drinking issues emerge, but they believe that they can rely on these private sources to test for drugs or drinking without incurring any legal repercussions.[7] When asked about this issue, some of the more privileged parents suggested that a referral to a family physician would be their preference over home drug testing. A white mother of two said that if she "felt [her] kids were using [drugs] and they were denying it, [she] would take them to [her] family physician and have a drug test." A Hispanic man, a college professor and father of four children, also said that he would not do drug testing at home because he could "see other tools [he] could use." He named both counseling and the pediatrician as options.

Professional middle-class parents view these outsiders—the doctor, the counselor—as resources who will help them keep the results of tests secret and away from formal agencies of social control. Thus, when they say that they do not want home drug testing to intrude in the relationship between themselves and their children, they do so with a unique consciousness about the available alternatives. These alternatives allow room to remain, as one woman implied, the "good cop": "[I would want to] take myself out of the equation but force [the drug testing] to happen. I would create the bad cop somewhere else."

In addition, a number of professional middle-class parents are casual, if not laissez-faire, in their attitude toward drug use.[8] A variety of reasons might stand behind this position: the professional middle-class parents have outlets for getting help (as just noted); they also know that the police are more likely to target lower-class youths (and people of color) than they are middle-class youth (and people who are white). Moreover, because drug use was common among the older generation of parents (and for some was the basis on which they challenged their own parents), they are open to acknowledging familiarity with illegal drugs. Some convey this familiarity—and their more permissive attitude—to their adolescent children.

Kristen Garner, a white, widowed mother of two children who lives in suburban Connecticut, said that she hopes for her children that "if they decide to try some sort of drug, . . . it's only marijuana" and then added that she also hopes "that they don't like it." And Jenna Hall, another white mother of two from across the country in Berkeley, openly acknowledged a bias toward drug use over drinking and admitted her own enjoyment of drugs (at least during her teen years):

> My husband drinks, and I really don't. And I think I've made it pretty clear to them [that] people don't really do great things when they're drunk. It's usually a bad situation. . . . And as far as drugs, you know, I think they've had stuff in school, and I kind of let it slip by. But if they were going to do something, I would kind of rather have them smoke pot than drink. Personal view. I know they'll try things, and it's just part of growing up. But, I mean, there's drugs and there's drugs. I don't want them doing heroin or anything, but I want them to have fun. That's kind of how I was. . . . They'll need to figure that out. I just hope that they use good judgment when the opportunities present themselves.

Jenna puts a higher premium on having fun than she does on abiding by the law: she believes that smoking pot is simply part of growing up. But Jenna has rules, even if they are unstated. She also has unstated expectations about her children's character. Just as Tom Audet said that pornography was okay if it didn't become an obsession, Jenna allows some drugs (marijuana) and not others (heroin). The trick for her children may be to figure out which revelations will confirm to their mother that they are using "good judgment."

As these examples suggest, professional middle-class parents respond to drug use within a very particular context. In comparison to the less privileged parents—and especially to parents with children of color—who have quite reasonable concerns about their children being targets of the criminal justice system, some parents can afford to be more lenient about drug use. This lenience rests, at least in part, on the awareness that should drug use become a problem within their families they will have the resources to turn to professionals for help and guidance.

"My Kids Are Good Kids": Heads in the Sand?

Over and over again professional middle-class parents insisted that their children were different from other children, that they were good kids who therefore deserved the "respectful" treatment of not being under technological surveillance. For example, when college professor Tom Audet was asked about drug testing, he suggested that it might be appropriate if "your daughter came home reeking of marijuana" or if her "behavior was erratic, doing cocaine or something like that." But he does not think that these conditions apply in his family; he said he wouldn't want to engage in drug testing "as a routine sort of thing," and he added, "not with *my* children." Other professional middle-class parents responded in similar language to questions about surveillance, whether through drug testing, GPS tracking, or keystroke monitoring: "Like I said, she's a good kid now, and I'm not concerned"; "I have good kids; they're not a surveillance problem. . . . I have very good kids."

The elite parents my research assistants and I interviewed may well be right about their kids. Indeed, we may have found the parents with perfect children in each of the various locales in which we conducted our interviews. It is worth noting, however, not only that some of the parents did say that they think or know that their children have tried drugs or engaged in other potentially problematic behavior but that the precise kids they are talking about—children from "good" homes, high-achieving students, suburban dwellers—are frequently crossing into behavior that some might view as problematic. One recent study, for example, suggests that rates of drinking, smoking, drug use, and sexual activity are high among all high school students and that they are equally high in suburban and urban areas. Three-quarters (74 percent) of suburban twelfth graders have tried alcohol more than two or three times, whereas 71 percent of urban twelfth graders have done so; two-thirds of all suburban and urban twelfth graders have "had sex" (and 43 percent of suburban and 39 percent of urban teenagers have had sex with a person with whom they did not have a romantic relationship); about four out of ten twelfth graders in suburban schools have used illegal drugs; the same statistics apply for urban twelfth graders.[9] (Moreover, if the adolescent children of the professional middle-class parents are not now drinking, using drugs, or having sex, they are likely to engage in these activities at the colleges to which they are headed.)[10] That is, the parents we interviewed *might* be right; they might also have their heads in the sand.

Knowing Anyway and Requiring Open Confession

Some of the professional middle-class parents acknowledged that they know that they might be "naive" about what their children are up to; most of them quickly backed off from an open acknowledgment of ignorance, however, claiming that their relationship with their children builds on intimacy and daily communication. They thus see home drug testing, GPS tracking, and spyware as being unnecessary. They assume that the hovering they do—which others might perceive as outright spying—provides sufficient protection. Additionally, these parents say they are less concerned with "deviant" behavior per se than they are with openness (confession) on the part of their children. A white father explained that he believes that his children have answered honestly his questions about drug use and drinking. Therefore, he said he has no reason to want to subject them to the surveillance of home drug testing. As he talked, he made it clear that he experiences no contradiction whatsoever between prying into his children's actions (and requiring confessions) and a stated commitment to respecting their privacy:

> I had no motivation for [drug testing my children]. One thing about our children, they've been very open and honest when we've sat them down and asked them questions. We asked [our son] in high school—we suspected some marijuana experimentation—and he was very honest and open and said, yes, he had been involved in a little bit of that. He told us the extent, and he told us his schoolmates' response to it, and we were very pleased that he could be that honest and share it and also pleased that that was what it was. It was a very brief experimentation. I felt that with the nature of our relationship, given his honesty, I didn't need to monitor or test; I just asked him. And he got into a little beer drinking in that high school period. . . . But again, my son was quite open and honest about that, and I figured if our children were open and honest about issues, we really didn't need to get into privacy or monitoring. You may not get the answers you want, but with the openness, you have a lot going for you.

Similarly, Jenna Hall (who expressed acceptance about drug use) said that the only conditions under which she would test her children for drugs at home would be "if they denied it." Like other elite parents, Jenna puts a higher premium on openness and honesty than she does on being drug free.

Trusting Children?

A third, and even more significant, theme in discussions about surveillance technologies has to do with what professional middle-class parents call "trust." Parents view the use of surveillance technologies—and particularly technologies that involve stealth—as indicating that they do not trust their children to do what they want and expect them to do. Technological surveillance is thus perceived as being a significant violation of the norms—friendship, respect, openness, and honesty—that prevail in parents' relationship with their adolescent children.

In Berkeley, Donna Gibson, a white, professional middle-class mother of two who works as an attorney, said that a GPS tracking system is a "big negatory [*sic*]" and that she and her husband "wouldn't do anything like that." And she continued, "See, our philosophy is, until our kids give us reason to mistrust them, we're going to function like we trust them and that they deserve our trust and that they know when they breach the trust thing will change. . . . We're not at that point. Let's hope we never get there."

Ellen Barnes, a married, professional middle-class mother of three who lives in rural Vermont and works on special projects at a liberal arts college, said that conversation should be sufficient and is a better way to interact with children rather than subjecting them to drug testing: "If there was an issue with drugs with our children, we would deal with it in other ways, not in a drug test. I can't imagine not trusting your child enough to have a conversation. I feel sorry for people who do [not have that trust]."

A DISCREPANCY BETWEEN PARENTS AND CHILDREN

While visiting colleagues in western Massachusetts one day, I asked their teenage daughter what she meant when she said "trust me" to her parents. She responded, "It does not mean that I won't do things that my parents don't want me to do, but it does mean that I will do them safely. It doesn't mean that I always do what my parents want, but it does mean that they can trust my character."[11] As her father, a sociologist, noted with mild contempt, this is an "essentialist" definition of trust: his daughter was proclaiming that she would always remain essentially the same—reliable, safe, self-protecting—and her parents had to respond to and respect her even when or if she were engaging in behaviors about which they had concerns (e.g., staying out late or visiting her boyfriend at his home) and even when or if she were not engaging in the behaviors they would like (e.g., getting to school on time or turning in her homework). Jenna Hall suggested that the older of her two daughters has precisely the same essentialist approach to trust. Jenna added that her daughter even believes that lying to her parents does not violate trust: "Like [my daughter] says, 'You don't have to believe me, but you have to trust me. And you can't always believe me because I'll not always tell the truth. But you've got to trust me with the big stuff that I've got my head on.'"

I think few parents would share in these young women's approach to the significant issue of trust. Indeed, Jenna responded to her daughter's declaration by stating, "I don't always buy into that." And like Jenna, most of the parents with whom I've spoken appear to hold dear a very different definition. For them, essentialism be damned—trust has to do with perceived *actions* rather than with *character* alone. In their minds, children could demonstrate trustworthiness (and thus *earn* a parent's trust) by doing precisely what my colleague's lovely daughter said was irrelevant to her understanding of trust: that is, both by not doing what parents didn't want their children to do and by doing that which the family morality prescribed. At the very least, professional middle-class parents of teens believe their children should freely and openly communicate about what is happening in their daily lives.

Of course, this parental definition leaves the determination of trustworthiness in the hands of the beholder (rather than the actor, which is where the teens would place it) because only the beholder knows for sure which actions cross the line from prescription to prohibition. In this context, consider Kristen Garner, a widowed, white mother of two children. Kristen blithely suggested that she assumes that her eighteen-year-old daughter Helen "must have tried something just because of her friends" and implied that "trying" a little something does not violate her more general prohibition against drinking or drug use. Kristen also said she doesn't have to worry because of all the years she has spent in an "open, honest, communicative relationship" with her daughters. Yet for all that, it might be that her children have good reason to conceal drinking, drug use, and sexual activity: the limits of trustworthy behavior (as was the case for Tom Audet and pornography) may not be openly discussed (and in fact the parents might be more open to a little experimentation than children believe), any more than is the definition of trust itself. Indeed, children might not know that telling (confession) may be more important than not doing and thus concealing what *appears* to be proscribed.

TRUST AS A TOGGLE

And there are good reasons for concealment, even if "confession" is urged by parents. As interpreted by the professional middle-class parents, trust is quite brittle and quite easily broken (even if the parameters of appropriate behavior might be looser than children know). Parents speak readily in the language of "broken" trust or of trust being "lost," thereby suggesting that their trust is neither elastic nor plastic. In the courts, it's three strikes and you're out—incorrigible, excluded, shut away for good. In the family, one strike alone may unalterably challenge a parent's trust.

Although, like their less privileged peers, the professional middle-class parents say there are a host of "signs and portents" that they rely on to assess whether their children are drinking or using drugs, among the professional middle class especially these signs and portents coalesce not just into a notion of change but into a description of the child having wandered off the acceptable path to fulfilling her or his potential. Not surprisingly, given how intensely privileged parents monitor academic achievement (even as they deny doing so), that achievement becomes one of the indicators on which they rely. One woman said she would know if her son were experimenting with legal or illegal substances if there were "a change in his personality, a change in his grades at school, a change in his appearance, the way he dresses, . . . any dramatic change from the status quo." Another woman responded that she would be concerned about her children "if their grades start dropping dramatically." Indeed, among these parents, a failure to maintain high achievement in school transforms a child into a "deviant" who is no longer worthy of parental trust. There were exceptions, but for the majority of parents trust is inelastic. Moreover, for the majority of parents, trust is not about character but about behavior, even though, like the winnings of a gambling spree, it can be won and lost. And maintaining high levels of academic achievement is key to ensuring winnings over losses.

PARENTS SPY

As we probe, we thus find that all this trust is something of a sham. Professional middle-class parents who talk at length about not wanting to enlist technology to help them spy because that would indicate that they do not trust their children also in the next breath talk about spying on their children. And many openly acknowledge that it is the spying (along with the confession) that leads them to hold the stance that they call "trust" in their children. The spying they do takes a variety of different forms, ranging from the covert glance at a diary left open in a daughter's room to the quite overt insistence that a son make available the password he uses on the computer. But it does not rely on technology. Indeed, for many of these professional middle-class parents *the technology itself—whether about drug testing, keystroke programs, or a GPS tracker—appears to be the issue.* This is what crosses an unacceptable line.

Kristen Garner, for example, insists that the behavior of her daughters fits within the limits she has set (which would allow an occasional drink for her eighteen-year-old daughter) and that the intimate and open relationship she has with her daughters ensures that they do not go beyond those limits. She also, astonishingly, assumes that the absence of boyfriends means that her daughters are not engaged in sexual activity (with either boys or girls), and she locates responsibility for drug use in her daughters' friends. Throughout her comments in response to a question about home drug testing, Kristen clearly made a distinction between what we can think of as monitoring (with a small "m"), which entails open conversation and taking a look at what her children place on social networking sites, and Monitoring (with a capital "M"), which entails actually going out and purchasing a piece of technology. The former occurs all the time, and Kristen believes it to be part of being a good parent. The latter she believes to be going too far, and she has never done that:

> I have never thought that I needed to scrutinize their actions. They're both doing quite well in school. . . . I don't think I need to monitor stuff like that. Maybe [I would] if I had seen anything that led me to believe that they weren't making good choices. And I could be a naive parent, but neither of them has ever had a boyfriend, so I don't have to worry about sexual activity. And I'm pretty certain neither of them has done drugs, and I'm pretty certain that Jennifer has never had a drink. I assume Helen must have tried something just because of her friends. So it's not like any of the stuff that I wouldn't want them to do is any aspect of their lives. So I don't need to monitor. And also because I've spent all of those years in an open, honest, communicative relationship, I don't think I need to do any monitoring. . . . We've had conversations about MySpace and Facebook, and I've seen both of their pages, and I don't think they're hiding anything from me. So I don't think I need to monitor.

Kristen sees no contradiction between asserting that she engages in close observation and denial that she monitors.

GETTING HELP IN SPYING

Although most parents see themselves as being alone in child rearing, there are exceptions. In small towns and tight social circles, parents can rely on others to report on their children. Indeed, some parents make it clear that their spies are everywhere and that their "trust" hinges on the fact that they will find out what their children are doing whether or not their children share that information. Paula Brown's initial answer about whether she would want to install a GPS tracking system in her car was both informed and negative: "I've heard of them. I can't imagine why I would need that." When asked whether there were any circumstances under which she might be interested in such a device, she responded, "If I thought my child was really not to be trusted at all times, . . . but man, I would just hope I would go on something very different to say [to my child], 'just be honest.'" Paula suggested initially, then, that she wants to trust her children to do what is right and good and to confess to her if that is not the case. But immediately after, she suggested that her trust is not very deep, that she engages in practices of finding out what it is her children are doing and therefore that they are controlled as much by her spying on them as she is by their honesty with her: "What we try to tell Emily and Josh is that we're in a small community. . . . Emily has been places, and she'll say, 'I saw so and so,' and I'll say, 'I know, they told me.' So it's almost like that's at work long before the GPS system." Under these conditions, when asked about a GPS for tracking, Paula is in a perfect position to claim that it is "extreme"; quite simply, she feels that she has no need for a device that will duplicate the arrangements she has already put in place to learn what her daughter is doing.

And technology can be an asset in this endeavor of keeping track within small circles of friends. Jeff Wright, the white, widowed father of a fourteen-year-old daughter, said that he wouldn't read his daughter's diary unless he had good reason to do so. But, in the next breath, he indicated that he is quite confident that his informal "spies" would alert him to problems; knowing that he has other ways of finding out what is going on and what his child is posting on her MySpace or Facebook account, he is comfortable "trusting" his child:

> I know that she has a MySpace account or a Facebook account—I can't remember which it is—and I would never [look at it]. There are times when

> I wonder what is she doing on there, but I also know that that's where she is, and *I also know that she has enough people on her list that if there was something wrong, they would probably tell me.* So I've got to give her as much trust as I can. (Emphasis added)[12]

SPYING ALL THE TIME

Even more commonly than professional middle-class parents indicated their reliance on others, they openly acknowledged that they spy all the time, even if they have not installed a device to record keystrokes. Checking the history on the computer seems to these parents to illustrate good sense, but they do not characterize it as being overly intrusive or demonstrating a lack of trust. A white mother of three, for example, said that although she is familiar with the software that enables one to read keystrokes, she doesn't use it because she trusts her teenage son and, perhaps even more significantly, because in checking histories on the computer she has never seen anything that would lead her to be suspicious.

For this elite group of parents, monitoring by having the computer in an open place or "coming across" private possessions does not count as demonstrating a lack of trust either. As one white mother of two said,

> I trust my kids a lot, and they have to be able to trust me. . . . I don't go through their room. Now, I come across stuff by accident sometimes. I went to pick out change, and there might be a note there, and I might open it up to see what is this. . . . And I never found anything that made me be suspicious that I needed to go more—I've never blocked anything [on the computer]. I don't know how to use it. I would have to get my kids to help me figure it out. I trust them—like with the TV programs. The computer is out in the open, so they weren't surfing for porn. It was right there in the family room. I just kind of trust them, given the kids that I have.

In a similar vein, consider Eve Todd, the white mother from rural Vermont, who wants to raise her children without fear, "to be encouraging and supportive in what their views are," and to support her daughter's ambition to be a rock star. The availability that she—and other parents—proclaim as a hallmark of the favored child-rearing style, has some ominous overtones. Eve said that trust depends on "being there" or, as she put it, being "not not there" so that you remain aware of what it is that your children are doing. If Eve monitors closely (she admits she checks the odometer after her daughter has borrowed the car) *and* trusts her children in the interstices, she doesn't need a GPS tracking system:

> But I think that you have to have some level of trust, and if there's a level of trust and it seems to be going okay and you're watching your kids and you're not not there, that you would pick up if there was something wrong or something askew, and then you would have to talk about it. But if we have her take a car, and she does what she says she's going to do, . . . there's no reason for me to track her.

Indeed, the parents suggest that going beyond these methods of keeping track (casual snooping, reliance on spies, checking the odometer) would make them confront and admit to their own intrusiveness.[13] The commitment to "trust" while not being trusting is so unselfconscious that parents who engage in actions that might easily be read as violations of trust still maintain that they have a trusting relationship with their children.

Marian English stumbled over herself as she sought to explain the circumstances under which she read her daughter's diary, while she insisted that she does not intrude into her daughter's private life. Marian finds herself in an awkward position when she learns more from reading the diary than she wants to know—and especially more than she wants her husband to know.[14] Still, Marian makes a distinction between casual reading prompted by the diary's being left open (monitoring) and purposeful reading prompted by her concern about her child's well-being (Monitoring):

> She does [keep a diary], and I read parts but not all. I would never tell her that. This is a hard area for me because you want to protect your kids, but you also want to protect their own privacy and ability to have their own lives; sometimes she would leave them out, and I would open to a page and read it. [But] if I thought there was something seriously wrong, if I thought she was going down a bad path, whether sexually, drugs, or that kind of thing, [then] I would probably find it and read it to find out what was going on. And in that case that is probably the only time I would justify doing it. The couple of times I found it and looked at a couple of pages

> I felt guilty, and I never told her I did it. And I would never say to her, "I read this in your diary. When did you do that?" But if I thought she was in some kind of danger, I would *find* them and read them. [When I did read them it was because] they were just there, and she just leaves them out because she's careless. And I was just cleaning her room one day, and there they were. And I read things that disturbed me, but I also didn't think I could say [anything to] her. But they weren't life threatening, and I didn't want to break her trust. I didn't want to lose her trust because of that—because there are other issues bigger than that that she still needs to be able to talk to me about. It wasn't something I felt like was going to result in some kind of dangers. . . . I didn't tell my husband because he would have probably gone berserk, freak out, ground her. . . . He does react differently. We have different parenting styles.

Professional middle-class parents thus not only suggest that trust is brittle and a bit of a sham, but they incorporate a fair degree of "spying" into trusting relationships. At the same time, they prefer not to reveal their snooping because they believe doing so will challenge the two-way relationship of trust and result in their children's not telling them things that, as Marian put it, her daughter "needs to" talk to her about. And the elite parents mostly do not choose to use those devices—a GPS tracking device, a keystroke reader, home drug testing—that could make that spying easier but would also make them acknowledge the spying they now do.

Few of the interviewed parents had ever used any of the new devices available for spying on their children. When asked about these devices, the parents imagined various situations they might face and then declared themselves willing—or unwilling—to deal with those situations through technological surveillance. These hypothetical responses are telling.

The professional middle-class parents adamantly rejected the devices that would enable them to spy on their children. They gave several different reasons for this response. The professional middle-class parents suggested that while the devices might be appropriate for other parents, they are unnecessary with their "good" children. As noted, it is likely that many of these parents are operating on the basis of a kind of denial: evidence shows that precisely these "good" kids are drinking, using drugs, and engaging in a wide range of sexual activities of which their parents are unaware and of which they might not approve.[15] But as parents who believe they have established intimate communication and who believe that their children will confess misdeeds, they have no basis on which to openly doubt their children's statements about what they are doing.

Moreover, the professional middle-class parents view these devices as violating some essential trust between parent and child. Yet it appears that parents and children may well have very different definitions of trust. For children, trust appears to be based on "essential" character and not incidental actions. For parents, the reverse is the case: trust builds on actions rather than character. Parental trust also operates as a toggle switch: parents trust their children until they don't trust them; there is no in-between point. Moreover, it turns out that among the elite, parental trust hardly exists, despite the image parents want to present. Parents engage in a wide range of "sneaky" behaviors to ensure that their children are doing what they want them to do (and not doing what they don't want them to do). But they appear reluctant to purchase a device that would force them to confront that sneakiness (and the ways they actually do violate trust); in this way they can maintain the illusion of a trusting relationship with their children. Yet this illusion requires that they be always alert and always available, since concealed spying takes more time and more subtlety than doing so out in the open. In their efforts to maintain this illusion parents, on occasion, act with questionable integrity.

When children break their parents' trust, professional middle-class parents are not unwilling to use technological devices to spy. Of course, the evidence for broken trust is in the hands of the parents. Although parents talk initially as if they would have to see quite dramatic changes in a child's behavior before instituting what one parent referred to as a "draconian measure," it turns out that parents such as Beth O'Brien are willing to abandon trust for relatively moderate alterations in behavior. Indeed, several parents suggested they would adopt a mechanism for spying if they simply believed that their child's academic status was in jeopardy.

In contrast to the subtle—but sharp—distinction made by professional middle-class parents between casual practices (such as reading a child's diary) and practices that rely on technology (such as a keystroke monitoring system), working-class and middle-class parents make little distinction between spying through technology and spying without it.[16] Because these parents have an enthusiastic impulse toward surveillance (at least under certain conditions) and because they are more ambivalent altogether about trust, the means may be a less important consideration than the ends. If a diary is there, the working-class and middle-class parents might very well read it (especially if they have grounds for suspicion that not all is well); if they can find some other mechanism for accessing concealed information, they might use that instead (or as well). When these parents talk about surveillance devices such as the keystroke reader, the GPS tracker, and home drug testing, they are less interested in the possibility of stealth (spying) per se than they are in deterrence and in keeping their children safe. They believe that teens are not yet self-disciplined: as one parent said, "Kids are kids. You can't just give the message that you're trusting them. You just have to watch them at all times." Eventually, they hope that discipline will be internalized; eventually they will be able to "trust" a young adult to act appropriately. During the teen years, however, these working-class and middle-class parents believe in maintaining an overt disciplinary gaze—both to induce self-control and to provide protection.

8 FROM CARE TO CONTROL

When the elite students on my college campus are asked about contact with their parents, they report that they initiate communication almost as much as their parents do. They report as well that they do not believe communicating with their parents more than ten times a week is too much. Indeed, they say they are "satisfied" with this level of interaction, and some report that they would prefer even more communication with their fathers.[1]

I've observed how this communication plays out in a number of different situations, even beyond my casual observations walking across the central quad. When I told a first-year advisee that she would probably not gain entry into an introductory psychology class during her initial semester on campus, tears welled up in her eyes. When I asked her to consider alternatives, she told me that she couldn't do so just then, that she would first have to talk to her "mom." Clearly, the patterns of parental responsiveness that began when they were infants in their cribs have now become taken-for-granted parts of my students' daily lives. When they have questions, meet difficulties, or simply want to report on their days, they reach out for their "moms" and, somewhat less often, their "dads." The (relatively few) less privileged students who take my classes and visit my office also own cell phones, and they too often describe themselves as being close to their parents. But they differ from the children of the professional middle class in the nature of their cell phone use and in the nature of this closeness. More of them have already assumed adult responsibilities of employment not just to support their pleasures but also to help put food on the table. They talk to their parents about financial aid forms and how they can reduce the economic burden that college tuition places on their families. And more of them know they have to handle incidental "crises" on their own.

Styles of Care

The summary characterizations captured in the phrases *parenting out of control* and *parenting with limits* help us think about the breadth and depth of parental influence and how this ultimately shapes the behavior of college-age students. Across the board, parents want children to internalize their values, embody their hopes, and fulfill their dreams. Parents who enroll their children in the full round of extracurricular activities, assess every academic achievement, and hoard advantages thereby create lives in which every moment is designed to contribute to privilege, to preserving a competitive place, to becoming the best. No sphere of life is untouched. Simultaneously there is a depth to this influence as parents build relationships with children based on intimacy, on being available, on staying connected, and on friendship. Among the nonelite, less structured lives leave more room for children to simply be; less intense relationships with parents allow children more occasions to demonstrate who they are (rather than who they might become).

The phrases *parenting out of control* and *parenting with limits* also refer to the absence—or presence—of external constraints imposed on children as part of a caregiving style. Elite parents have concerns about children who wander off an acceptable path; they do set some limits for their children. But some of those limits go unstated, and at least some of those limits are up for grabs—as Anna Benton said, her approach is "1-2-3 maybe." Children who sense (or know) that their parents are hesitant to stay firm may very well respond by wheedling and whining. Parents acknowledge that wheedling and whining sometimes make their job a nightmare. But their commitment to flexibility allows for the negotiation that engenders such behaviors. Less elite parents who make clear that there are limits to what kinds of behavior they will allow may also be confronted with wheedling and whining. They are more likely, however, to nip it in the bud—to tell and yell instead of negotiate. For the working-class and middle-class parents who live with more present dangers, limits are seen as lifesavers, rather than as barriers to free expression or as premature restrictions on potential.

Finally, the phrases make reference to the absence—or presence—of external constraints of time and money that frame styles of care. Almost by definition, privilege carries with it a certain freedom. Professionals are often in a position of authority; they make decisions themselves rather than enact those made by others. Parents with professional training are often also in the position to make the decision to devote themselves to their children. Even jobs that are intensely demanding—being a college professor, an attorney, or the CEO of a camping-goods business—contain at least some flexibility for those at the top, and parents can opt to work that flexibility to serve the end of being available to their children. In the process they may also work themselves into exhaustion. Having chosen the path of intense responsiveness, they may not know just when to cut short their engagement with their children. They may feel that their parenting has gotten out of control.

For many of the elite parents, few economic constraints exist to help them define limits. Substantial financial resources allow them to purchase whatever it takes to ensure their children's social, psychological, and academic well-being. Here also they may feel that their parenting has gotten out of control as they indulge their children's every whim. Quite obviously, and by definition, less privileged adults function within more serious constraints. Less flexible jobs and lesser financial resources circumscribe the style of parenting that can be adopted.

Parenting Styles Meet Technology

A parent commenting about the delights of her baby monitor wrote on Epinions.com that she had extended its use to engage in concealed observation of her older children:

> This is also a great monitor to hide in the playroom. I can put the transmitter in the room and when I hear them getting too rowdy, I just push the button and tell them to simmer down. It's great because they think God told me they were acting up and I don't have to walk all the way upstairs![2]

The control strategy is (like the Almighty) simultaneously omnipresent and invisible. As this mother likened herself to a god in both her omniscience and her invisibility, she illustrated just how easily care could shade into control. Like this mother, the professional middle-class parents interviewed for this study generally began with a concern about care when they explained why they eagerly use devices of connection such as baby monitors and cell phones. As they talked more freely, they provided evidence for the dialectical relationship that exists between seemingly disparate impulses.

The more privileged parents also indicated that they found the level of care abetted by these devices—being able to hear every whimper and sigh made by an infant or being able to keep track of a teen's whereabouts and activities from morn to night—to be especially compatible with other aspects of what they choose as a style for raising their children. These parents actively want to remain close to their children, and they equally actively want to respond to needs and concerns as they arise. The professional middle-class parents praise baby monitors and cell phones for helping them to establish this desired closeness and responsiveness and for enabling them to use the knowledge thus obtained to better control their children. In contrast, the working-class and middle-class parents praise these devices because they ensure safety.

Even sharper class differences emerge with respect to the devices that openly seek to constrain behaviors—a child locator that lets parents know where a child is, a filtering device that stops wandering to an array of websites on the computer, and a mechanism that blocks television programs. In general, the professional middle-class parents are least inclined to report that they find these useful; the working-class and middle-class parents are more inclined to view such devices favorably. Among the professional middle class, parents' objections rest on a number of grounds, including the sense (and this is especially the case for the child locator) that these devices are an unwelcome substitute for parental responsibility. Professional middle-class parents are willing—even eager—to manage their children's behavior, and they view doing so as part of the definition of being a parent. They want to remain intensely involved; they want to know what is happening; they want to "be there." One aspect of what Annette Lareau calls "concerted cultivation" or what Sharon Hays calls "intensive mothering," then, is ongoing, continuous involvement in children's lives.[3] This is time-consuming parenting.

In contrast, the working-class and middle-class parents want to limit parenting both in space and in time. Recall that more of these parents indicated that they find parenting to be burdensome in some way. Recall as well that more of these parents assume that intensive responsibility will end by the time their children graduate from college. On a day-to-day basis, they know that they cannot always be home, and when they are home they want to free themselves from negotiations and arguments about appropriate behavior. Quite simply, if the technology will help them keep their children safe and enable the implementation of clear limits, they are interested in using it.

Discussions with parents about these constraining devices illuminate some deeper aspects of parental relationships with teenage children, and some other key differences between parenting out of control and parenting with limits.

Professional middle-class parents discuss how their role as parents involves shaping and guiding their children to help them fulfill their boundless potential and become the best they can be. Of course, they can describe their children as having rather distinctive and rather set personalities—one child is compassionate, one is athletic, one is a good student—just as the less privileged parents do when asked to describe their children. But the professional middle-class parents also understand their parental responsibility to include gaining intimate knowledge of what their children are capable of and "imposing" their values through (sometimes coerced) conversation. When they talk about why they wouldn't want to have a child locator, they talk about "working with" their young children to teach them not to wander off, they talk about helping a child "to be able to internalize . . . safety behaviors," and they talk about traumatic events (e.g., when a child is lost) as "learning opportunities." Professional middle-class parents of older children talk about how they negotiate the transition to more adult content in the media. They watch television with their children, and they discuss the significance and meaning of what they have seen; they check histories on the computer and ask about Internet activities. And as they do, they continue their efforts to shape their children in their own likeness.

Erica Harper, who had different rules for her three children and required her sixteen-year-old son to watch R-rated movies with her, spoke about how she simultaneously allowed that son to have access to his PlayStation and his video games (as a reward) when he was younger and about how she still wants to change who he is so that he can achieve a perfect "balance" in his leisure activities:

> Back when Nate was younger he was really into PlayStation and video games, and I consider that just sitting in front of a screen. We would limit that to chunks of time. We actually tried to keep that a privilege for him, so if he got his responsibilities concluded, . . . then he could earn himself the privilege of being on for x amount of time. . . . It wasn't good for his brain; it wasn't good for his temperament. . . . We worked really hard to encourage our kids to have a balance in what they do with their free time. Nate is so incredibly drawn towards technology. . . . He is one of those kids that would sit in front of [a screen] and rarely do much more. . . . To this day we have to say, "You've been on a long time."

That perfect "balance," of course, is far more difficult to establish than are clear and straightforward limits on the number of hours a child can sit in front of a screen.

And rather than allowing "freedom" within identifiable constraints, the professional middle-class parents constantly shift the constraints themselves. Working-class mother Danielle Jones relies on the cell phone to augment the parental gaze, "to find out where [her children] are" and "remind them of their curfew." In contrast to Danielle, a professional middle-class mother uses the cell phone to negotiate about appropriate behavior. Recall, for example, Anna Benton, who first encouraged her daughter to attend a party and then called her home. Or consider Donna Gibson, who described herself as being both permissive and protective. She discussed the intense negotiation that took place, with her daughter and with the parents of her daughter's friends, about whether to allow her child to attend an underage club in San Francisco (they live across the Bay in Berkeley). The rules about what is or is not acceptable behavior might quite appropriately be outside this sixteen-year-old's control; even so, she is subject to a considerable period of indecision and a negotiated settlement as her parents find the best midpoint between their concerns about safety and their desire to nurture their child's emerging independence, and between their own attitudes and those of other parents:

> You just get a feeling about balancing safety and their desire to be independent and what is okay and what is not okay. My daughter wanted to take BART [the Bay Area's transit system] into the city to go to an underage club and come home on BART, and it was a big brouhaha for a week. And what finally happened was we let her go in with her friends in daylight, but a parent had to escort them back at night; it was going to be like midnight or one—she's sixteen. It goes on and on, these issues.

During this period of indecision, a child is subject to changing rules:

> I was very insistent about the girls' being accompanied by an adult on the way home on the BART. [The] other adults were not as concerned about it. They would probably have let them come home alone, and it was out of the question for me. In fact, I did insist for a while that they be accompanied to the club and ultimately backed down because all the other parents

> said they can make it okay on their own, so I say, "okay in the daylight." So I think in the area of security I'm more protective than what I see are the average parents.

Indeed, one of the technologies examined here—the cell phone that remains so present in the lives of college students—becomes a key tool for this shifting, as children negotiate freedom and independence against parental restraint.[4] The child at the other end of the conversation does not know whether she or he will be allowed to engage in a desired activity but must remain in constant contact and participate in constant discussion. Parental control abetted by technology thus operates like a "sieve whose mesh will transmute from point to point"; the actions of an individual child may—or may not—be allowed at any given time; and since the power lies with the parent, whose rules change and shift as children mature or as the parents themselves change their perceptions, the privileged child's world is full of unexpected and unanticipated shifts.[5]

Working-class and middle-class parents talk with a greater clarity about rules. In keeping with their standpoint of "predestination," they also demonstrate a greater acceptance of who their children are at any given moment. Recall that Yvonne Wood said that she would have used a child locator with Samantha because "her mind was like somewhere else all the time." In addition, there appears to be a greater acceptance by these parents of the sheer likelihood of misbehavior. Because children "cheat," parents put a code in their television to block out certain channels; because children will be curious and look at pornography, parents put a filter on the computer to prevent wandering onto questionable websites. The parent does not try so hard to change her or his children or to encourage the internalization of the family morality; the parent accommodates who her or his children are by adopting technologies that allow for the implementation of clear, unchanging, and obvious rules. These technologies also ensure compliance, whether children want to comply or not. In short, middle- and working-class parents adopt fundamentally different styles than do their more privileged peers; these different styles do not *depend* on technology but work in conjunction with—or sometimes against—new developments.

Taken as a whole, then, the working-class and middle-class parents regard both the devices of containment and the devices of surveillance more favorably. They are more likely to use filtering devices on the television and computer, and they think that if they could afford it, they would purchase some of the new surveillance devices. They speak with more open acknowledgment that teens are *not* to be trusted and that it is better to know where they are and what they are doing than to ignore the possibility that they might be getting into trouble. They also view these devices as good substitutes for parental discipline when parents can't be at home and when parents are too busy to engage in personal monitoring.

Inclusionary and Exclusionary Control

In the discussion of surveillance technologies, professional middle-class parents suggest that they will not impose "draconian measures" such as drug testing because they have good kids who confess to them and whom they therefore trust. Of course, parents are not unanimous in their determination of what constitutes trustworthy behavior. Some parents might be accepting of an occasional drink or even experimentation with illegal drugs; other parents would find these same behaviors unacceptable. But as long as children remain openly confessional and apparently trustworthy, the "good kids" of elite parents are subject to the individualized control and oversight that their parents prefer to the straightforward discipline emerging from the use of technological devices. Professional middle-class parents communicate, remain involved, and allow freedom within personalized and very intense surveillance. Through these methods the parents hope to stay close enough to know what is going on with their children and to ensure that their children pursue behaviors that will preserve an elite class position down the road. The professional middle-class parents also rely on these methods of engagement to monitor well-being and self-confidence. The simultaneous demands of accomplishment and happiness, and of working hard while appearing to find work effortless, exist as enormous pressures in the lives of successful adolescent children.[6] The fact that the parents themselves may not know how to produce the children they want and hold out highly elusive and indefinite goals (e.g., how do you know when your children are happy and passionate?) constitute all the more reason for parents to remain intensely attentive.

The contemporary social theorist Nikolas Rose describes two sets of control strategies: inclusion and exclusion.[7] Inclusionary control, he explains, relies on *constant* evaluation according to rules that can change without warning. In such a system, evaluation is ongoing and built into all activities. In this context, the process of becoming is perpetual, and surveillance is both built into everyday existence and "dispersed across the time and space of ordinary life."[8] Thus, surveillance may be less apparent in control strategies than in disciplinary ones such as Bentham's panopticon (as analyzed by Foucault).[9] But the surveillance is no less real.

Exclusionary control stands in contrast to inclusionary control. And Rose suggests that it can take two different forms. In some cases, "excluded" individuals are subject to "reeducation" and then reincorporated into civil society: an example would be when drug-using teens are sent to "treatment centers" for rehabilitation. In more extreme cases, the "excluded" remain confined and separate: an example would be when "hardened" criminals are locked in jail for life.[10]

On a daily basis, it would appear that the professional middle-class family operates far more often on the principles of inclusionary control than of exclusionary control.[11] In turn, inclusionary control rests equally on the assumption of intimacy, as well as on the veneer of goodness (on the part of the kids) and the veneer of trust (on the part of the parents). Professional middle-class parents engage in negotiation with their children, shift the rules as their children mature, and subject children to ongoing assessments, the terms of which may be unclear. The professional middle-class parents indicate that in their households control is a constant process: every activity at every moment—from school to soccer to watching movies—becomes an opportunity for children to reveal themselves, a mechanism for self-improvement, and a means through which a child can discover her or his own potential.[12] Moreover, inclusionary control is an endless project: children are not "finished" when they head for college or even when they graduate. In fact, as with the first-year student in my office who needed to discuss her course options with her mother before making a decision, control remains a persistent and ongoing strategy, abetted by the constant electronic communication between parents and children.[13]

The practices of inclusionary control are burdensome. From time to time professional middle-class parents might attempt to relieve themselves of these burdens in their dealings with their teenage children. They might, for example, opt for some kinds of formal enclosures such as a gated community or a private boarding school. But for the most part, professional middle-class parents appear to welcome the burdens of parenting out of control and choose the ongoing construction of (and negotiation about) the limits of what constitutes acceptable behavior.

As professional middle-class parents talk about how they decide whether to engage in the disciplinary practices of technological surveillance, they suggest that they would need to see some significant shift in behavior from that which they find acceptable and especially about which their children have not confessed. Only a few of those who were interviewed had relied on such devices as the keystroke reader or had instituted a policy of home drug testing with a teen. However, professional middle-class parents contradict their own preferences when they discuss their reasons for these actions. Then they suggest that something as ordinary as obstinate behavior or nighttime wandering provided the basis for making the shift from inclusionary strategies of control to those that might appear more exclusionary or even more traditionally "disciplinary" or punishing.[14]

The sociologists Dawn Moore and Kevin Haggerty have identified home drug testing as an appropriate part of a strategy of inclusionary control (at least in relation to other antidrug strategies). They write,

> In keeping with the disease trope, home drug testing is a strategy of inclusion, situating the detection and punishment of criminal behaviors in the compassionate embrace of the family. In contrast, the state's anti-drug policies constitute a strategy of exclusion, which follows the trope of criminality, to remove individuals from their usual social settings, subjecting them to more intensive forms of repression.[15]

Moore and Haggerty thus view *the family* as being a single unit, and a "compassionate" one at that. But to think this way is to ignore the ways in which the family itself can operate on the basis of both inclusion and exclusion and can simultaneously embody different modes of control in addition to both discipline and punishment.

As the discussion in chapter 7 showed, professional middle-class families do want to contain deviance within the embrace of the family, and, to be sure, they also view professionals standing outside the family—the doctors, the counselors—as essentially on their side, as operating with their interests at heart, and therefore as worthy of their confidences. But from the perspective of the *usual* practices of the professional middle-class family, home drug testing is viewed not as a part of an inclusionary strategy of control but as a disciplinary one that might result in the implementation of exclusionary strategies. The teen who might need drug testing is no longer acting like himself or herself but has become the "other." The same is true of the notion of tracking driving with a GPS system or reading keystrokes on the computer. These are looked at askance, at least in part because they overtly shift the mode of parenting from control to discipline with clear limits. And even when used, these (potentially stealth) technologies—along with the drug testing—are often hopefully temporary expedients: children who meet their parents' expectations for good behavior and clean drug tests are returned to the embrace of the family; they move, then, from being one of them—the other—to being one of us (again). This was the case for Beth O'Brien, who used the keystroke program secretly to gather information in order to better control her daughter Melissa: "It made us aware of how to manage her differently."

◈ CONCLUSION

The Consequences of Parenting Out of Control

I vividly remember the moment when I first conceived of this project. As I was standing at my kitchen counter, eating a bowl of cereal, and glancing at the local newspaper, I came across one of those small "human interest" articles that described a "smart card" parents could use to track lunchtime purchases by their children. Do you know whether your children are buying nutritious meals? Are you concerned about why your daughter is gaining so much weight? Do you wonder why your son is so hungry when he gets home from school? No problem. You can find out what is happening, each day, even though you are not there.

As I read this piece, I wondered about the motivations of parents who so strongly believed that they had to know about their children's every move that they would buy into a piece of technology that secured that knowledge. And I wondered whether these parents were the same ones who, it seemed to me from casual observation, were so intently engaged in hypervigilant practices, so controlling of their children, and seemingly so unwilling to launch them into adulthood. Although ultimately I decided not to include the smart card within the range of devices explored (because I wanted only those technologies potentially available to all parents rather than being dependent on what a school system had to offer), as I have shown, the answers to these two questions are more complex than I originally believed.[1]

I found that within what I have called the professional middle class, parents do, indeed, adopt a style of parenting that has as its key features constant oversight, belief in children's boundless potential, intimacy with children, claims of trust, and delayed launching. And I found that this style of care emerges from anxieties about their children's future, from nostalgia for the way they imagine families used to live, and from assessments of dangers to childhood in the world today. I found as well that this distinctive style of parenting gives rise to enthusiasm for technologies of connection that allow for both care and control, even as it creates ambivalence toward technologies of straightforward constraint and distaste toward technologies of surveillance. Indeed, most professional middle-class parents might look at the new smart card with some horror, seeing it as too clumsy a mechanism for parental control and as something that would overtly challenge the trust they have appeared to place in their children to do the right thing.

It is different among the working class and middle class, where parenting styles draw on concerns about concrete dangers, an awareness of youthful indiscretions, and a desire to see children mature sooner, rather than later. These parents might very well be grateful for the smart card—along with the full range of connection, constraint, and surveillance technologies—if they believe it could help them keep their children safe and operating within parental limits. Our sociological answers often challenge our simple commonsense assumptions about the world.

The Dimensions of Class

My use of social class throughout this book distinguishes little among material, social, and cultural meanings. Each of these is relevant to how I believe it is that parents choose among competing strategies and among existing technologies. Recall, for example, Peter Chaplin, the divorced, middle-class father of a thirteen-year-old. Peter is tempted by private school and expensive sports programs for his son; he believes he lacks the economic resources to enable him to afford those special privileges; he also lacks the social resources that would enable him to evaluate which privileges might be most effective in achieving the goals he wants; and he questions the necessity of this kind of "concerted cultivation."[2] But we can go beyond this one example to see how all these elements are relevant to parenting styles.

Quite obviously, material conditions allow for greater freedom not only to consider the range of privileges about which Peter was so concerned but also to imagine a future that puts self-confidence, happiness, and passion ahead of the necessity of earning a living. Professional middle-class parents envision a long period of dependence for their children in part because they can afford to do so. Ultimately, of course, elite parents believe their children will settle down and find a career, but they are in no rush to push them out of the nest.

In addition, the daily circumstances of everyday life give rise to different sets of concerns and opportunities. Professional middle-class parents might worry about the safety of their children as they traverse busy streets in urban and suburban neighborhoods, travel in cars with friends in suburban and rural areas, and hang out in empty houses in the full range of locales. But taken as a whole, these privileged parents need not worry about the same level of danger from the outside as do parents whose children live in neighborhoods with high crime rates. Of course, there are exceptions. One professional middle-class mother talked about a child who had been regularly harassed by a man on her block as she walked to and from school; another talked about a shooting in the neighborhood. However, these stories were rare. In contrast, for quite a few of the less privileged parents harassment and shooting were evoked more commonly as dangers to which they have to be attentive on a daily basis.

Material conditions matter in other ways as well. Most of those who were interviewed work full-time outside the home. This is as true for the working-class and middle-class parents as it is for the professional middle-class parents. However, working-class and middle-class respondents have considerably less flexible schedules than do their professional middle-class peers, and they feel less able to "be there" to supervise their children's activities. Hence, they rely more often on technology as a substitute.

At the same time, many of the professional middle-class parents hold very demanding jobs; it might very well be the case that these individuals are working *more* hours than are their less privileged peers.[3] In this context, parents' clear-cut decisions to make themselves available to watch every move become significant. Furthermore, we cannot ignore the influence of social factors and of cultural attitudes as they circulate in the media, among groups of young mothers gathering on the playground or among the telephone trees of the parents of teens as they make decisions about what to allow.[4] The practices that get established—the degree to which parents begin to use a language of "choice," for example—may have less to do with what can be afforded than with what other people within one's social group find appropriate.[5]

Among the respondents in this study the professional middle-class parents are, on average, four years older than their less privileged peers. This small average difference has large ramifications. The older parents had a particular set of cultural experiences when they were young. And although many participants in the sixties rejected the counterculture activities of drug use, protest, and antimaterialist values (and many adopted a far more conservative political position later in life), the experience of an acute generational divide ("don't trust anyone over thirty") may have left many in that generation with a sense that connection could be found more readily by looking down to one's children than up to one's parents. These privileged adults are also highly mobile and thus often live at a distance from their own parents. In contrast, the middle-class and working-class adults, who remain both ideologically and geographically closer to their own parents, might have less of a psychic need to find connection in the next generation.

In short, the attentive hovering of the professional middle-class parents both requires and builds on a vast array of material resources, even though it does not necessarily rely on all available technology; simultaneously, the attentive hovering has roots and dynamics that emerge from, and are sustained by, cultural and social practices.

Concerns about Children

Cracks in a World View

No matter what the origins of the parenting style of the professional middle-class parents with whom I spoke, those parents appear to doubt themselves more often than do the working-class and middle-class parents. Indeed, the latter sets of parents often seem quite confident about their child-rearing approach.[6] The style I call *parenting with limits* is in many ways straightforward and unselfconscious. But professional middle-class parents, who adopt *parenting out of control,* worry a lot about the consequences of their own actions: they worry about the pressure their children face in school and on the athletic field; they worry that there is not time for their children simply to "be" children; they worry about material and psychological "overindulgence"; and they worry that the hovering they do might have problematic consequences. As postmodern parents, they are committed to a therapeutic approach to daily life—to improving their children and to improving themselves.[7] Not surprisingly, they are particularly concerned about their performance as parents.

Recall that when Jenna Hall was asked about her approach to raising children, she said she worries that there is too much "celebration for these things that aren't that great" and that "later on these kids are going to be really disappointed [because] things aren't going to be fun enough." Even more openly,

Susan Chase said she worries about "hoarding advantage" as parents eagerly seek out opportunities to provide "every little thing that will give [their children] some sort of little edge in this competitive and uncertain world." Jeff Wright, the widower, after talking about how much delight he had found in being able to maintain contact with his daughter once she had a cell phone, speculated about whether it may have become too much of a crutch for her:

> It almost makes it too easy at some times to ask for help instead of trying to [manage on her own]. . . . It can be an easy way out for her, [and] it raises expectations sometimes: "Well I can call you and tell you I need to be picked up right now." [And I'm thinking], "Well, no, you don't." So it can increase her expectations inappropriately.

Similarly, one parent realized that even as a cell phone enables her children to range more widely than they might have without that device, her children have a delayed experience of autonomy: "You know, you're not as independent because of the cell phone. Your parents can get a hold of you."

Independence and Autonomy

The murmurings of concern expressed by these parents are echoed by those who (whether or not they are parents themselves) have taken a more critical approach to the new practices of parenting among the professional middle class. In fact, commentators seem almost universally critical of this new approach to parenting. The titles of their books convey their distaste: *A Nation of Wimps: The High Cost of Invasive Parenting*; *Parenting, Inc.*; *Worried All the Time: Rediscovering the Joy in Parenthood in an Age of Anxiety*; *The Price of Privilege: How Parental Pressure and Material Advantage Are Creating a Generation of Disconnected and Unhappy Kids*; and *Perfect Madness: Motherhood in the Age of Anxiety*.[8]

Some of these commentators share the concern about delayed independence and autonomy. Researchers in the field of psychology measure emotional autonomy with concepts such as *de-idealization* (ceasing to perceive parents as perfect and seeing them as people with lives apart from parenting), *individuation* (the degree to which one sees oneself as separate from others), and *nondependence* (the degree to which one can make decisions oneself).

The psychologist Barbara Hofer and her colleagues at Middlebury College use this array of standard measures in a series of interesting studies, one of which found high levels of communication between college students and their parents. Hofer et al. also report that "hovering" hinders the development of autonomy, and they note both that "a high frequency of communication [is] related to parental regulation of academics and behaviors, as well as to increased parental dependency," and that students "who are in *frequent* contact with their parents may be less emotionally autonomous than individuals in either the low or medium groups."[9]

But are delayed independence and low autonomy necessarily bad? Perhaps and perhaps not. And while there are many people ready to assert that "'helicopter parents' . . . stunt student growth," the National Survey of Student Engagement found that "children of helicopter parents were more satisfied with every aspect of their college experience, gained more in such areas as writing and critical thinking, and were more likely to talk with faculty and peers about substantive topics."[10] If columnists argue that "letting go is the final frontier for boomer parents, who've made child rearing a major focus of their adult lives," many parents—and their children—believe that the electronic tether should remain in good working form.[11]

We might remember as well that there is no set time when children *should* be independent and autonomous, in the sense of being free from the interest, concern, and advice of the older generation. And, as I discussed earlier, what is seen as being appropriate moments for independence and autonomy changes over time and differs across social groups. Although some people might have been bemused by the *New York Times* story about a couple who bought a second home so that they could more easily attend their daughter's field hockey games when she was in college, "both General Douglas MacArthur and President Franklin Delano Roosevelt had mothers who moved to be near them when they went to college."[12] At elite institutions, college students today, even if they no longer live with strict parietal rules, do live in surroundings where all the accouterments of daily life are taken care of for them, while their working-class peers might well be earning sufficient money to provide for themselves (and possibly for a spouse and children as well). When privileged students graduate from college they are likely to move away from their families even if they still draw on family resources to supplement internships, graduate education, or meager initial earnings. But today, as in the past, less privileged youth might well remain closer to ongoing support structures even if they are expected to meet more of their own material needs. These different experiences make it difficult to conclude if *either* group of young adults is fully independent or truly autonomous.[13]

Unequal Outcomes

Social class differences in child-rearing practices have been clearly linked to differences in educational achievement as measured by grades, standardized test scores, and college attendance; in turn, these differences in educational achievement give rise to enormously unequal life chances.[14] Interestingly, now that the "hovering" of professional middle-class parents does not appear to end when children move out of the home and into college, social class might continue to matter in new ways. Indeed, the research by Barbara Hofer and her colleagues also demonstrates that the academic assistance parents offer to their children continues during the college years:

> In terms of academic regulation, some parents are maintaining their involvement and monitoring. Proofing papers and editing papers are not uncommon, reported at 19% and 14% respectively, and 8% of the students responded that "my parent contacts my professors or deans when I have a problem," although they do so infrequently. Some parents check to see if the students are keeping up with homework (32%), and check to make sure that students have written papers that are due (14%).[15]

If professional middle-class parents are now using their privileges to help their children not just to get into college but also to wend their way through college (and, as some commentators have suggested, in the years beyond), these class differences might have significant impacts that challenge whatever notions of meritocracy and individual achievement we might still hold dear.[16]

And What about the Parents?

For much of the foregoing analysis I have not distinguished between the parenting approaches of mothers and fathers. Indeed, men and women expressed many similar attitudes during the interviews. Occasionally differences emerged within couples, but even these were not consistent: for example, although some mothers said that their husbands are stricter than they are, other mothers said that precisely the opposite is the case in their homes. Of course, had I studied the number of hours put into providing child care and the degree of effort put into sustaining daily life, I would most certainly have found more significant differences between mothers and fathers. A substantial body of research demonstrates that rather than sharing equally in these efforts, women work far harder than do men.[17]

If parenting out of control is even more time-consuming and emotionally demanding than other parenting styles, the inequity between men and women might have particularly devastating consequences for women. This is precisely what a series of influential books and popular articles suggest, that at least some women in the professional middle class find the conflict between the demands of the workplace and the demands of rearing children so acute that they abandon highly successful careers.[18] Although it is easy to overstate the numbers and misinterpret the data on this issue, the narratives of such women suggest two causes for "opting out": the workplace has not proved to be particularly flexible, and parenting has become more intensive and more demanding than ever before.[19] Time-use statistics support this assertion about the increasing intensity of parenting practices: since 1965 the amount of time mothers spend on all child care activities has risen even though the majority of mothers are now in the labor force. The increase in time devoted to parenting is true across the board; it is especially the case for the highly educated adults who are also putting in more time at work.[20] Professional middle-class mothers thus appear to have few options: they can opt out, or they can overwork themselves.[21] Those who do opt out may need to justify that decision: defining child rearing as a full-time, totally consuming job can provide precisely that justification. Moreover, professional middle-class mothers might have considerable managerial skills to enhance that activity of raising children, and they may well set trends for other parents both within and outside their circle of peers.

In addition, I suggest that if mothers in the professional middle class find themselves in a difficult spot, their marriages might bear the costs of those difficulties. The excessive attention paid to one's children might leave little time for the maintenance and repair of adult relationships; in turn, the unsettled state of many marriages might lead adults to conclude that the only reliable, and persistent, relationships are those with their children. A study by

Robin Wilson at the Washington and Lee University School of Law reports that "huge numbers of female, and male, professionals who remain in the workplace . . . opt out of family" and that "these men and women forego parenting and stable, long-term relationships in surprisingly high numbers, believing they cannot have both." More specifically, using data from the 2003 National Survey of College Graduates, Wilson shows that women with MBAs are divorced or separated more often than those who have only a bachelor's degree and that women with JDs and MDs "are also more likely to divorce or separate than their male counterparts in the same profession."[22] In short, when women have serious career obligations a high divorce rate might be both a cause and a consequence of intense devotion to one's children.

The sociologist Rosanna Hertz makes the following provocative statement in the introduction to her compelling book, *Single by Chance, Mothers by Choice: How Women Are Choosing Parenthood without Marriage and Creating the New American Family*:

> The bottom line of this book is clear: we can no longer deny that the core of family life is the mother and her children. Marriage was once the only socially sanctioned way to have a child, just as sex was once coupled with procreation. Even though it still takes both sexes to create a baby, only the availability of both sets of gametes is essential. This sea change is rendering sexual intimacy between husbands and wives obsolete as *the* critical family bond. . . . While this begs the question of where men fit in, it is the reality of the new family, built on the assumption that romantic ties are no longer the foundation of family life. Caregiving and nurturing, which have always long been the responsibility of women, are at the center of U.S. family life in the twenty-first century.[23]

Hertz reaches this conclusion through an investigation of sixty-five women who sought artificial insemination as a way to become mothers even though it would mean raising their children outside marriage. The women in Hertz's study thus are not the stereotypical single mothers who arrive at that status as a result of divorce, separation, or abandonment by men. At least theoretically, they might say that they value marriage as much as or even more than they value children but were simply (or not so simply) unable to sustain (or even achieve) the former in their own lives.

Interestingly, however, Kathryn Edin and Maria Kefalas—in *Promises I Can Keep: Why Poor Women Put Motherhood before Marriage,* a very different investigation of single motherhood that builds on interviews with 162 low-income single mothers—say that these less privileged women also place motherhood at the center of family life and that remaining single protects marriage as a goal to be achieved when (and if) one is able. Indeed, Edin and Kefalas insist that low-income women do not marry because they value marriage *too much* to risk it when the marriage vow is not a "promise" they (or their male partners) can keep. However, because these young women also value children—and believe in their capacity to keep the promise to care for and raise those children to adulthood—they go ahead with the decision to have children outside marriage and often before "the public" believes it is appropriate. It could thus be argued that like the more privileged single mothers Hertz interviewed, low-income women regard men as optional, while they regard children as essential.

Similarly, it could be argued that the high rates of divorce among all social classes, which produce intense struggles by both men and women to maintain custody of dependent children, provide evidence that mothers and fathers alike view their children as being more essential to their happiness than they do life with a (particular) spouse. Of course, I do not mean to imply that divorce is either taken lightly or that it is always a matter of choice.[24] Rather, I mean to suggest that in contemporary times children often appear to be valued more deeply than are the relationships that produced them.

When I raised this issue of the irrelevance of spouses (at least in comparison with the importance of children) with friends and colleagues, an immediate response was to refer to the recent rise of lavish weddings. Precisely. The elaborate white weddings underwritten by the paychecks of parents like those interviewed for this study might be evidence of attempts to shore up a dying institution, to put front and center the romance of marriage, and to invest with significance something that contemporary statistics suggest is unlikely to last very long.[25]

But we needn't be quite so cynical to note that the *central* obsession of many parents is the safety and psychological well-being of their children rather than the current status of their adult relationships. Indeed, it is a commonplace truism that raising children wreaks havoc on relationships, especially during the early years. Moreover, the same parents who are spending more time with their children are spending less time with their spouses: the time-use data analyzed by the sociologists Suzanne Bianchi, John Robinson, and Melissa Milkie demonstrate that married adults spent 20 percent less time with their spouses in 2000 than did adults in 1975, even as parents today spend more time with their children.[26]

In a maybe not atypical moment of prying, I asked a colleague about whether she is able to spend time with friends as she sustains her highly successful professional life while running her (equally successful) home. She blanched. Friends? And well might she blanch. As Bianchi, Robinson, and Milkie report, both married fathers and married mothers spend less time visiting other people than did similar adults a generation ago. These declines are actually quite dramatic: married fathers spend three hours less per week visiting in 2000 than they did in 1964 (from 7.7 hours to 4.7 hours), and married mothers have reduced the time they devote to that social activity by almost the same amount (from 9.3 hours to 6.4 hours). (The statistics for single mothers also show declines, though not as significant: from 7.1 hours to 5.4 hours.) It would appear that the intensity of daily life might offer parents few opportunities to pursue friendship unless those friendships come "free" (e.g., with attendance at children's sporting events or through contacts in the workplace). The opportunities for simple sociability might be particularly rare in the lives of members of the professional middle class who devote especially long hours to both work and children.

Children, then, may have become the new companions, the promises adults believe that they can keep. And it's not *just* that this relationship, as Sharon Hays suggests, "comes to stand as a central symbol of the sustainable human ties, free of competition and selfish individualism, that are meant to preserve us . . . from an unbearable moral solitude."[27] It may also be that this relationship saves one from *literal* solitude. Mobile, career-driven adults find new forms of companionship in the parent-child relationship, and this relationship now appears to last (as an intimate relationship, even as it changes over time) far longer than it did in the relatively recent past.[28]

What Lies Ahead?

I see no reason to believe that cell phones and baby monitors will cease to remain popular devices among all groups of parents. And why not? Safety and responsiveness are likely to remain significant concerns. New models of baby monitors solve older problems of poor reception; some now offer video as well as sound. And cell phones are being promoted for ever younger children and with ever more varied innovations.[29]

I also anticipate that among the professional middle class the current aversion to some of the other devices discussed here will disappear. Recently child locators got a major sales boost when they were advertised with Duracell batteries.[30] And the insurance industry now promotes GPS tracking in cars as a way of keeping children safe.[31] On the other hand, home drug testing seems to be in disgrace and may therefore be less likely to be used in the future by the professional middle class than are referrals to physicians and counselors.[32]

When I began this study newspapers reported frequently—almost daily it seemed—about predators and other dangers on the Internet; the frequency of those reports appears to be diminishing.[33] Our moral panics are often time bound—here today, gone tomorrow.[34] This panic may have subsided because more and more adults are themselves becoming comfortable with the new technologies of the World Wide Web. And I suspect that as anxiety decreases, parents will feel less compelled to adopt technologies that constrain Internet usage.[35] (Moreover, as children become more adept themselves, they will be able to get around whatever devices their parents have chosen to use.)

There is already evidence that parents are becoming inured to sexuality and violence on television: fewer parents said they are "very concerned" about sex, violence, and adult language on television in 2006 than did in 1998, and fewer parents said they rely on ratings for television programs and movies (though more said they rely on music advisories and video game advisories).

In a 2008 piece in the *New York Times*, the popular mystery writer Harlen Coben described how a friend of his had put spyware on a teen's computer. Coben suggested that, in spite of his initial revulsion, he had come around to believing this was a "good idea." He explained: "This isn't the government we are talking about—this is your family. . . . Loving parents are doing the surveillance here, not faceless bureaucrats. And most parents already monitor their children, watching over their home environment, their school."[36] Whether bringing this kind of activity out into the open and condoning it will produce more purchases of spyware among the professional middle class, I don't know. With so many parents teetering on the brink, it just might be the case that a number of people will be persuaded by this kind of commentary. But, no matter what the outcome, these devices will be used within the framework of control itself, at least by the professional middle class.

Is control here to stay? Will parents continue to hover?[37] In spite of some pushback in the encouragement of what is referred to as "free-range children," hovering has roots in parental perceptions of where the burden for keeping children safe and secure rests *and* on parental perceptions of the consequences of educational and occupational failure.[38] I argue that unless there are changes—in neighborhoods, in workplaces, in communities, in state actions—that demonstrate that child care is a community responsibility, and as long as our society continues to be marked by an extreme income inequality that makes consequences of "failure" so severe, it is likely that control is here to stay. Moreover, current parents—of emerging adults, of teens, and even of younger children—are modeling parenting styles for their peers, their younger friends, and, of course, the next generation. Whether that next generation—raised through control—will take it upon themselves to resist that control and raise *their* children some other way is impossible to predict. What is clear, however, is that to do so they will have to grow up enough to know their own minds.

◈ APPENDIX A

Methods

In this book I rely on information collected during in-depth interviews with ninety-three parents.[1] I asked parents to answer a series of questions about the two main issues of concern in this research: first, parenting practices and, second, attitudes toward and use of various new technologies of connection, constraint, and surveillance. In addition, I asked parents to answer questions about what worries, difficulties, and satisfactions they encounter as they raise their children today and to compare those with the worries, difficulties, and satisfactions they believe their own parents faced. I also asked some broader questions that were designed to shed light on motivations for parenting practices: for example, "What do you think are the greatest problems facing parents today?" "Do you think it is important to raise children within a religion of some sort or another?" and "Do you think there is too much surveillance in the United States today?"

I was interested in how parents across the country and parents from a variety of demographic groups would respond to these questions. In order to gain access to this broad range of respondents, I hired a team of research assistants to conduct interviews in places with which I was less familiar and to which I might not have ready access. Nine of these interviewers were young men and women who had very recently been my undergraduate students; one was a woman who had been my student several years before, another was a woman who had been my student over a decade before, and another was an adult friend trained as a speech pathologist. Among the relatively recent students, five were teaching through subsidized programs such as Teach for America and Teach Kentucky. Several of these individuals conducted interviews in both their hometowns and in the places where they were working. In the latter sites, they drew on colleagues and friends as well as the parents of children in the schools where they were teaching. All but two of the interviewers were women.

Although hiring others to conduct interviews often results in the loss of appropriate follow-up to questions of interest, the reverse can be the case as well: some of the interviewers had broader interests than I did and were quick to pick up on interesting issues I might have overlooked. In addition, these particular interviewers had access to populations with whom I might have had a far more difficult time establishing rapport. These populations include African American mothers in inner-city Philadelphia; Hispanics living in San Antonio, Texas; and whites living in rural (and semiurban) Kentucky.

Respondent Characteristics

Although only a relatively small proportion of the respondents are given pseudonyms in the text, the majority of those who were interviewed are mentioned in other ways (e.g., with the use of quotes or as examples). An overview of the entire sample of respondents is provided in table A.1. Altogether, four-fifths of the sample are women; a similar proportion of respondents are partners in heterosexual married couples.[2] Among those who indicated race/ethnicity on a brief questionnaire that respondents were asked to complete after the interview, 70 percent identified themselves as being white, 16 percent as black or African American, 10 percent as Hispanic, and 4 percent as Asian American. The parents ranged in age from thirty-one to fifty-nine; the average age was forty-seven, and the median was somewhat lower, at forty-six.

TABLE A.1

Sample Characteristics

Gender	Working Class and Middle Class	Professional Middle Class	Total
Female	88%	66%	79%
Male	13%	34%	21%
Total	101%	100%	100%
(N)	(57)	(36)	(93)
Marital Status			
Divorced	7%	0%	4%
Married	76%	84%	79%
Single	13%	13%	13%
Widowed	4%	3%	4%
Total	100%	100%	100%
(N)	(57)	(36)	(93)

TABLE A.1
Sample Characteristics (continued)

Race/Ethnicity	Working Class and Middle Class	Professional Middle Class	Total
Black/African American	17%	14%	16%
White	70%	71%	70%
Hispanic	13%	4%	10%
Asian	0%	11%	4%
Total	100%	100%	100%
(N)	(57)	(36)	(93)
Age			
Median age	44	48	46
Mean age	45	49	47
Median age at first birth	28	31	29
Mean age at first birth	27	31	30
Number of Children			
1	24%	3%	16%
2	43%	56%	48%
3 or more	33%	41%	36%
Total	100%	100%	100%
(N)	(57)	(36)	(93)
Mean	2.3	2.4	2.4
Median	2	2	2

TABLE A.1

Sample Characteristics (continued)

Income	Working Class and Middle Class	Professional Middle Class	Total
Less than $50,000	17%	7%	14%
$50,000–$99,000	33%	26%	30%
$100,000–$149,000	26%	15%	22%
$150,000 or more	24%	52%	34%
Total	100%	100%	100%
(N)	(46)	(27)	(73)

Education	Working Class	Middle Class	Professional Middle Class	Total
High school or less	12%			3%
Some college or associate's degree	88%			23%
Bachelor's degree		100%		35%
Graduate degree			100%	39%
Total	100%	100%	100%	100%
(N)	(24)	(33)	(36)	(93)

Approximately half the respondents said that they live in a suburban area; another 29 percent said that they live in an urban area, and one-fifth live in either a small town or a rural area. The vast majority of those who were interviewed own their own home—only 11 percent are renters.

On average, the interviewed parents have 2.4 children; the median number of children is 2.0. All but 13 percent of the parents have at least one child who is a teenager; one-quarter of the parents have at least one child who has passed beyond her or his teen years as well as a teenager still living at home.

With regard to both income and education, the sample is a relatively privileged one. Only 14 percent of all parents have an annual household income of less than $50,000, and one-third of the parents have incomes over $150,000. In 2005, the median income for all U.S. families with children under eighteen was $56,886, and the mean was $74,037.[3]

As noted in the introduction, I divide the sample into three subgroups: I identify as working class those whose education does not include a bachelor's degree, as middle class those with a bachelor's degree but no higher education, and as professional middle class those who have some postgraduate degree. This latter group includes two MDs, four JDs, and three PhDs. (For most of the analysis I combine the working and middle class.) Taken as a whole, the study population is well educated: only 3 percent of those interviewed have no more than a high school education, 23 percent have some college credit or an associate's degree, 35 percent have a bachelor's degree, and 39 percent have a graduate degree. By way of comparison, in the United States as a whole in 2005, 40.7 percent had no more than a high school education, 25.4 percent had some college credit or an associate's degree, 18.1 percent had a bachelor's degree, and 9.5 percent had a graduate degree.[4]

Of course, there are many "deviant" cases within the groupings I identify for purposes of analysis. Among the sample, for example, are a woman who has achieved high educational status but lives on an extremely low income and a woman who, although she has but a bachelor's degree herself, lives with a man whose professional position secures a very high income. Because I do not adjust for these exceptions, numerical differences in practices and attitudes (see, for example, the tables in appendix B) may often be smaller than if my measure were more precise or took into account more factors of class (e.g., by including income and occupation as well). However, because for the most part I rely on qualitative data, I can look at general trends and also highlight occasions when a respondent fits better within a different grouping than the one to which she or he has formally been assigned. The messiness that remains both within the categories of respondents—and within any given respondent's approach to parenting—reminds us that in the United States at least, social classes are not neatly bounded and that ideal types are figments of our (sociological) imaginations.

Comparing Social Classes

None of the three social class groupings is exclusively made up of white respondents; in fact, the racial/ethnic distribution is fairly consistent across the social groups. The only exceptions to this generalization are that the working-class and middle-class group includes a more substantial Hispanic population than does the professional middle-class group, and the few Asian respondents were all members of the professional middle class.

The groups do differ in other ways, as might be expected. Not only on average do the professional middle-class respondents have higher incomes than do those who are working class or middle class, but on average the professional middle-class respondents are also older than the middle-class and working-class respondents. The professional middle-class respondents were also older than their less privileged peers when they had their first child. Moreover, the professional middle-class respondents were least likely to have only one child and most likely to have the modal number of two children.

Race/Ethnicity and Gender

Not surprisingly, there are demographic differences within the sample with respect to race/ethnicity: more of the African American respondents were single parents at the time of the interview, and more of this group of respondents lived in an urban area. At the same time, as noted, the professional middle-class and the working-class/middle-class groupings had equal proportions of white and African American respondents. Needless to say, there were occasions when race/ethnicity seemed of particular relevance: for example, African American mothers expressed more overt concern than did other mothers about the possibility that their children would get in trouble with the police. However, for most of the issues with which this study is concerned, race/ethnicity seemed if not irrelevant, then at least insignificant in its effects.[5]

Intentionally I collected more information from mothers (who are generally more engaged in the hands-on care of children) than from fathers, and I interviewed more professional middle-class fathers than fathers in the other social groupings. Once again, however, I found that with respect to attitudes, class was more important than gender: within each social class mothers and fathers gave quite similar answers with respect to most of the questions. I did not examine differences in responses by the gender of children.[6] However, when an issue seemed to be of particular concern with respect to children of one gender or the other (e.g., sexual images), I have discussed that in the text.

From Qualitative to Quantitative Data

With the exception of the brief questionnaire asking for information about demographic characteristics, I collected only qualitative data. In several places in the text and notes, and especially in appendix B, I do convert these data into numerical form. All tables should be interpreted with a grain of salt. Indeed, a handful of that salt might be applied to the data concerning adoption of the devices under consideration in part II. Respondents were asked if they had ever heard of these devices and if they had any interest in using them. Although some respondents gave clear positive or negative answers to the latter question, most answers could not be easily coded. Many parents hedged in their responses: that is, they would start by saying no, they would not use such a device, but then introduce a qualification. "Well," they would say, "if this or that situation arose, I would consider it." Indeed, the line between a negative response and an "interested" response was often merely temporal (that is, respondents started out saying no and then moved into a consideration of the conditions under which they might engage in this form of surveillance). For example, Patsy Doria, a working-class single mother of one teenage boy and two considerably older children, said the following about the GPS tracking system:

> I've heard of it; I heard about it when a friend of mine was telling me about her husband [tracking her]. . . . *No I would not* [*use it*]. *I should back up on that—I probably would* for the same reasons I would read his diary . . . if I were concerned about drug use or a predator or something where I felt he could be in danger. . . . Currently I don't feel I have a need to. (Emphasis added)

The relatively straightforward categories of "No," "Conditional No," and "Would Use or Did Use" represent my best attempt to translate these complex responses into a tabular form. The text discussion of the kinds of issues that arose as respondents thought about the issues represents more fully the complexity of parental attitudes.

◈ APPENDIX B

Data Analysis

Educational Aspirations

Table B.1 shows responses to the question of how much education parents want their children to obtain (an issue discussed in chapter 2). The "college plus" category indicates that the respondent suggested that it might well be desirable to have education that extends beyond a bachelor's degree; the "more than college" category indicates parents who named a professional degree or who were relatively insistent that their children continue their education beyond college. Because this table builds on qualitative responses, these categories are illustrative rather than definitive. I divide the working class from the middle class here to show how aspirations for children increase with the parents' own level of education.

TABLE B.1

Parents' Expectations Concerning the Future Education of Their Children

How Much Education They Want for Their Own Children	Parents' Own Level of Education		
	Less than College (Working Class)	College (Middle Class)	Graduate Degree (Professional Middle Class)
Associate's degree	0%	5%	0%
College	40%	15%	0%
College plus	35%	70%	55%
More than college	25%	10%	45%
Total	100%	100%	100%
(N)	(24)	(30)	(35)

Technological Choices

Tables B.2–B.10 all show responses to questions concerning the devices of connection, constraint, and surveillance (discussed in chapters 5–7). Once again I caution that because these tables build on qualitative responses, the categories are meant to be illustrative rather than definitive. In addition, not all respondents gave responses to all questions.

Devices of Connection

TABLE B.2

Baby Monitor Ownership by Social Class

	Working Class and Middle Class	Professional Middle Class	Total
Didn't have one	19%	22%	20%
Would have wanted one	0%	6%	2%
Had one	81%	72%	78%
Total	100%	100%	100%
(N)	(55)	(34)	(89)

TABLE B.3

Cell Phone Ownership by Age of Child

Age of Child	No Cell Phone	Not Yet Purchased	Has Cell Phone
Six to twelve	25%	78%	9%
Thirteen to seventeen	50%	22%	51%
Eighteen and older	25%	0%	39%
Total	100%	100%	100%
(N)	(4)	(9)	(74)

TABLE B.4

Child's Cell Phone Ownership by Social Class

	Working Class and Middle Class	Professional Middle Class	Total
No cell phone	7%	3%	6%
Will get cell phone	11%	7%	9%
Has cell phone	82%	90%	85%
Total	100%	100%	100%
(N)	(56)	(34)	(90)

Devices of Constraint

TABLE B.5

Attitudes toward Child Locator by Social Class

	Working Class and Middle Class	Professional Middle Class	Total
Might use; would have used	42%	19%	33%
Would not use	58%	81%	67%
Total	100%	100%	100%
(N)	(51)	(33)	(84)

TABLE B.6

Software Filter Ownership by Social Class

	Working Class and Middle Class	Professional Middle Class	Total
Had or currently have	60%	40%	52%
Will get or might get	16%	16%	16%
No interest in owning	24%	44%	32%
Total	100%	100%	100%
(N)	(52)	(31)	(83)

Devices of Surveillance

TABLE B.7

Attitudes toward Keystroke Monitor Ownership by Social Class

	Working Class and Middle Class	Professional Middle Class	Total
No interest in owning	28%	53%	37%
Conditional interest	58%	44%	53%
Would use or did use	14%	3%	10%
Total	100%	100%	100%
(N)	(54)	(33)	(87)

TABLE B.8

Attitudes toward GPS Tracking Ownership by Social Class

	Working Class and Middle Class	Professional Middle Class	Total
No interest in owning	48%	63%	54%
Conditional interest	40%	30%	36%
Would use or did use	12%	7%	10%
Total	100%	100%	100%
(N)	(54)	(33)	(87)

TABLE B.9

Attitudes toward Home Drug Testing by Social Class

	Working Class and Middle Class	Professional Middle Class	Total
No interest	25%	44%	32%
Conditional no	68%	53%	62%
Would or did use	7%	3%	6%
Total	100%	100%	100%
(N)	(52)	(34)	(86)

TABLE B.10

Attitudes toward Reading Diary versus Using Keystroke Monitoring System by Social Class

	Working Class and Middle Class	Professional Middle Class
Would never use keystroke monitoring system	28%	53%
Would never read diary	17%	10%
Difference (preference for reading diary)	11%	43%

◈ NOTES

NOTES TO THE INTRODUCTION

1. For the new possibilities for tracking children's school performance, see Pearson's PowerSchool website, http://www.pearsonschoolsystems.com/; Edline website, http://www.edline.com/; Linton Weeks, "How'd You Do in School Today? With Edline Online, the Report Card Goes 24/7 and Every Test Is an Open Book," *Washington Post,* April 30, 2008; Jan Hoffman, "I Know What You Did Last Math Class," *New York Times,* May 4, 2008.

2. The term "hypervigilance" comes from Cindi Katz, "The State Goes Home: Local Hyper-Vigilance of Children and the Global Retreat from Social Reproduction," *Social Justice* 28, no. 3 (2001): 47–56. For parenting books, see David Anderegg, *Worried All the Time: Rediscovering the Joy in Parenthood in an Age of Anxiety* (New York: Free Press, 2003); Judith Warner, *Perfect Madness: Motherhood in the Age of Anxiety* (New York: Riverhead Books, 2005). For journalists, see Hara Estroff Marano, "A Nation of Wimps," *Psychology Today,* November–December 2004; Peter Applebome, "How We Took the Child Out of Childhood," *New York Times,* January 8, 2006; Pamela Paul, *Parenting, Inc.* (New York: Times Books, 2008); Madeline Levine, *The Price of Privilege: How Parental Pressure and Material Advantage Are Creating a Generation of Disconnected and Unhappy Kids* (New York: Harper, 2008); Lisa Belkin, "Let the Kid Be," *New York Times,* May 31, 2009. And for academics, see Peter N. Stearns, *Anxious Parents: A History of Modern Childrearing in America* (New York: NYU Press, 2004); Ann Hulbert, *Raising America: Experts, Parents and a Century of Advice about Children* (New York: Knopf, 2003). Newspaper columns on the topic engender a vociferous response. See, for example, the website Marano has entitled "A Nation of Wimps," http://www.nationofwimps.com/, and the many letters generated by Applebome's article in the *New York Times,* "Readers Respond: Taking the Child Out of Childhood," *New York Times,* January 14, 2006, www.nytimes.com/2006/01/14/nyregion/14towns-readers.html. See also the review essay in the *New Yorker,* Joan Acocella, "The Child Trap: The Rise of Overparenting," *New Yorker,* November 17, 2008. That review referred to the following books: Hara Estroff Marano, *A Nation of Wimps: The High Cost of Invasive Parenting* (New York: Broadway Books, 2008); Levine, *The Price of Privilege*; Gary Cross, *Men to Boys: The Making of Modern Masculinity* (New York: Columbia University Press, 2008); Carl Honore, *Under Pressure: Rescuing Our Children from the Culture of Hyper-Parenting* (New York: HarperOne, 2009).

3. Wikipedia, "Helicopter Parent," http://en.wikipedia.org/wiki/Helicopter_parent.

4. There is almost no scholarly commentary on "helicopter parenting," though researchers at the University of Texas are exploring this phenomenon: University of Texas at Austin, "Mom Needs an 'A,'" 2007, http://www.utexas.edu/features/2007/helicopter/. So too is my colleague Barbara Hofer at Middlebury College: Barbara Hofer et al., "The 'Electronic Tether': Communication and Parental Monitoring during the College Years," in *Who's Watching? Daily Practices of Surveillance among Contemporary Families*, ed. Margaret K. Nelson and Anita Ilta Garey, 277–94 (Nashville, TN: Vanderbilt University Press, 2009). At the same time, college administrators are certain that this phenomenon exists, and they create sessions during orientation to deal with parents who they believe will tend to hover. For discussions, see, for example, "Colleges Cope with 'Helicopter Parents,'" *Buffalo News,* July 23, 2008, http://buffalonews.typepad.com/inside_the_news/2008/07/colleges-cope-w.html; National Resource Center Listservs; "'Helicopter' Parents at Orientation," http://www.sc.edu/fye/listservs/archives/HelicopterParentsatOrientation.html.

5. National Survey of Student Engagement, "Experiences That Matter: Enhancing Student Learning and Success; Annual Report 2007," 2007, http://nsse.iub.edu/NSSE_2007_Annual_Report/docs/withhold/NSSE_2007_Annual_Report.pdf.

6. Ibid., 25.

7. Hofer et al., "The 'Electronic Tether,'" 284.

8. Ibid.

9. Janine DeFao, "Parents Turn to Tech Toys to Track Teens," *San Francisco Chronicle*, July 9, 2006; Chris Jenks, "Editorial: Children at Risk?" *Childhood* 10, no. 1 (2003): 5–8; Lydia Martens, "Gender, Power, and the Household (Book Review)," *Sociology* 35, no. 1 (February 2001): 241; Amy Harmon, "Lost? Hiding? Your Cellphone Is Keeping Tabs," *New York Times*, December 21, 2003; Larry Magid, "GPS Chips in Cellphones Track Kids and Help Navigate, Too," *International Herald Tribune*, July 19, 2007. In England, one parent even had a microchip implanted in her daughter so that her movements could be traced if she were abducted. Jamie Wilson, "Girl to Get Tracker Implant to Ease Parents' Fears," *Guardian*, September 3, 2002.

10. These devices are described more fully in part II.

11. Presumably many elite parents are also engaged in electronic surveillance of their nannies. Julia Wrigley, *Other People's Children: An Intimate Account of the Dilemmas Facing Middle-Class Parents and the Women They Hire to Raise Their Children* (New York: Basic Books, 1995); Julia Wrigley, "Hiring a Nanny: The Limits of Private Solutions to Public Problems," *Annals, AAPSS* 593 (May 1999): 162–74. See also the frequency with which this practice is mentioned on the website I Saw Your Nanny, http://isawyournanny.blogspot.com/. For a discussion of this phenomenon, see Margaret K. Nelson, "'I Saw Your Nanny': Gossip and Shame in the Surveillance of Child Care," in *Who's Watching? Daily Practices of Surveillance among Contemporary Families,* ed. Margaret K. Nelson and Anita Ilta Garey, 219–38 (Nashville, TN: Vanderbilt University Press, 2009).

12. Most famously, perhaps, the term "professional middle class" has been used by Barbara Ehrenreich to describe that version of the middle class "whose economic and social status is based on education, rather than on the ownership of capital or property." Barbara Ehrenreich, *Fear of Falling: The Inner Life of the Middle Class* (New York: HarperCollins, 1990), 12.

13. Miller McPherson, Lynn Smith-Lovin, and James M. Cook, "Birds of a Feather: Homophily in Social Networks," *Annual Review of Sociology* 27 (2001): 415–44.

14. Thanks to Anita Garey for helping me see this.

15. For a fuller discussion of these issues, see the introduction to part I.

16. I conducted this research before the recession in 2008; even so, I argue that economic uncertainty was a feature of the lives of even the most privileged parents among my sample of respondents.

17. Pierre Bourdieu, "Cultural Reproduction and Social Reproduction," in *Knowledge, Education, and Cultural Change*, ed. Richard Brown, 487–507 (London: Tavistock, 1973).

18. Benjamin Spock, *Dr. Benjamin Spock's Baby and Child Care* (New York: Pocket Book, 1959).

19. I also assumed that the cost of these technologies would be well within the reach of professional middle-class parents' budgets but outside that of their less wealthy peers.

20. Hofer et al., "The 'Electronic Tether.'"

21. I discuss both these issues in the conclusion.

22. This design was originally developed by Jeremy Bentham. See Michel Foucault, *Discipline and Punish: The Birth of the Prison*, trans. A. M. Sheridan (New York: Pantheon, 1977).

23. David Lyon, *Surveillance Studies: An Overview* (Cambridge, UK: Polity, 2007), 59.

24. This discussion of control is based on the work of Deleuze and Rose. Gilles Deleuze, "Postscript on the Societies of Control," *October* 59 (Winter 1992): 3–7; Nikolas Rose, *Governing the Soul: The Shaping of the Private Self* (London: Free Association Books, 1989); Nikolas Rose, *Powers of Freedom: Reframing Political Thought* (Cambridge: Cambridge University Press, 1999); Nikolas Rose, "Government and Control," *British Journal of Criminology* 40 (2000): 321–39. See also the interpretation in J. Macgregor Wise, "Assemblage," in *Gilles Deleuze: Key Concepts*, ed. Charles J. Stivale, 77–87 (Montreal: McGill-Queen's University Press, 2005), 86.

25. Hence, Nikolas Rose, for example, writes, "Community is not simply the territory within which crime is to be controlled; it is itself a *means* of governments: its ties, bonds, forces and affiliations are to be celebrated, encouraged, nurtured, shaped and instrumentalized in the hope of enhancing the security of each and of all." Rose, *Powers of Freedom*, 250. However, the parents with whom I spoke, rather than trusting "community" to help in the difficult job of raising children, see themselves as

being very much on their own. And rather than trusting institutions, families today mainly trust themselves. In this context the family becomes the gated community or the fortress city. Edward J. Blakeley, *Fortress America: Gated Communities in the United States* (Washington, DC: Brookings Institution Press, 1999).

26. Making these links, however, is not meant as an assertion of similar causes (beyond broad cultural patterns): different domains within society respond (in particular ways) to the *particular* configurations of issues affecting them. Hence, even shared phenomena (e.g., growing rates of poverty) will have different manifestations within different institutions (e.g., the family, the school, the state) even as shared cultural attitudes affect the form and content of those manifestations. For issues relating to the criminal justice system, see David Garland, "The Culture of High Crime Societies: Some Preconditions of Recent 'Law and Order' Policies," *British Journal of Criminology* 40 (2000): 347–75.

NOTES TO THE INTRODUCTION TO PART I

1. John Nagy and Tiffany Danitz, "Parental Fears Heightened by Columbine, Poll Shows," *Stateline.org,* April 20, 2000, http://www.stateline.org/live/ViewPage.action?siteNodeId=136&languageId=1&contentId=13994; Alexandra Starr, "'Security Moms': An Edge for Bush?" *Business Week*, December 1, 2003, 60; R. Burns and C. Crawford, "School Shootings, the Media, and Public Fear: Ingredients for a Moral Panic," *Crime Law and Social Change* 32, no. 21 (1999): 147–68.

2. David L. Altheide, "Children and the Discourse of Fear," *Symbolic Interaction* 25, no. 2 (2002): 229–50; Barry Glassner, *The Culture of Fear: Why Americans Are Afraid of the Wrong Thing* (New York: Basic Books, 1999); Joel Best, *Threatened Children: Rhetoric and Concern about Child-Victims* (Chicago: University of Chicago Press, 1990); David Anderegg, *Worried All the Time: Rediscovering the Joy in Parenthood in an Age of Anxiety* (New York: Free Press, 2003).

3. Ulrich Beck, *Risk Society: Towards a New Modernity* (London: Sage, 1992); Anderegg, *Worried All the Time*, 26–36.

4. Viviana A. Zelizer, *Pricing the Priceless Child: The Changing Social Value of Children* (New York: Basic Books, 1985).

5. Frank Furedi, *Paranoid Parenting: Abandon Your Anxieties and Be a Good Parent* (London: Allen Lane/Penguin Press, 2001), 31.

6. Anthony Giddens, "Risk and Responsibility," *Modern Law Review* 62, no. 1 (1999): 1–10; Beck, *Risk Society.*

7. Giddens, "Risk and Responsibility," 3.

8. Deborah Lupton and John Tulloch, "'Risk Is Part of Your Life': Risk Epistemologies among a Group of Australians," *Sociology* 36, no. 2 (2002): 318. See also Marianne Cooper, "'Doing Security' in Insecure Times: Class and Family Life in Silicon Valley" (PhD diss., Sociology, University of California at Berkeley, 2008).

9. Kathryn Backett-Milburn and Jeni Hardin, "How Children and Their Families Construct and Negotiate Risk, Safety and Danger," *Childhood* 11, no. 4 (2004): 429–47; Gill Valentine, "'My Son's a Bit Dizzy.' 'My Wife's a Bit Soft': Gender, Children and Cultures of Parenting," *Gender, Place and Culture* 4, no. 1 (1997): 37–62; Gill Valentine, "'Oh Yes I Can.' 'Oh No You Can't': Children and Parents' Understandings of Kids' Competence to Negotiate Public Space Safely," *Antipode* 29, no. 1 (1997): 65–89; Gill Valentine and John McKendrick, "Children's Outdoor Play: Exploring Parental Concerns about Children's Safety," *Geoforum* 28, no. 2 (1997): 219–35.

10. Cooper, "'Doing Security' in Insecure Times." Whatever the cause, commentators are ready to offer solutions. Some suggest that the problem of parental anxiety could be "solved" if there were more social responsibility for children. See, for example, Judith Warner, *Perfect Madness: Motherhood in the Age of Anxiety* (New York: Riverhead Books, 2005). For a more "academic" version of this argument, see Cindi Katz, "The State Goes Home: Local Hyper-Vigilance of Children and the Global Retreat from Social Reproduction," *Social Justice* 28, no. 3 (2001): 47–56; and Dawn Moore and Kevin D. Haggerty, "Bring It on Home: Home Drug Testing and the Relocation of the War on Drugs," *Social & Legal Studies* 10, no. 3 (2001): 377–405. Others, from a more conservative point of view, suggest the solution might be found in having more mothers leave the workplace to watch children themselves and to practice "appropriate" family values. See, for example, "Readers Respond: Taking the Child Out of Childhood," *New York Times*, January 14, 2006, www.nytimes.com/2006/01/14/nyregion/14towns-readers.html.

11. Public Agenda, "A Lot Easier Said than Done," 2002, http://www.publicagenda.org/files/pdf/easier_said_than_done.pdf (June 2, 2008).

12. Sharon Hays, *The Cultural Contradictions of Motherhood* (New Haven, CT: Yale University Press, 1996), 128–29.

13. Ibid., 175.

14. Ibid., 212n. 12.

15. Annette Lareau, *Unequal Childhoods: Class, Race, and Family Life* (Berkeley: University of California Press, 2003), 260–61.

16. Ibid., 31.

17. For a good review, see David H. Demo and Martha J. Cox, "Families with Young Children: A Review of Research in the 1990s," *Journal of Marriage and the Family* 62 (November 2000): 876–95.

18. Hays, *The Cultural Contradictions of Motherhood*, 51.

19. Basil Bernstein, *Class, Codes, and Control* (London: Routledge and Kegan Paul, 1971); Francesca M. Cancian, "Defining 'Good' Child Care: Hegemonic and Democratic Standards," in *Child Care and Inequality: Rethinking Carework for Children and Youth*, ed. Francesca M. Cancian et al., 65–82 (New York: Routledge, 2002); Hays, *The Cultural Contradictions of Motherhood*; Lareau, *Unequal Childhoods*.

20. Bernstein, *Class, Codes, and Control*; Betty Hart and Todd R. Risley, *Meaningful Differences in the Everyday Experience of Young American Children* (Baltimore: Paul H. Brookes, 1995); Shirley Brice Heath, *Ways with Words: Language, Life and Work in Communities and Classrooms* (New York: Cambridge University Press, 1996); Pierre Bourdieu and Jean Claude Passeron, *Reproduction in Education, Culture and Society* (Beverly Hills, CA: Sage, 1977); Nan Dirk De Graaf, Paul M. De Graaf, and Gerbert Kraaykamp, "Parental Cultural Capital and Educational Attainment in the Netherlands: A Refinement of the Cultural Capital Perspective," *Sociology of Education* 73 (2000): 92–111; Paul DiMaggio, "Cultural Capital and School Success: The Impact of Status Culture Participation on the Grades of U.S. High School Students," *American Sociological Review* 47 (1982): 189–201; Lareau, *Unequal Childhoods*. These different strategies can be seen as part of parents' efforts to prepare children for different social class positions. See Melvin Kohn, *Class and Conformity: A Study in Values* (Homewood, IL: Dorsey, 1969). Especially in the contemporary world, where institutions follow the model used in the middle class, these different styles have quite different outcomes for children. For example, Lareau's central interest is in the differential advantage that middle-class child rearing has for a range of outcomes—educational success being among the most important (Lareau, *Unequal Childhoods*).

NOTES TO CHAPTER I

1. All names are pseudonyms.

2. E. S. Browning, "Exorcising Ghosts of Octobers Past," *Wall Street Journal Online,* October 15, 2007, http://online.wsj.com/public/article_print/SP119239926667758592.html; National Bureau of Economic Research, "U.S. Business Cycle Expansions and Contractions," 2008, www.nber.org/cycles/main.html. This research was conducted *before* the stock market fell so drastically in 2008, but talk of a recession was already in the winds.

3. Between 1975 and 2005, U.S. households in the bottom 80 percent income bracket saw their share of national income actually fall; "only the top 20 percent of households experienced an increase in their share of the total national income; much of that went to households in the highest 5 percent of the income bracket." Uri Berliner, "Have and Have-Nots: Income Inequality in America," *NPR.org,* February 5, 2007, www.npr.org/templates/story/story.php?storyId=7180618. See also Carmen DeNavas-Walt, Bernadette D. Proctor, and Cheryl Hill Lee, *Money Income in the United States: 2005,* Current Population Reports P60-231, U.S. Census Bureau (Washington, DC: U.S. Government Printing Office, 2006).

4. The number of college applicants is expected to decline between 2009 and 2015. Alan Finder, "Elite Colleges Reporting Record Lows in Admission," *New York Times,* April 1, 2008.

5. Karen W. Arenson, "Applications to Colleges Are Breaking Records," *New York Times,* January 17, 2008; Kate Stone Lomardi, "High Anxiety of Getting into College," *New York Times,* April 8, 2007; Michael Winerip, "Young, Gifted, and Not Getting into Harvard," *New York Times,* April 29, 2007; Sam Dillon, "A Great Year for Ivy League Colleges, but Not So Good for Applicants to Them," *New York Times,* April 4, 2007.

6. For a similar argument about how educational concerns transcend class divisions, see Annette Lareau, *Home Advantage: Social Class and Parental Intervention in Elementary Education* (Lanham, MD: Rowman & Littlefield, 2000); Heather Beth Johnson, *The American Dream and the Power of Wealth: Choosing Schools and Inheriting Inequality in the Land of Opportunity* (New York: Routledge, 2007). In 2005, 69 percent of all high school completers made the immediate transition to college; among white students that figure was an all-time high of 73 percent. National Center for Education Statistics, "Student Effort and Educational Progress: Transition to College," in *The Condition of Education,* 2007, http://nces.ed.gov/programs/coe/2007/section3/indicator25.asp.

7. For specific studies on this issue, see Stephen J. Ball, *Class Strategies and the Education Market: The Middle Classes and Social Advantage* (London: RoutledgeFalmer, 2003); Ellen Brantlinger, *Dividing Classes: How the Middle Class Negotiates and Rationalizes School Advantage* (London: RoutledgeFalmer, 2003); Annette Lareau, *Unequal Childhoods: Class, Race, and Family Life* (Berkeley: University of California Press, 2003); Lareau, *Home Advantage*; H. Johnson, *The American Dream and the Power of Wealth.* For an excellent overview, see Joel Spring, *American Education,* 13th ed. (New York: McGraw-Hill, 2007).

8. Peter Cookson and Caroline Persell, *Preparing for Power* (New York: Basic Books, 1985); H. Johnson, *The American Dream and the Power of Wealth.*

9. For interesting discussions of learning disabilities and the uses made of them by children, parents, and educators, see Peter Conrad, "Medicalization and Social Control," *Annual Review of Sociology* 18 (1992): 209–32; Peter Conrad and D. Potter, "From Hyperactive Children to ADHD Adults: Observations on the Expansion of Medical Categories," *Social Problems* 47, no. 4 (November 2000): 559–82; Linda Feldmeier White, "Learning Disability, Pedagogies, and Public Discourse," *College Composition and Communication* 53, no. 4 (2002): 705–38; Ruth Shalit, "Defining Disability Down: Why Johnny Can't Read, Write, or Sit Still," *New Republic,* August 25, 1997.

10. Private school enrollment at both the elementary and secondary level rises with family income. Stacey Bielick and Chris Chapman, "Trends in the Use of School Choice," *Education Statistics Quarterly* (National Center for Education Statistics) 5, no. 2 (2003).

11. Lareau, *Home Advantage*; Lareau, *Unequal Childhoods.*

12. In 2008, the average for the average household income among the communities in which the interviewed parents live was $109,758 for the professional middle-

class parents and $97,497 for the middle-class and working-class parents. In the same year, the average for the average home sales price among the communities in which the interviewed parents live was $462,716 for the professional middle-class parents and $351,295 for the middle-class and working-class parents. The average proportion of the total population with graduate degrees ranged from 16.9 percent for those communities in which professional middle-class parents live to 12.3 percent in the areas in which middle-class and working-class parents live. These data are available for communities identified by zip codes from Move.com, Homefair, City Profile Report, http://www.homefair.com/real-estate/city-profile/.

13. For statistics showing the per-student expenditures in different districts, as divided by the percent of children in the school district at different poverty levels, see National Center for Education Statistics, "Student Effort and Educational Progress." See also H. Johnson, *The American Dream and the Power of Wealth*.

14. For evidence that social class is related to extracurricular activities, see Amanda M. White and Constance T. Gager, "Idle Hands and Empty Pockets? Youth Involvement in Extracurricular Activities, Social Capital, and Economic Status," *Youth and Society*, September 2007, 75–111; Alyce Holland and Thomas Andre, "Participation in Extracurricular Activities in Secondary School: What Is Known, What Needs Be Known?" *Review of Educational Research* 57, no. 4 (Winter 1987): 437–66.

15. Manuel Castells, *The Rise of the Network Society*, vol. 1 (Oxford, UK: Blackwell, 2000).

16. Michael J. Carter and Susan Boslego Carter, "Women's Recent Progress in the Professions, or, Women Get a Ticket to Ride after the Gravy Train Has Left the Station," *Feminist Studies* 73, no. 3 (Autumn 1981): 477–504.

17. Yelizavetta Kofman, "Preschool and the PMC: How Professional Middle Class Parents Negotiate Advantages for Their Children in the Early Education Market," senior thesis, Department of Sociology/Anthropology, Middlebury College, Middlebury, VT, 2007, 37.

18. On this point, Lareau argues that class differences in child-rearing styles depend more on resources than on cultural attitudes. Lareau, *Unequal Childhoods*.

19. National Center for Education Statistics, "Parent Expectations and Planning for College: Statistical Analysis Report," April 2008, http://nces.ed.gov/pubsearch/pubsinfo.asp?pubid=2008079.

20. Table B.1 in appendix B shows these various responses; because this table, like other tables in appendix B, builds on qualitative responses, the categories are illustrative rather than definitive.

21. Patricia M. McDonough, *Choosing Colleges: How Social Class and Schools Structure Opportunity* (Albany: State University of New York Press, 1997); Don Vossler, Jack Schmit, and Nick Vesper, *Going to College: How Social, Economic, and Educational Factors Influence the Decisions Students Make* (Baltimore: Johns Hopkins University Press, 1999).

22. In thinking this way, they may be in line with the staff of liberal arts colleges, who often explain during orientation that they do not offer vocational training.

23. These issues are discussed in note 13 of the conclusion.

24. WelcomeHomeFizber.com, March 12, 2009, http://www.fizber.com (suburb name concealed). A website explains the prices in Martha's Vineyard; most of these are second homes rather than year-round residences:

> The 2002 median single-family home price on Martha's Vineyard averaged $661,900 ($1,183,750 for Aquinnah, $1,200,000 for Chilmark, $485,000 for Edgartown, $325,000 for Oak Bluffs, $337,000 for Tisbury, and $440,000 for West Tisbury). The entire range of prices can be found here, from a cape cod at $429,000 to secluded estates in the millions.

EscapeHomes.com, "Martha's Vineyard," http://www.escapehomes.com/main.aspx?Tabid=46&EscapeTownID=102.

25. Indeed, more of the professional middle-class parents than middle- or working-class parents insisted that they were *not* concerned with the financial aspects of whatever it was their children decided to do but that they *were* concerned that their children have meaningful careers.

26. Todd Gitlin, *The Sixties: Years of Hope, Days of Rage,* rev. ed. (New York: Bantam, 1993).

27. Jerry A. Jacobs and Kathleen Gerson, *The Time Divide: Work, Family, and Gender Inequality* (Cambridge, MA: Harvard University Press, 2004), 47.

> Couples in which the wife had completed four years of college were working 2.1 hours more in 2000 than in 1970, while couples in which the husband had not completed high school were working 0.5 hours more. A 3.4 hour difference in favor of the most educated couples in 1970 grew to become a 5.0 hour difference by 2000. These changes principally reflect the growing hours of working women. Employed wives with at least some college increased their working hours by nearly two hours per week during this period. . . . Those putting in longer workweeks may face time squeezes and domestic conundrums, but those putting in shorter ones likely face other difficulties, such as insufficient income and blocked work opportunities. (Ibid., 47–49)

28. University of Texas at Austin, "Mom Needs an 'A,'" 2007, http://www.utexas.edu/features/2007/helicopter/; "Do 'Helicopter Moms' Do More Harm than Good?" *ABC News,* October 21, 2005, http://abcnews.go.com/2020/print?id=1237868; Stephanie Armour, "'Helicopter' Parents Hover When Kids Job Hunt," *USA Today,* April 23, 2007, http://www.usatoday.com/money/economy/e,ployment/2007-05-23-helocopter-parents.

NOTES TO CHAPTER 2

1. While some working-class and middle-class parents believe their parents neither understood nor supported them when they were young, others hold themselves responsible for every mistake they made as risk-taking and exuberant adolescents.

And whether or not they believe their parents approached the task of raising their teens in an appropriate manner, some still can turn to their parents for advice and help as they face the challenges of child rearing in contemporary times. In fact, the working-class and middle-class parents we spoke with, like their peers everywhere, were likely to rely on family members to care for their young children. Indeed, so common was that pattern that some parents were surprised that my research assistants and I would ask about how they chose this form of child care. Although a few professional middle-class parents—most notably a woman from California whose mother came and lived with her during her triplets' infancy—called on members of their families of origin for help with child care, most of the women in these families either stayed home themselves or relied on some form of paid care such as a nanny or a day care center. See Julia Overturf Johnson, *Who's Minding the Kids? Child Care Arrangements: Winter 2002* (Current Population Reports P70-101, U.S. Census Bureau, Department of Commerce, Washington, DC, October 2005); Valerie E. Lee and David T. Burkman, *Inequality at the Starting Gate* (Washington, DC: Economic Policy Institute, 2002); Lynet Uttal, "Custodial Care, Surrogate Care, and Coordinated Care: Employed Mothers and the Meaning of Child Care," *Gender & Society* 10, no. 3 (June 1996): 291–311; Karen V. Hansen, *Not-So-Nuclear Families: Class, Gender and Networks of Care* (New Brunswick, NJ: Rutgers University Press, 2004).

2. In Paula's suburb the murder rate is well below the national average; where Martha lives, the year before we spoke with her, there were no murders, no robberies, and no assaults. Statistics for individual locations can be found on WelcomeHomeFizber.com, March 12, 2009, http://www.fizber.com.

3. This latter theme is common in statements made over the past several decades by working-class and poor African Americans who believe that their neighborhoods—abetted by the rise of crack cocaine, the work requirements of new social welfare legislation, and the engagement of increasing numbers of women in the labor force—have ceased being communities in which one can count on "othermothers" as well as one's own mother to instill correct behavior. For the classic statement of "othermother" support, see Carol Stack, *All Our Kin: Strategies for Survival in a Black Community* (New York: Harper and Row, 1974). For other references, see Patricia Hill Collins, *Black Feminist Thought: Knowledge, Consciousness, and the Politics of Empowerment* (New York: Routledge, 2008); Theodore Sasson and Margaret K. Nelson, "Danger, Community, and the Meaning of Crime Watch: An Analysis of the Discourses of African American and White Participants," *Journal of Contemporary Ethnography* 259, no. 21 (1996): 171–200. For a contemporary fictional reference to the sense of change in neighborhoods, see Stephen Carter's description of an area called "The Nest" in his fictional Elm City. Stephen L. Carter, *New England White* (New York: Vintage Books, 2008).

4. For a thorough statement of this idea, particularly as it relates to children, see Lee Rainwater and Timothy M. Smeeding, *Poor Kids in a Rich Country: America's Children in Comparative Perspective* (New York: Russell Sage Foundation, 2003). For

an argument that the state has retreated, see Cindi Katz, "The State Goes Home: Local Hyper-Vigilance of Children and the Global Retreat from Social Reproduction," *Social Justice* 28, no. 3 (2001): 47–56. For a discussion of how this phenomenon has shaped dynamics within the home, especially around issues of security, see Marianne Cooper, "'Doing Security' in Insecure Times: Class and Family Life in Silicon Valley" (PhD diss., Sociology, University of California at Berkeley, 2008).

5. I do not assume from most of the parents' sense of personal responsibility that they would not appreciate more state support such as parental leaves or better health insurance. Instead, I am arguing that they do not see a change from the past, and they do not currently view the state as playing a significant role in their daily lives.

6. Ulrich Beck, *Risk Society: Towards a New Modernity* (London: Sage, 1992); Anthony Giddens, "Risk and Responsibility," *Modern Law Review* 62, no. 1 (1999): 1–10.

7. Barry Glassner, *The Culture of Fear: Why Americans Are Afraid of the Wrong Thing* (New York: Basic Books, 1999); Frank Furedi, *Paranoid Parenting: Abandon Your Anxieties and Be a Good Parent* (London: Allen Lane/Penguin Press, 2001); David L. Altheide, "Children and the Discourse of Fear," *Symbolic Interaction* 25, no. 2 (2002): 229–50; Joel Best, *Threatened Children: Rhetoric and Concern about Child-Victims* (Chicago: University of Chicago Press, 1990).

8. For an interesting, contemporary discussion of how much children should be allowed to roam, see Louise Crawford, "Helicopter Moms vs. Free-Range Kids," *Newsweek,* April 21, 2008, hhtp://www.newsweek.com/id/133103.

9. Today, fewer than 15 percent of children get to school under their own steam, in contrast with half of all children just forty years ago. Jane E. Brody, "Turning the Ride to School into a Walk," *New York Times*, September 11, 2007, http://www.nytimes.com/2007/09/11/health/11brod.html. For an innovative attempt to encourage children to walk, see R. A. Kearns, D. C. A. Collins, and P. M. Neuwelt, "The Walking School Bus: Extending Children's Geographies?" *Area* 35, no. 3 (2003): 285–92.

10. Gill Valentine and John McKendrick, "Children's Outdoor Play: Exploring Parental Concerns about Children's Safety," *Geoforum* 28, no. 2 (1997): 219–35; Gill Valentine, "'Oh Yes I Can.' 'Oh No You Can't': Children and Parents' Understandings of Kids' Competence to Negotiate Public Space Safely," *Antipode* 29, no. 1 (1997): 65–89.

11. Sharon R. Cohany and Emy Sok, "Trends in Labor Force Participation of Married Mothers of Infants," *Monthly Labor Review,* February 2007, 9–16.

12. It also is seen as a *private problem* affecting individual families, rather than a social issue to which the government might respond with more fully supportive services.

13. For discussions about how we often remember a world that never existed, see Stephanie Coontz, *The Way We Never Were: American Families and the Nostalgia Trap* (New York: Basic Books, 1992); Anita Ilta Garey, *Weaving Work and Motherhood* (Philadelphia: Temple University Press, 1999).

14. Kathryn Edin and Maria Kefalas, *Promises I Can Keep: Why Poor Women Put Motherhood before Marriage* (Berkeley: University of California Press, 2005). For a

piece in the popular press that suggests that parents are spending less time with their children, see Laura Shapiro, "The Myth of Quality Time: How We're Cheating Our Kids, What You Can Do," *Newsweek*, May 12, 1997, 64–69. For an argument that this is not the case, see Liana C. Sayer, Suzanne M. Bianchi, and John P. Robinson, "Are Parents Investing Less in Children? Trends in Mothers' and Fathers' Time with Children," *American Journal of Sociology*, July 2004, 1–43. For some negative accounts of the time parents spend with their children, see Michael Bittman and Judy Wajcman, "The Rush Hour: The Quality of Leisure Time and Gender Equity," in *The Social Organisation of Care*, ed. Nancy Folbre (New York: Routledge, 2004); Arlie Russell Hochschild, *The Time Bind: When Work Becomes Home and Home Becomes Work* (New York: Metropolitan Books, 1997).

15. Suzanne M. Bianchi, John P. Robinson, and Melissa A. Milkie, *Changing Rhythms of American Family Life* (New York: Russell Sage Foundation, 2006), 61, 76.

16. Ibid., 75.

17. Jonathan Guryan, Erik Hurst, and Melissa Schettini Kearney, "Parental Education and Parental Time with Children" (Working Paper 13993, National Bureau of Economic Research, Cambridge, MA, May 2008), 38.

18. Ibid., 39.

19. Mary Blair-Loy, *Competing Devotions: Career and Family among Women Executives* (Cambridge, MA: Harvard University Press, 2003).

20. Bianchi, Robinson, and Milkie, *Changing Rhythms of American Family Life*, 95–96; Robert D. Putnam, *Bowling Alone: The Collapse and Revival of American Community* (New York: Simon and Schuster, 2001). See also Miller McPherson, Lynn Smith-Lovin, and Matthew E. Brashears, "Social Isolation in America: Changes in Core Discussion Networks over Two Decades," *American Sociological Review* 71 (June 2006): 353–75.

21. Baumrind identified three basic child-rearing styles, which she termed *authoritative, authoritarian,* and *permissive* parenting. D. Baumrind, "Current Patterns of Parental Authority," *Developmental Psychology Monographs* 4 (1971): 1–103; D. Baumrind, "Child Care Practices Anteceding Three Patterns of Preschool Behavior," *Genetic Psychology Monographs* 75 (1967): 43–88. Maccoby and Martin redefined and expanded this categorization and classified parents as high or low on each of two dimensions—responsiveness and demandingness—yielding a total of four parenting styles: (a) authoritative, (b) authoritarian, (c) indulgent, and (d) neglectful parents. E. D. Maccoby and J. A. Martin, "Socialization in the Context of the Family," in *Handbook of Child Psychology,* vol. 4, *Socialization, Personality and Social Development,* 4th ed., ed. P. H. Mussen and E. Hetherington (New York: Wiley, 1983).

22. I am not saying here that having children at a young age necessarily has negative effects for low-income women; I *am* saying that having children at a young age shapes one's life in significant ways and that some of the women who were interviewed did not want their own children to have the same experience. For discussion of this topic, see Edin and Kefalas, *Promises I Can Keep*. See also Frank F. Fursten-

berg, Jr., *Destinies of the Disadvantaged: The Politics of Teenage Childbearing* (New York: Russell Sage Foundation, 2007).

23. Heather Beth Johnson, *The American Dream and the Power of Wealth: Choosing Schools and Inheriting Inequality in the Land of Opportunity* (New York: Routledge, 2007); Teresa Toguchi Swartz, "Family Capital and the Invisible Transfer of Privilege: Intergenerational Support and Social Class in Early Adulthood," in *New Directions for Child and Adolescent Development, 119*, ed. J. T. Mortimer, 11–24 (New York: Wiley, 2008).

24. For a classic account, see Todd Gitlin, *The Sixties: Years of Hope, Days of Rage*, rev. ed. (New York: Bantam, 1993).

25. I might note that less privileged youth were less likely to be involved in the protest activities of the sixties. For an interesting response to those activities by a young woman who was growing up poor, see Mary Childers, *Welfare Brat: A Memoir* (Edinburgh, UK: Bloomsbury, 2005).

26. But even if the parents we interviewed shared this sense of isolation, as I show in the next chapter, parents from different social groupings identified different threats to the contemporary well-being of their children.

27. Jason P. Schachter, *Geographical Mobility: 2002 to 2003* (Current Population Reports P20-549, U.S. Census Bureau, U.S. Department of Commerce, Washington, DC, March 2004).

28. See the professional middle-class couple described in Hansen, *Not-So-Nuclear Families*.

29. Bianchi et al. also refer to "the pervasive ideal of 'intensive mothering.'" However, to cite this ideology is not to explain it. Bianchi, Robinson, and Milkie, *Changing Rhythms of American Family Life*, 127.

30. Ibid.; Putnam, *Bowling Alone*.

NOTES TO CHAPTER 3

1. Anita Chandra et al., "Does Watching Sex on Television Predict Teen Pregnancy? Findings from a National Longitudinal Survey of Youth," *Pediatrics* 122 (2008): 1047–54.

2. Victoria Rideout, "Parents, Children & Media: A Kaiser Family Foundation Survey," Kaiser Family Foundation, June 2007, http://www.kff.org/entmedia/upload/7638.pdf.

3. Philippe Ariès, *Centuries of Childhood* (New York: Vintage Books, 1962). See also Owen Jones, "Naturally Not! Childhood, the Urban and Romanticism," *Human Ecology Review* 9, no. 2 (2002): 17–30.

4. For information on child care arrangements, see Julia Overturf Johnson, *Who's Minding the Kids? Child Care Arrangements: Winter 2002* (Current Population Reports P70-101, U.S. Census Bureau, Department of Commerce, Washington, DC, October 2005).

5. Henry C. Lajewski, "Working Mothers and Their Arrangements for Care of Their Children," *Social Security Bulletin,* August 1959; Henry C. Lajewski, *Child Care Arrangements of Full-Time Working Mothers* (Washington, DC: Children's Bureau, 1959).

6. Stephanie Coontz, *The Way We Never Were: American Families and the Nostalgia Trap* (New York: Basic Books, 1992); Stephanie Coontz, *The Way We Really Are: Coming to Terms with America's Changing Families* (New York: Basic Books, 1997).

7. Nancy Lesko, "Denaturalizing Adolescence: The Politics of Contemporary Representations," *Youth and Society* 28, no. 2 (December 1996): 138–61; Nancy Lesko, *Act Your Age! A Cultural Construction of Adolescence* (New York: RoutledgeFalmer, 2001); G. S. Hall, *Adolescence: Its Psychology and Its Relation to Physiology, Anthropology, Sociology, Sex, Crime, Religion and Education* (New York: Appleton, 1904).

8. J. J. Arnett, "Emerging Adulthood: A Theory of Development from the Late Teens through the Twenties," *American Psychologist* 55, no. 5 (2000): 469–80. See also the discussions of this issue in Barrie Thorne, *Gender Play* (New Brunswick, NJ: Rutgers University Press, 1983); C. J. Pascoe, *Dude, You're a Fag* (Berkeley: University of California Press, 2007). It might be noted that from the other end of life there are changes as well. As life expectancy has shifted upward, those who were previously considered elderly are now considered in their prime. "Sixty is the new forty," those approaching retirement proclaim, as they enjoy the energy and engagement of a time of life that was previously denoted old age. Darrell Laurant, "The Re Generation," *Science & Spirit,* 2008, http://www.science-spirit.org/printerfriendly.php?article_id=676. Meanwhile, the media refers to the employment of those eligible for Social Security as "productive aging" and "retirement jobs." Dan Kadlec, "Making Flexible Retirements Work," *Time,* May 10, 2008, http://www.time.com/time/magazine/article/0,9171,1619545,00.html.

9. Mary Childers, *Welfare Brat: A Memoir* (Edinburgh, UK: Bloomsbury, 2005).

10. For a discussion that argues that "childhood for the middle class is a state to be preserved, free from economic intrusion and producing the possibility of the rational and playful child who will become a rational, educated professional, a member of the 'new middle class,'" see Valerie Walkerdine, "Safety and Danger: Childhood, Sexuality, and Space at the End of the Millennium," in *Governing the Child in the New Millennium*, ed. Kenneth Hultquist and Gunilla Dahlberg, 15–34 (New York: RoutledgeFalmer, 2001), 31.

11. See the memoir by Laura Shane Cunningham, *Sleeping Arrangements: A Memoir* (New York: Knopf, 1989). See also Judith Levine, *Harmful to Minors: The Perils of Protecting Children from Sex* (New York: Thunder's Mouth, 2003); and Joan D. Atwood, "Mommy's Little Angel, Daddy's Little Girl: Do You Know What Your Pre-Teens Are Doing?" *American Journal of Family Therapy* 34 (2006): 447–67.

12. James Kincaid, *Erotic Innocence: The Culture of Child Molesting* (Durham, NC: Duke University Press, 1998); Henry A. Giroux, *Stealing Innocence: Corporate Culture's War on Children* (New York: Palgrave, 2001).

13. Neil Postman, *The Disappearance of Childhood* (New York: Delacorte, 1982).

14. A concern with sex is especially acute among parents who have daughters, but the concern is not exclusive to them. And while it is a particular concern for men (who may be disturbed by the budding sexuality of their adolescent daughters), it is not exclusive to them either.

15. I am not implying that these images were not traumatic but rather that they weren't aimed at children specifically—and especially not at this woman's children specifically.

16. Annette Lareau, *Unequal Childhoods: Class, Race, and Family Life* (Berkeley: University of California Press, 2003). Suzanne Bianchi, John Robinson, and Melissa Milkie note, "As early as 1939, an associate of the Child Study of America bemoaned what it called the extinction of children's leisure time by the increase in scheduled and organized activities." And they also note that "these concerns are strikingly similar across the decades—suggesting that there will always be worries about children's use of time." Suzanne M. Bianchi, John P. Robinson, and Melissa A. Milkie, *Changing Rhythms of American Family Life* (New York: Russell Sage Foundation, 2006), 143. On this issue, see William A. Corsaro, *We're Friends, Right? Inside Kids' Culture* (Washington, DC: Joseph Henry Press, 2003).

17. The information is provided for various communities by Simply Hired: Job Search Made Simple, http://www.simplyhired.com/.

18. Allison Pugh writes that indulging children's consumption desires is a way to indulge children's need to belong. She also sees this happening in a wide range of social contexts. Allison J. Pugh, *Longing and Belonging: Parents, Children, and Consumer Culture* (Berkeley: University of California Press, 2009). I do not mean to imply here that the less privileged parents do *not* indulge some of their children's desires. But those parents talked less about these concerns—and they were less likely, for example, to have bought each of their children a laptop computer.

19. When the working-class parents talked about these issues, it was more that they could not afford to give what others offer; their opposition to materialism and affluence has a different flavor to it.

20. Again, a class bias is obvious here. It doesn't take much to recall that not all kids (including those in the sample) had the time to "screw around"; indeed, among the working-class and middle-class parents there are those who had children before completing high school, and one man talked about coming home every day and helping his parents on the farm.

21. For an article that says that children's fears may be quite closely tied with real dangers, see Rachel Pain, "Paranoid Parenting? Rematerializing Risk and Fear for Children," *Social & Cultural Geography* 73, no. 21 (April 2006): 221–43. See also Kathryn Edin and Maria Kefalas, *Promises I Can Keep: Why Poor Women Put Motherhood before Marriage* (Berkeley: University of California Press, 2005).

22. The average personal crime risk—defined as the combined risks of rape, murder, assault, and robbery—for those communities in which professional middle-

class parents live (as indicated by zip codes) is 89.6; the median personal crime risk 63.0. The average personal crime risk for those communities in which middle-class and working-class parents live is 109.0, and the median is 97.5. The average for the United States as a whole is 100. These data are available from Move.com, Homefair, City Profile Report, http://www.homefair.com/real-estate/city-profile/.

23. Edin and Kefalas, *Promises I Can Keep*; Mary Pattilo-McCoy, *Black Picket Fences: Privilege and Peril among the Black Middle Class* (Chicago: University of Chicago Press, 1999).

24. According to a Public Agenda report, this issue is the only one that is regarded similarly by high-income and low-income parents. Public Agenda, "A Lot Easier Said than Done," 2002, http://www.publicagenda.org/files/pdf/easier_said_than_done.pdf.

NOTES TO CHAPTER 4

1. Basil Bernstein, *Class, Codes, and Control* (London: Routledge and Kegan Paul, 1971); Francesca M. Cancian, "Defining 'Good' Child Care: Hegemonic and Democratic Standards," in *Child Care and Inequality: Rethinking Carework for Children and Youth*, ed. Francesca M. Cancian et al. (New York: Routledge, 2002), 65–82; Sharon Hays, *The Cultural Contradictions of Motherhood* (New Haven, CT: Yale University Press, 1996); Annette Lareau, *Unequal Childhoods: Class, Race, and Family Life* (Berkeley: University of California Press, 2003).

2. Lareau, *Unequal Childhoods.*

3. Basil Bernstein's discussion of progressive education is one of the best descriptions of this process; see Basil Bernstein, "Class and Pedagogies: Visible and Invisible," in *Class, Codes and Control,* vol. 3, ed. Basil Bernstein, 116–56 (London: Routledge and Kegan Paul, 1975).

4. As shown by the data from Suzanne M. Bianchi, John P. Robinson, and Melissa A. Milkie, *Changing Rhythms of American Family Life* (New York: Russell Sage Foundation, 2006), fathers are spending far more time with their children than was the case a generation ago (see notes 15, 16, and 18 in chapter 2). However, these attitudes of engagement are not unique to fathers.

5. Thomas W. Phelan, *1-2-3 Magic: Effective Discipline for Children* 2–12 (Glen Ellyn, IL: ParentMagic, 2004).

6. Allison J. Pugh, *Longing and Belonging: Parents, Children, and Consumer Culture* (Berkeley: University of California Press, 2009); Pamela Paul, *Parenting, Inc.* (New York: Times Books, 2008).

7. Margaret K. Nelson and Rebecca N. Schutz, "Day Care Differences and the Reproduction of Social Class," *Journal of Contemporary Ethnography* 36 (2007): 281–317.

8. Lareau, *Unequal Childhoods.*

9. Ibid.

NOTES TO THE INTRODUCTION TO PART II

1. Diana Ray, "Big Brother Is Watching You," *Insight on the News*, July 23, 2001, 18.

2. Good reviews can be found in David Lyon, *Surveillance Studies: An Overview* (Cambridge, UK: Polity, 2007). See also the essays in *Contemporary Sociology* 36, no. 2 (2007), which included David Cunningham, "Surveillance and Social Movements: Lenses on the Repression-Mobilization Nexus," 120–25; Valerie Jenness, David A. Smith, and Judith Stepan-Norris, "Editor's Note: Taking a Look at Surveillance Studies," vii–viii; David Lyon, "Sociological Perspectives and Surveillance Studies: 'Slow Journalism' and the Critique of Social Sorting," 107–11; Gary T. Marx, "Desperately Seeking Surveillance Studies: Players in Search of a Field," 125–30; John Torpey, "Through Thick and Thin: Surveillance after 9/11," 116–19; and Elia Zureik, "Surveillance Studies: From Metaphors to Regulation to Subjectivity," 112–15.

3. For a fuller discussion of this oversight, see Margaret K. Nelson and Anita Ilta Garey, "Who's Watching? An Introductory Essay," in *Who's Watching? Daily Practices of Surveillance among Contemporary Families,* ed. Margaret K. Nelson and Anita Ilta Garey, 1–16 (Nashville, TN: Vanderbilt University Press, 2009).

4. William G. Staples, *Everyday Surveillance: Vigilance and Visibility in Postmodern Life* (Lanham, MD: Rowman & Littlefield, 2000), 3.

5. Ibid., 143. See also Gary T. Marx, "What's New about the 'New Surveillance'? Classifying for Change and Continuity," *Surveillance & Society* 1, no. 2 (2002): 9–29.

6. Dawn Moore and Kevin D. Haggerty, "Bring It on Home: Home Drug Testing and the Relocation of the War on Drugs," *Social & Legal Studies* 10, no. 3 (2001): 377–405; Cindi Katz, "The State Goes Home: Local Hyper-Vigilance of Children and the Global Retreat from Social Reproduction," *Social Justice* 28, no. 3 (2001): 47–56.

7. The first reference I have been able to find to baby monitors occurred in July 1984. See Jane C. Cable, "Bringing Home Baby—and Monitor Too," *American Baby*, July 1984, 18–21. Cell phones became widely used in the United States within the past decade. For a history, see Tom Farley, "The Cell-Phone Revolution," *AmericanHeritage.com,* 2007, http://www.americanheritage.com/events/articles/web/20070110-cell-phone-att-mobile-phone-motorola-federal-communications-commission-cdma-tdma-gsm.shtml.

8. As my research assistants and I were conducting our interviews, GPS on cell phones became more commonplace. Only one parent indicated that she had this device; other parents might have as well but did not say. See Larry Magid, "GPS Chips in Cellphones Track Kids and Help Navigate, Too," *International Herald Tribune*, July 19, 2007; Barry Levine, "Meet the Cell-Phone Tracking Parents," *NewsFactor Network,* June 5, 2006, http://www.newsfactor.com/story.xhtml?story_id=01100000A9QB.

9. "Wireless Child Locator," Übergizmo website, July 4, 2008, http://www.ubergizmo.com/15/archives/2008/07/wireless_child_locator.html.

10. Advertisements for child locators prey on parents' fears about lost or snatched children:

> Have you ever been on a shopping trip with your child, and you take a look at an item for just a second, then look back to see that your wandering toddler child has vanished? One second he's under your feet, the next, he is gone. It has happened to every parent! We have the answer! Our Teddy Bear Child Locator! Our child locator—child personal safety alarm—will beep where your child is located. ("Child Locator," My Precious Kid: Child Safety Products, 2008, http://www.mypreciouskid.com/child-locator.html)

Advertisements also prey on fears of abduction (omitting the data indicating that the vast majority of all abductions are by someone related to the child):

> Over seven hundred and twenty five thousand children are reported lost every year in the United States, while shopping or out in public with their parents and-or legal guardians. This leads to over FIFTY TWO THOUSAND REAL ABDUCTIONS! It doesn't matter how good of a parent you are. (Mommy I'm Here Child Locator, 2009, http://www.mommyimhere.com/)

Some advertisements particularly target children with special needs:

> Do you have a child with special needs? Down Syndrome? Autism? Non-verbal? This child personal safety alarm is the perfect solution to bring you peace of mind. Non-verbal children (such as Autistic or Down Syndrome) greatly benefit from wearing a child locator every day. ("Child Locator," http://www.mypreciouskid.com/child-locator.html)

Debates about the ethics of attaching such devices to such individuals as the elderly with dementia or people with learning disabilities are now appearing in the literature. See S. Welsh et al., "Big Brother Is Watching You: The Ethical Implications of Electronic Surveillance Measures in the Elderly," *Aging & Mental Health* 73, no. 5 (September 2004): 372–75.

11. The V-chip reads encoded television material and blocks entire shows based on predetermined parental controls. The Federal Communications Commission (FCC) mandated in the 1996 Telecommunications Act that all televisions bigger than thirteen inches have a V-chip. The FCC's mandate coincided with broadcasting companies rating television programs and posting their ratings during the first fifteen seconds of all television shows. The ratings scale begins with TV-Y, which is supposed to contain content suitable for all children, and ends with TV-MA, which includes shows that are intended for mature audiences only.

12. Software filters block computer users' access to specified Internet material. Filter programs use a range of sorting techniques including object analysis, URL-based identification, keyword-based identification, and "dynamic categorization." With these tools, software filters can block anything from chat rooms to designated websites and keywords to peer-to-peer music sharing to e-mails and personal informa-

tion. Even basic software programs, such as the Internet Explorer web browser, have simple filter options.

Children and adults who wish to escape filter restrictions can accomplish successful evasion: information on software filter resistance is readily obtainable. Numerous websites document methods of discovering and circumventing parent-installed software filters. One particularly informative video demonstrates how to disable a software filter with step-by-step instructions. Blogs such as Computer.Blogspot.com also document how to discover and disable software filters.

13. Some of the devices are even more sophisticated and can offer some control of a vehicle from a distance, enabling a parent to disable the ignition, lock the car, honk the horn, or flash the lights. Youth Driving Safe, 2008, http://www.youthdrivingsafe.org/state.php.

14. "Safe Teen Vehicle Tracker: How Does It Work," Safe Teen Driving Club website, 2009, http://www.safeteendrivingclub.org/proddetail_vt.php.

15. "SafeTrak—Teen Driver Tracking for Your Peace of Mind," 2009, GPS Technologies, June 2, 2009, http://www.gpstechnologies.net/products/safetrak.asp?gclid=CKOvgc3rj5QCFQSwFQodwhfAhA.

16. Timothy, "GPS Tracking Device Beats Radar Gun in Court," *Slashdot,* July 18, 2009, http://tech.slashdot.org/article.pl?sid=08/07/18/0318228; Lisa Leff, "Teen's Ticket Hinges on GPS vs. Radar," Associated Press, October 25, 2007; Dave Carpenter, "Car Insurers' Devices Track Teen Drivers," Associated Press, October 10, 2007.

17. According to Moore and Haggerty ("Bring It on Home," 382),

> The extent of home drug testing in America is difficult to gauge. There are no national statistics on such tests, and home tests are frequently a subcomponent of corporations that market drug tests to industry and government. This makes it difficult to disaggregate the specific number of home tests. The testing industry is also highly competitive, a fact which fosters a degree of secrecy. Industry representatives who are otherwise very forthcoming generally have refused to provide precise sales figures for their tests. Nonetheless, one gains the impression that this is a small but growing sector. One company spokesperson suggested that home test kits might come close to representing 10 percent of their $20 million testing business. Another representative claimed sales of approximately 3,000 units a month, a figure that was rising steadily. Only six weeks after introducing its home drug test nationally, ChemTrac Inc. had shipped more than 10,000 units to American drug stores. Recent decisions by major American retailers, such as Walgreen's, to stock home test kits will likely result in increased sales.

18. Two extreme positions can be found in debates about the role and impact of technology. Those who can be dubbed "technological determinists" argue for the autonomous role of technology in producing and creating new sets of social relations; those who are called "social determinists" essentially reduce technologi-

cal developments to preexisting sets of social relationships. Most theorists who explore the effects of the new surveillance technologies argue for a more nuanced and dynamic view that acknowledges both sides simultaneously, even as they stress the manner in which technologies "serve systems of imperceptible social classification and purposes that they come to embody." David Lyon, *Surveillance Society: Monitoring Everyday Life* (Philadelphia: Open University Press, 2001), 27. This dynamic approach, Torin Monahan argues, also helps move discussions of the kinds of surveillance technologies with which this book is concerned (that is, those that are used within the boundaries of the family) beyond simple examinations of efficiency and trade-offs, to probe the more subtle ways in which relationships are affected by the introduction of new technologies; this approach does not assume that these consequences are either anticipated or understood by those participating in the use of the new technologies. Torin Monahan, *Surveillance and Security: Technological Politics and Power in Everyday Life* (New York: Routledge, 2006).

NOTES TO CHAPTER 5

1. Jane C. Cable, "Bringing Home Baby—and Monitor Too," *American Baby*, July 1984, 18–21.
2. Marvin B. Scott and Lyman M. Stanford, "Accounts," *American Sociological Review* 33, nos. 1–2 (1968): 46.
3. Margaret K. Nelson, "Watching Children: Describing the Use of Baby Monitors on Epinions.com," *Journal of Family Issues* 29, no. 4 (April 2008): 531.
4. In my discussion of baby monitors as described on Epinions.com, I note that the respondents are likely to be "economically upscale." Ibid., 521.
5. Although this response might indicate disinterest in having a monitor, the parents who did not use a monitor all mentioned the small size of their house or apartment; many of them said that they would use a monitor if they lived in a larger house.
6. Ulrich Beck, *Risk Society: Towards a New Modernity* (London: Sage, 1992); Anthony Giddens, "Risk and Responsibility," *Modern Law Review* 62, no. 1 (1999): 1–10; Deborah Lupton and John Tulloch, "'Risk Is Part of Your Life': Risk Epistemologies among a Group of Australians," *Sociology* 36, no. 2 (2002): 318.
7. Advertisements for monitors stress safety:

> The UltraClear II Baby Monitor is a portable, reliable way to check up on your baby without waking her. It has a soft glow nightlight that illuminates Baby's room as she settles herself in for sleep time, then shuts itself off automatically after 15 minutes. ("Graco Ultra Clear II 49mhz Baby Monitor," Amazon.com, http://www.amazon.com/Graco-Ultra-Clear-49mhz-Monitor/dp/B000E0KN5I/ref=sr_1_1?ie=UTF8&s=baby-products&qid=1230895876&sr=1-1)

> The Safety 1st High-Def Digital Monitor provides a 100% clear connection anytime, anywhere. It is the next leap in digital audio clarity, providing parents ease of mind that they have distinguished between a gurgle and a whimper. This unit, from Safety 1st utilizes the DECT 6.0 frequency for guaranteed clear and private connection with no interference. ("Safety 1st High-Def Digital Monitor," Amazon.com, http://www.amazon.com/Safety-1st-High-Def-Digital-Monitor/dp/B00101TXPG/ref=sr_1_2?ie=UTF8&s=baby-products&qid=1230895876&sr=1-2)

For a general statement about how much parents are now spending on baby "equipment," see Pamela Paul, *Parenting, Inc.* (New York: Times Books, 2008).

8. There was very little class difference in ownership of baby monitors. See table B.2 in appendix B.

9. Because some of the middle-class parents also speak in a language of responsiveness to infants but have a different approach to the care of older children, these links are not inevitable: among the professional middle class they are sustained; among those who are less privileged they may be fractured in later childhood or adolescence.

10. See tables B.3 and B.4 in appendix B.

11. Tracy L. M. Kennedy et al., "Networked Families" (report, Pew Internet & American Life Project, October 19, 2008), http://www.pewinternet.org/~/media/Files/Reports/2008/PIP_Networked_Family.pdf.pdf. See also www.cmch.tv/mentors/hotTopic.asp?id=70.

12. For similar findings, see Kerry Devitt and Debi Roker, "The Role of Mobile Phones in Family Communication," *Children & Society*, 2008: 189–202. On the basis of interviews with sixty families of teens (aged eleven to seventeen), these authors report that mobile phones were seen as a way to keep in touch and to monitor and ensure young people's safety. For questions emerging about mobile use and relations between parents and children, see Leslie Haddon, "The Social Consequences of Mobile Telephony: Framing Questions," paper presented at the Sosiale Konsekvenser Av Mobiltelfoni, Oslo, Telenor, June 16, 2000.

13. In the conclusion I discuss the more negative viewpoint as expressed by some of the parents.

14. Kurz found the same pattern in her study of parental monitoring. Demie Kurz, "'I Trust Them but I Don't Trust Them: Issues and Dilemmas in Monitoring Teenagers," in *Who's Watching? Daily Practices of Surveillance Among Contemporary Families*, ed. Margaret K. Nelson and Anita Ilta Garey, 260–76 (Nashville, TN: Vanderbilt University Press, 2009). Interestingly, as Beth discussed this event as an example of how useful a cell phone is for her child, she switched at the end of her comment from the advantage of having her child be able to reach her to the advantage of her being able to reach her child, showing that she makes little differentiation between the need for contact on the part of herself and her children.

15. Ironically, having a cell phone itself can increase, rather than diminish, those dangers. As one working-class mother explained, when asked whether there were any disadvantages associated with having a cell phone, her son was beaten up in his neighborhood when a gang of boys tried to wrest his cell phone from him:

> He was with his friends [and some kids tried to take his cell phone]. Terrence was not letting go of the phone, and I told him, "Terrence, if somebody wants your cell phone, give it to him." They had him down on the ground, kicking him. . . . That was a disadvantage as far as I'm concerned, and it's the same thing with his clothes, his sneakers. . . . I want to reward my children for doing well, but I don't want that to be something [that would cause them to get hurt].

16. For discussions of how cell phones enable responsiveness and how parents are learning to keep up with their children, see Laura M. Holson, "Text Generation Gap: U R 2 Old (JK)," *New York Times,* March 9, 2008; AT&T, "AT&T Shares Results from 2008 Parent-Child Texting Survey," October 8, 2008, http://www.att.com/gen/press-room?pid=4800&cdvn=news&newsarticleid=26157.

17. David Lyon, *Surveillance Society: Monitoring Everyday Life* (Philadelphia: Open University Press, 2001), 27.

18. Interestingly, with respect to baby monitors, the reverse is true: parents gain independence while being tethered to their children. See Nelson, "Watching Children." For a discussion about how having a cell phone can induce college-age students to engage in riskier behavior than they would otherwise, see J. Nasar, P. Hecht, and R. Wener, "'Call If You Have Trouble': Mobile Phones and Safety among College Students," *International Journal of Urban and Regional Research* 31, no. 4 (2007): 863–73.

19. According to the Center on Media and Child Health, "the Pew Internet & American Life Project found that 39 percent of cell users ages 18–29 say that they are not always truthful about where they are when they are on the phone." "Cell Phones," cmchmentors website, www.cmch.tv/mentors/hotTopic.asp?id=70.

20. For a similar discussion, see Kurz, "I Trust Them but I Don't Trust Them."

NOTES TO CHAPTER 6

1. This advertisement can be see on YouTube: http://www.youtube.com/watch?v=DrzOBLDYi-U&NR=1.

2. See table B.5 in appendix B.

3. Anita Chandra et al., "Does Watching Sex on Television Predict Teen Pregnancy? Findings from a National Longitudinal Survey of Youth," *Pediatrics* 122 (2008): 1047–54.

4. My research assistants and I did not ask parents specifically about their use of the V-chip on televisions; the discussion of this device is based on the kinds

of issues that came up with parents in discussions about how they control the number of hours their children spent watching television and the content of the television programs their children watch. According to the Kaiser Family Foundation, only 15 percent of all parents have used the V-chip, which was required to be included in all television sets over thirteen inches after January 2000. Much of the nonuse is based on ignorance: almost 40 percent of those who have bought a new television don't think it includes a V-chip. Among those who have a V-chip and know it, two-fifths have used it; nearly two-thirds of parents who have used the V-chip say they have found it "very" useful. Victoria Rideout, "Parents, Children & Media: A Kaiser Family Foundation Survey," Kaiser Family Foundation, June 2007, http://www.kff.org/entmedia/upload/7638.pdf. For information about how rules about television vary by social class, see Elizabeth A. Vandewater et al., "'No—You Can't Watch That': Parental Rules and Young Children's Media Use," *American Behavioral Scientist* 48, no. 5 (January 2005): 608–23; T. Lugaila, "A Child's Day: 2000 (Selected Indicators of Child Well-Being)," U.S. Census Bureau, 2003. http://www.census.gov/prod/2003pubs/. Parents are advised in the media to make their own determinations of whether the industry guidelines are appropriate. Julie Salamon, "The Rating Says PG, but Is That Guidance Enough?" *New York Times*, January 17, 2005.

5. Kimberly J. Mitchell, David Finkelhor, and Janis Wolak, "Protecting Youth Online: Family Use of Filtering and Blocking Software," *Child Abuse & Neglect* 29 (2005): 753–65.

6. Rong Wang, Suzanne M. Bianchi, and Sara B. Raley, "Teenagers' Internet Use and Family Rules: A Research Note," *Journal of Marriage and Family* 67 (December 2005): 1257.

7. See table B.6 in appendix B.

8. Margaret K. Nelson and Rebecca N. Schutz, "Day Care Differences and the Reproduction of Social Class," *Journal of Contemporary Ethnography* 36 (2007): 281–317.

9. Many sources offer parents advice on how to monitor children's Internet use, including the U.S. Department of Justice, which has "A Parent's Guide to Internet Safety" (2006, http://www.fbi.gov/publications/pguide/parentsguide.pdf), and popular periodicals such as *Working Mother* (C.H., "Keeping Kids Safe Online," *Working Mother*, October 2004, 186). According to a study commissioned by the New York City–based Conference Board, about three-quarters of parents report that they remain in the room while their children use the Internet, and more than a third of the parents surveyed check the web browser history after their children have been online. Jessica L. Tonn, "Online Monitoring," *Education Week*, January 19, 2005, 12.

10. For a humorous discussion of parents joining Facebook so that they can see what their children have on that site (and sometimes being blocked by their children), see Lisa Belkin, "When Your Kid Won't Friend You," *New York Times,* October 14, 2008, http://parenting.blogs.nytimes.com/2008/10/14/when-your-kid-wont-friend-you/.

11. A clear filter allows for clear resistance. There are many websites where teens can learn how to disable the various filters and devices put on a computer. It may be less clear how to "disable" parental vigilance.

12. Arlie Russell Hochschild, *The Second Shift*, updated ed. (New York: Penguin Books, 2003; first published 1989).

NOTES TO CHAPTER 7

1. As Beth O'Brien explained why she used the software, she used the language of "management" as a way to indicate her parenting style: professional middle-class parents are managers, not bosses. I return to this idea later in this chapter.

2. "I Am Big Brother Software," Spying-Software.com, http://www.spying-software.com/keylogger/iambigbrother-keylogger.html.

3. For complete responses, see tables B.7, B.8, and B.9 in appendix B.

4. The popular press and popular websites tell you what to look for. See, for example, Denise Witmer, "Warning Signs of Teenage Drug Abuse," About.com, http://parentingteens.about.com/cs/drugsofabuse/a/driug_abuse20.htm:

> Signs in the Home: loss of interest in family activities; disrespect for family rules; withdrawal from responsibilities; verbally or physically abusive; sudden increase or decrease in appetite; disappearance of valuable items or money; not coming home on time; not telling you where they are going; constant excuses for behavior; spending a lot of time in their rooms; lies about activities; finding the following: cigarette rolling papers, pipes, roach clips, small glass vials, plastic baggies, remnants of drugs (seeds, etc.).
>
> Signs at School: sudden drop in grades; truancy; loss of interest in learning; sleeping in class; poor work performance; not doing homework; defiant of authority; poor attitude towards sports or other extracurricular activities; reduced memory and attention span; not informing you of teacher meetings, open houses, etc.
>
> Physical and Emotional Signs: changes friends; smell of alcohol or marijuana on breath or body; unexplainable mood swings and behavior; negative, argumentative, paranoid or confused, destructive, anxious; over-reacts to criticism; acts rebellious; sharing few if any of their personal problems; doesn't seem as happy as they used to be; overly tired or hyperactive; drastic weight loss or gain; unhappy and depressed; cheats, steals; always needs money, or has excessive amounts of money; sloppiness in appearance.

The CDC suggests that it takes but six of these signs to indicate that there may well be a problem. For a study of public service announcements about drug use, see Michael T. Stephenson, "Anti-Drug Public Service Announcements Targeting Parents," *Southern Communication Journal* 67, no. 4 (Summer–Fall 2002): 335–50.

5. Ryan S. King, "Disparity by Geography: The War on Drugs in America's Cities" (report, The Sentencing Project, Washington, DC, May 2008); Michael Tonry, *Malign Neglect: Race, Crime, and Punishment in America* (New York: Oxford University Press, 1996).

6. Only the professional middle-class parents (and there were several of these) mentioned that drug testing of their teenage children at home was irrelevant because their children's participation in sports requires drug testing in some other location and as a routine matter. As one African American, professional middle-class mother of two said, "My kids are really into sports, so they are always tested. . . . I think that automatically they test for drugs when they take their blood, so they have a physical every year." Of course, this may be the case also for working-class and middle-class children, even if no parents mentioned it.

7. This is part of the Moore and Haggerty argument that I also challenge in the following chapter. Dawn Moore and Kevin D. Haggerty, "Bring It on Home: Home Drug Testing and the Relocation of the War on Drugs," *Social & Legal Studies* 10, no. 3 (2001): 377–405.

8. Recall that some said they would be casual about pornography as well.

9. Jay P. Greene and Greg Forster, "Sex, Drugs, and Delinquency in Urban and Suburban Public Schools" (Education Working Paper 4, Manhattan Institute, January 2004), http://www.manhattan-institute.org/cgi-bin/apMI/print.cgi. For a study about the sexual activity of preadolescent girls (which argues that these children are no "angels"), see Joan D. Atwood, "Mommy's Little Angel, Daddy's Little Girl: Do You Know What Your Pre-Teens Are Doing?" *American Journal of Family Therapy* 34 (2006): 447–67.

10. For a discussion of sex in college, see Kathleen A. Bogle, *Hooking Up: Sex, Dating, and Relationships on Campus* (New York: NYU Press, 2008). For a discussion of drinking in college, see Henry Wechsler et al., "Trends in College Binge Drinking during a Period of Increased Prevention Efforts: Findings from 4 Harvard School of Public Health College Alcohol Study Surveys: 1993–2001," *Journal of American College Health* 50, no. 5 (2002): 203–17; "Editorial: Binge Drinking on Campus," *New York Times*, July 1, 2009.

11. In a similar way, Giddens describes trust as "confidence in the reliability of a person or system, regarding a given set of outcomes or events, where that confidence expresses a faith in the probity or love or another, or in the correctness of abstract principles (technical knowledge)." Anthony Giddens, *The Consequences of Modernity* (Palo Alto, CA: Stanford University Press, 1990), 34.

12. I recently asked a highly educated, white woman whether she went to her daughter's Facebook page; she gave almost exactly the same response as the father quoted in the text. She said that her daughter did not allow her to be her "friend" on the site but that there were enough other people (including cousins) who were her daughter's friend that she was certain she would be alerted if there were something inappropriate there.

13. Some parents feel that because they are less adept at technology than their children are, they are wiser to remain with what it is they know how to do than to adopt a strategy that might put their children in a position of being able to get around and dismantle their surveillance; dislike of these technologies is multifaceted and multilayered.

14. For a similar account, see Joyce Maynard, "My Secret Left Me Unable to Help," *New York Times*, July 26, 2009, Sunday Styles: 8.

15. Greene and Forster, "Sex, Drugs, and Delinquency in Urban and Suburban Public Schools."

16. See table B.10 in appendix B.

NOTES TO CHAPTER 8

1. Barbara Hofer et al., "The 'Electronic Tether': Communication and Parental Monitoring during the College Years," in *Who's Watching? Daily Practices of Surveillance among Contemporary Families*, ed. Margaret K. Nelson and Anita Ilta Garey, 277–94 (Nashville, TN: Vanderbilt University Press, 2009).

2. Margaret K. Nelson, "Watching Children: Describing the Use of Baby Monitors on Epinions.com," *Journal of Family Issues* 29, no. 4 (April 2008): 525. See also Mark Leyner, "Tinker, Tailor, Toddler," *Esquire*, July 1997, 120–21.

3. Annette Lareau, *Unequal Childhoods: Class, Race, and Family Life* (Berkeley: University of California Press, 2003); Sharon Hays, *The Cultural Contradictions of Motherhood* (New Haven, CT: Yale University Press, 1996).

4. See, for example, Jennie Carroll and Elizabeth Hartnell-Young, "Available Just Enough: The Mobile Phone as a Safety Net for Parents and Their Teenage Children," *Proceedings of the Life of Mobile Data Conference,* 2004, 1–7; Trine Fotel and Thyra Uth Thomsen, "The Surveillance of Children's Mobility," *Surveillance & Society* 1, no. 4 (2004): 535–54; and Leslie Haddon, "The Social Consequences of Mobile Telephony: Framing Questions" (paper presented at the Sosiale Konsekvenser Av Mobiltelfoni, Oslo, Telenor, June 16, 2000).

5. Gilles Deleuze, "Postscript on the Societies of Control," *October* 59 (Winter 1992): 3–7.

6. Sara Rimer, "For Girls, It's Be Yourself, and Be Perfect, Too," *New York Times*, March 31, 2007.

7. Nikolas Rose, "Government and Control," *British Journal of Criminology* 40 (2000): 321–39; Nikolas Rose, *Powers of Freedom: Reframing Political Thought* (Cambridge: Cambridge University Press, 1999).

8. Rose, *Powers of Freedom,* 234.

9. Michel Foucault, *Discipline and Punish: The Birth of the Prison*, trans. A. M. Sheridan (New York: Pantheon, 1977).

10. Rose, *Powers of Freedom,* 240.

11. Because the middle-class and working-class parents rely on traditional disciplinary practices, their style of care is not evaluated here.

12. Rose describes this process as evaluation through the "logics immanent within all networks of practice," Rose, "Powers of Freedom," 234.

13. Hofer et al., "The 'Electronic Tether'"; National Survey of Student Engagement, "Experiences That Matter: Enhancing Student Learning and Success; Annual Report 2007," 2007, http://nsse.iub.edu/NSSE_2007_Annual_Report/docs/withhold/NSSE_2007_Annual_Report.pdf.

14. And they reveal that status anxiety—are their children doing well in school and applying to college?—is a primary, if not *the* primary, concern.

15. Dawn Moore and Kevin D. Haggerty, "Bring It on Home: Home Drug Testing and the Relocation of the War on Drugs," *Social & Legal Studies* 10, no. 3 (2001): 383.

NOTES TO THE CONCLUSION

1. For the same reason, I also chose not to examine mechanisms for tracking children's school performance. See Pearson's PowerSchool website, http://www.pearsonschoolsystems.com/; Edline website, http://www.edline.com/; Linton Weeks, "How'd You Do in School Today? With Edline Online, the Report Card Goes 24/7 and Every Test Is an Open Book," *Washington Post,* April 30, 2008; Jan Hoffman, "I Know What You Did Last Math Class," *New York Times,* May 4, 2008.

2. Annette Lareau, *Unequal Childhoods: Class, Race, and Family Life* (Berkeley: University of California Press, 2003).

3. Jerry A. Jacobs and Kathleen Gerson, *The Time Divide: Work, Family, and Gender Inequality* (Cambridge, MA: Harvard University Press, 2004).

4. Holly Blackford, "Playground Panopticism: Ring-Around-the-Children, a Pocketful of Women," *Childhood* 2 (2004): 227–49. Many parents refer to blogs for advice about how early, for example, to allow a child to walk to school. See Berkeley Parents Network, "When Is It Safe for Kids to Walk Alone?" 2005, http://parents.berkeley.edu/advice/worries/walking.html.

5. Blackford, "Playground Panopticism"; Margaret K. Nelson and Rebecca N. Schutz, "Day Care Differences and the Reproduction of Social Class," *Journal of Contemporary Ethnography* 36 (2007): 281–317.

6. To be sure, some working-class parents worry that their use of physical punishment leaves them vulnerable to criticism. Even so, they appear to know how they want to approach disciplinary issues.

7. Nikolas Rose, *Governing the Soul: The Shaping of the Private Self* (London: Free Association Books, 1989).

8. David Anderegg, *Worried All The Time: Rediscovering the Joy in Parenthood in an Age of Anxiety* (New York: Free Press, 2003); Madeline Levine, *The Price of Privilege: How Parental Pressure and Material Advantage Are Creating a Generation of*

Disconnected and Unhappy Kids (New York: Harper, 2008); Hara Estroff Marano, *A Nation of Wimps: The High Cost of Invasive Parenting* (New York: Broadway Books, 2008); Pamela Paul, *Parenting, Inc.* (New York: Times Books, 2008); Judith Warner, *Perfect Madness: Motherhood in the Age of Anxiety* (New York: Riverhead Books, 2005).

9. Barbara Hofer et al., "The 'Electronic Tether': Communication and Parental Monitoring during the College Years," in *Who's Watching? Daily Practices of Surveillance among Contemporary Families*, ed. Margaret K. Nelson and Anita Ilta Garey (Nashville, TN: Vanderbilt University Press, 2009), 286. See also Valerie Strauss, "Putting Parents in Their Place: Outside Class; Too Much Involvement Can Hinder Students' Independence, Experts Say," *Washington Post,* March 21, 2006, http://www.washingtonpost.com/wp-dyn/content/article/2006/03/20/AR2006032001167.html.

10. Brittany Whitlow, "Helicopter Parents Limit, Stunt Student Growth," *Webster University Journal,* March 6, 2008, http://media.www.webujournal.com/media/storage/paper245/news/2008/03/06/Opinioneditorial/helicopter.Parents.Limit.Stunt.Student.Growth-3253679.shtml; Jay Matthews, "New Study Gives Hovering College Parents Extra Credit," *Washington Post,* November 5, 2007, http://www.washingtonpost.com/wp-dyn/content/article/2007/11/04/AR2007110401754.html.

11. Barbara Kantrowitz and Peg Tyre, "The Fine Art of Letting Go," *Newsweek,* May 22, 2006.

12. Louise Tutelian, "Following the Kids to College," *New York Times*, August 22, 2008; Kantrowitz and Tyre, "The Fine Art of Letting Go."

13. College administrators, counselors, and public health officials report on a set of disturbing behaviors on college campuses. Rates of binge drinking (defined as "the consumption of five or more drinks in a row by men—or four or more drinks in a row by women—at least once in the previous 2 weeks" ["Binge Drinking," KidsHealth website, http://kidshealth.org/teen/drug_alcohol/alcohol/binge_drink.html]) appear to have increased or held steady over the past decade in spite of considerable efforts to reduce that phenomenon. Lloyd D. Johnston et al., *Monitoring the Future: National Survey Results on Drug Use, 1975–2006,* NIH Publication No. 07-6206, U.S. Department of Health and Human Services, National Institutes of Health, National Institute on Drug Abuse, 2007, http://monitoringthefuture.org/pubs/monographs/vol2_2006.pdf. See also Henry Wechsler et al., "Trends in College Binge Drinking during a Period of Increased Prevention Efforts: Findings from 4 Harvard School of Public Health College Alcohol Study Surveys: 1993–2001," *Journal of American College Health* 50, no. 5 (2002): 203–17; "Editorial: Binge Drinking on Campus," *New York Times*, July 1, 2009. In addition, the number of students "coming to campus with concurrent psychological problems has grown dramatically" in recent years, and according to the National College Health Assessment (2003), which is sponsored by the American College Health Association, nearly 40 percent of students "have frequently felt so depressed they could not function." Keith J. Anderson, "Challenges and Opportunities," *Student Health Spectrum,* March 2004, 2.

Are these behaviors (binge drinking) and attitudes (depression) related to shifts in parental behavior? Perhaps. In fact, some commentators focus on the demands parents place on children to be "perfect" and on the intentional challenge of family beliefs by engaging in risky sexual behaviors, drinking excessively, and taking illicit drugs. Richard Kadison and Theresa Foy DiGeronimo, *College of the Overwhelmed: The Campus Mental Health Crisis and What to Do about It* (New York: Wiley, 2004). We can also imagine that adolescents who have had their actions intimately shaped by parental interventions, once free to "control" themselves, might find that they don't quite know how to do that. These explanations suggest a link between the professional middle-class approach to parenting and problematic behaviors on campus. But the jury is still out on this connection.

14. Lareau, *Unequal Childhoods*; Joel Spring, *American Education,* 13th ed. (New York: McGraw-Hill, 2007).

15. Hofer et al., "The 'Electronic Tether,'" 286.

16. Sue Shallenbarger, "Helicopter Parents Go to Work: Moms and Dads Are Now at the Office," *Wall Street Journal* (Eastern edition), March 16, 2006, D1; Kathryn Tyler, "The Tethered Generation," *HRMagazine*, 2007, http://www.gendiff.com/docs/TheTetheredGeneration.pdf.

17. For a popular discussion of this issue, see Lisa Belkin, "When Mom and Dad Share It All," *New York Times Magazine,* June 15, 2008, 44. Much of the new information about how to monitor children on the Internet is explicitly directed at women. On this issue, see Jane Long, "Be [Net] Alert, but Not Alarmed? Regulating the Parents of Generation MSM," *Media International Australia Incorporating Culture and Policy*, 2005, 122–34.

18. Mary Blair-Loy, *Competing Devotions: Career and Family among Women Executives* (Cambridge, MA: Harvard University Press, 2003); Pamela Stone, *Opting Out: Why Women Really Quit Careers and Head Home* (Berkeley: University of California Press, 2007); Lisa Belkin, "The Opt-Out Revolution," *New York Times Magazine*, October 26, 2003, 42–47, 85–86.

19. Heather Boushey, "Opting Out? The Effect of Children on Women's Employment in the United States," *Feminist Economics* 14, no. 1 (January 2008): 1–36.

20. Suzanne M. Bianchi, "The Changing Demographic and Socioeconomic Characteristics of Single Parent Families," in *Single Parent Families: Diversity, Myths and Realities*, ed. Shirley M. H. Hanson et al. (New York: Haworth, 1995), 64.

21. Not surprisingly, some of the professional middle-class women who were interviewed for this study recognize the burdensome nature of parenting out of control; even so, they seem unable to resist its claims.

22. Robin Fretwell Wilson, "Keeping Women in Business (and Family)," *Social Science Research Network,* April 1, 2008, http://ssrn.com/abstract=1115468. See also Sandra Tsing Loh, "Let's Call the Whole Thing Off," *Atlantic Online*, July–August 2009.

23. Rosanna Hertz, *Single by Chance, Mothers by Choice* (New York: Oxford University Press, 2006), xviii.

24. For a discussion of the gender issues (and violence) that stands behind many divorces, see Demie Kurz, *For Richer, for Poorer: Mothers Confront Divorce* (New York: Routledge, 1995).

25. Chrys Ingraham, *White Weddings: Romancing Heterosexuality in Popular Culture* (New York: Routledge, 1999).

26. Suzanne M. Bianchi, John P. Robinson, and Melissa A. Milkie, *Changing Rhythms of American Family Life* (New York: Russell Sage Foundation, 2006), 104.

27. Sharon Hays, *The Cultural Contradictions of Motherhood* (New Haven, CT: Yale University Press, 1996).

28. The professional middle-class women I know suggest that they are not nearly as close to their mothers as they report that their children are to them.

29. Associated Press, "Cell Phone Makers Target 'Tween' Market," *FoxNews.com*, March 22, 2005, http://www.foxnews.com/story/0,2933,151014,00.html.

30. BrickHouse Security, "Overwhelming Consumer Demand for Child Safety Device Sells Out Four Months of Inventory Creating Wait List for New Product," news release, July 9, 2008.

31. Joseph B. White, "Technology Allows Monitoring of Teen Drivers, Raising Questions," *Wall Street Journal*, December 3, 2007.

32. Sharon Levy, Shari Van Hook, and John Knight, "A Review of Internet-Based Home Drug-Testing Products for Parents," *Pediatrics* 113, no. 4 (April 2004): 720–26.

33. As an example of the kind of stories that would have awakened parental fears, see Kurt Eichenwald, "Through His Webcam, a Boy Joins a Sordid Online World," *New York Times*, December 19, 2005. I conducted a quick search of the *New York Times* in the years 2003 to the present asking for content that included the words *Internet, pornography,* and *youth*. The number of pieces fluctuated between 2005 and 2006 before dropping off sharply in 2007.

Year	Number of Pieces with Content Including the Words "Internet," "Pornography," and "Youth"
2003	32
2004	30
2005	18
2006	60
2007	26
2008	12
2009 (until June 1)	2

34. Erich Goode and Nachman Ben-Yehuda, *Moral Panics: The Social Construction of Deviance* (New York: Wiley-Blackwell, 1994).

35. In addition, some people are concerned that filters screen out credible health resources. Todd Melby, "See No Evil: Internet Filters Block More than Porn," *Contemporary Sexuality* 37, no. 2 (2003): 1, 4–5.

36. Harlan Coben, "The Undercover Parent," *New York Times*, March 16, 2008, http://www.nytimes.com/2008/03/16/opinion/16coben.html.

37. For another set of predictions, see Lisa Belkin, "America and the Alpha Mom," *Motherlode: Adventures in Parenting*, October 20, 2008, http://parenting.blogs.nytimes.com.

38. For more nuanced discussions of "helicopter parenting" and for discussions of the "pushback," see Lisa Belkin, "In Defense of Helicopter Parents," *New York Times*, March 4, 2009; Susan Newman, "When Does Mothering Become Smothering? Part 1," *Psychology Today*, April 23, 2009; Susan Newman, "When Does Mothering Become Smothering? Part 2," *Psychology Today*, April 23, 2009; Don Aucoin, "For Some, Helicopter Parenting Delivers Benefits," *Boston Globe*, March 31, 2009; Tom Hodgkinson, *The Idle Parent: Why Less Means More When Raising Kids* (London: Hamish Hamilton, 2009); Lenore Skenarzy, *Free-Range Kids: Giving Our Children the Freedom We Had without Going Nuts with Worry* (New York: Jossey-Bass, 2009).

NOTES TO APPENDIX A

1. This research was approved by the Institutional Review Board at Middlebury College. Each respondent signed an informed consent form, which was kept on file in my office.

2. By chance, rather than by design, I did not interview any members of same-gender couples; I did not ask respondents about their sexual orientation, believing that issue to be irrelevant to the broader issues at hand.

3. "Annual Demographic Survey: March Supplement," U.S. Census Bureau, http://pubdb3.census.gov/macro/032006/hhinc/new04_006.htm.

4. "Highest Level of Educational Attainment of U.S. Population, 2005," U.S. Census Bureau, *Current Population Survey*, March 2005, available online at http://www.infoplease.com/ipa/A0908670.html.

5. It may well be, as Lareau suggests in *Unequal Childhoods*, for many issues having to do with raising children, class, and not race/ethnicity, is the critical variable. Annette Lareau, *Unequal Childhoods: Class, Race, and Family Life* (Berkeley: University of California Press, 2003).

6. For a discussion of how parents' perceptions of risk are gendered, see Gill Valentine, "'My Son's a Bit Dizzy.' 'My Wife's a Bit Soft': Gender, Children and Cultures of Parenting," *Gender, Place and Culture* 4, no. 1 (1997): 37–62.

◈ BIBLIOGRAPHY

Acocella, Joan. "The Child Trap: The Rise of Overparenting." *New Yorker,* November 17, 2008.

Altheide, David L. "Children and the Discourse of Fear." *Symbolic Interaction* 25, no. 2 (2002): 229–50.

Anderegg, David. *Worried All the Time: Rediscovering the Joy in Parenthood in an Age of Anxiety.* New York: Free Press, 2003.

Anderson, Keith J. "Challenges and Opportunities." *Student Health Spectrum,* March 2004, 2.

Applebome, Peter. "How We Took the Child Out of Childhood." *New York Times,* January 8, 2006.

Arenson, Karen W. "Applications to Colleges Are Breaking Records." *New York Times,* January 17, 2008.

Ariès, Philippe. *Centuries of Childhood.* New York: Vintage Books, 1962.

Armour, Stephanie. "'Helicopter' Parents Hover When Kids Job Hunt." *USA Today,* April 23, 2007. http://www.usatoday.com/money/economy/e,ployment/2007-05-23-helocopter-parents.

Arnett, J. J. "Emerging Adulthood: A Theory of Development from the Late Teens through the Twenties." *American Psychologist* 55, no. 5 (2000): 469–80.

Associated Press. "Cell Phone Makers Target 'Tween' Market." *FoxNews.com,* March 22, 2005. http://www.foxnews.com/story/0,2933,151014,00.html.

AT&T. "AT&T Shares Results from 2008 Parent-Child Texting Survey." October 8, 2008. http://www.att.com/gen/press-room?pid=4800&cdvn=news&newsarticleid=26157.

Atwood, Joan D. "Mommy's Little Angel, Daddy's Little Girl: Do You Know What Your Pre-Teens Are Doing?" *American Journal of Family Therapy* 34 (2006): 447–67.

Aucoin, Don. "For Some, Helicopter Parenting Delivers Benefits." *Boston Globe,* March 31, 2009. http://www.boston.com/lifestyle/family/articles/2009/03/03/for_some_helicopter_parenting_delivers_benefits/.

Backett-Milburn, Kathryn, and Jeni Hardin. "How Children and Their Families Construct and Negotiate Risk, Safety and Danger." *Childhood* 11, no. 4 (2004): 429–47.

Ball, Stephen J. *Class Strategies and the Education Market: The Middle Classes and Social Advantage.* London: RoutledgeFalmer, 2003.

Baumrind, D. "Child Care Practices Anteceding Three Patterns of Preschool Behavior." *Genetic Psychology Monographs* 75 (1967): 43–88.

———. "Current Patterns of Parental Authority." *Developmental Psychology Monographs* 4 (1971): 1–103.

Beck, Ulrich. *Risk Society: Towards a New Modernity*. London: Sage, 1992.

Belkin, Lisa. "America and the Alpha Mom." *Motherlode: Adventures in Parenting*, October 20, 2008. http://parenting.blogs.nytimes.com.

———. "In Defense of Helicopter Parents." *New York Times*, March 4, 2009. http://parenting.blogs.nytimes.com/2009/03/04/in-defense-of-helicopter-parents/.

———. "Let the Kid Be." *New York Times*, May 31, 2009. http://www.nytimes.com/2009/05/31/magazine/31wwln-lede-t.html?_r=1.

———. "The Opt-Out Revolution." *New York Times Magazine*, October 26, 2003, 42–47, 85–86.

———. "When Mom and Dad Share It All." *New York Times Magazine*, June 15, 2008, 44.

———. "When Your Kid Won't Friend You." *New York Times*, October 14, 2008. http://parenting.blogs.nytimes.com/2008/10/14/when-your-kid-wont-friend-you/.

Berkeley Parents Network. "When Is It Safe for Kids to Walk Alone?" 2005. http://parents.berkeley.edu/advice/worries/walking.html.

Berliner, Uri. "Have and Have-Nots: Income Inequality in America." *NPR.org*, February 5, 2007. www.npr.org/templates/story/story.php?storyId=7180618.

Bernstein, Basil. "Class and Pedagogies: Visible and Invisible." In *Class, Codes and Control*, vol. 3, edited by Basil Bernstein, 116–56. London: Routledge and Kegan Paul, 1975.

———. *Class, Codes, and Control*. London: Routledge and Kegan Paul, 1971.

Best, Joel. *Threatened Children: Rhetoric and Concern about Child-Victims*. Chicago: University of Chicago Press, 1990.

Bianchi, Suzanne M. "The Changing Demographic and Socioeconomic Characteristics of Single Parent Families." In *Single Parent Families: Diversity, Myths and Realities*, edited by Shirley M. H. Hanson, Marsha L. Heims, Doris J. Julian, and Marvin B. Sussman, 71–98. New York: Haworth, 1995.

Bianchi, Suzanne M., John P. Robinson, and Melissa A. Milkie. *Changing Rhythms of American Family Life*. New York: Russell Sage Foundation, 2006.

Bielick, Stacey, and Chris Chapman. "Trends in the Use of School Choice." *Education Statistics Quarterly* (National Center for Education Statistics) 5, no. 2 (2003).

Bittman, Michael, and Judy Wajcman. "The Rush Hour: The Quality of Leisure Time and Gender Equity." In *The Social Organisation of Care*, edited by Nancy Folbre. New York: Routledge, 2004.

Blackford, Holly. "Playground Panopticism: Ring-Around-the-Children, a Pocketful of Women." *Childhood* 2 (2004): 227–49.

Blair-Loy, Mary. *Competing Devotions: Career and Family among Women Executives*. Cambridge, MA: Harvard University Press, 2003.

Blakeley, Edward J. *Fortress America: Gated Communities in the United States*. Washington, DC: Brookings Institution Press, 1999.

Bogle, Kathleen A. *Hooking Up: Sex, Dating, and Relationships on Campus*. New York: NYU Press, 2008.

Bourdieu, Pierre. "Cultural Reproduction and Social Reproduction." In *Knowledge, Education, and Cultural Change*, edited by Richard Brown, 487–507. London: Tavistock, 1973.

Bourdieu, Pierre, and Jean Claude Passeron. *Reproduction in Education, Culture and Society*. Beverly Hills, CA: Sage, 1977.

Boushey, Heather. "Opting Out? The Effect of Children on Women's Employment in the United States." *Feminist Economics* 14, no. 1 (January 2008): 1–36.

Brantlinger, Ellen. *Dividing Classes: How the Middle Class Negotiates and Rationalizes School Advantage*. London: RoutledgeFalmer, 2003.

BrickHouse Security. "Overwhelming Consumer Demand for Child Safety Device Sells Out Four Months of Inventory Creating Wait List for New Product." News release, July 9, 2008.

Brody, Jane E. "Turning the Ride to School into a Walk." *New York Times*, September 11, 2007. http://www.nytimes.com/2007/09/11/health/11brod.html.

Browning, E. S. "Exorcising Ghosts of Octobers Past." *Wall Street Journal Online,* October 15, 2007. http://online.wsj.com/public/article_print/SP119239926667758592.html.

Burns, R., and C. Crawford. "School Shootings, the Media, and Public Fear: Ingredients for a Moral Panic." *Crime Law and Social Change* 32, no. 21 (1999): 147–68.

Cable, Jane C. "Bringing Home Baby—and Monitor Too." *American Baby*, July 1984, 18–21.

Cancian, Francesca M. "Defining 'Good' Child Care: Hegemonic and Democratic Standards." In *Child Care and Inequality: Rethinking Carework for Children and Youth*, edited by Francesca M. Cancian, Demie Kurz, Andrew S. London, Rebecca Reviere, and Mary C. Tuominen, 65–82. New York: Routledge, 2002.

Carpenter, Dave. "Car Insurers' Devices Track Teen Drivers." Associated Press, October 10, 2007.

Carroll, Jennie, and Elizabeth Hartnell-Young. "Available Just Enough: The Mobile Phone as a Safety Net for Parents and Their Teenage Children." *Proceedings of the Life of Mobile Data Conference*, 2004, 1–7.

Carter, Michael J., and Susan Boslego Carter. "Women's Recent Progress in the Professions, or, Women Get a Ticket to Ride after the Gravy Train Has Left the Station." *Feminist Studies* 73, no. 3 (Autumn 1981): 477–504.

Carter, Stephen L. *New England White*. New York: Vintage Books, 2008.

Castells, Manuel. *The Rise of the Network Society*, vol. 1. Oxford, UK: Blackwell, 2000.

C.H. "Keeping Kids Safe Online." *Working Mother*, October 2004, 186.

Chandra, Anita, Steven C. Martino, Rebecca L. Collins, Marc N. Elliott, Sandra H. Berry, David E. Kanouse, and Angela Miu. "Does Watching Sex on Television Predict Teen Pregnancy? Findings from a National Longitudinal Survey of Youth." *Pediatrics* 122 (2008): 1047–54.

Childers, Mary. *Welfare Brat: A Memoir*. Edinburgh, UK: Bloomsbury, 2005.

Coben, Harlan. "The Undercover Parent." *New York Times,* March 16, 2008. http://www.nytimes.com/2008/03/16/opinion/16coben.html.

Cohany, Sharon R., and Emy Sok. "Trends in Labor Force Participation of Married Mothers of Infants." *Monthly Labor Review,* February 2007, 9–16.

"Colleges Cope with 'Helicopter Parents.'" *Buffalo News,* July 23, 2008. http://buffalonews.typepad.com/inside_the_news/2008/07/colleges-cope-w.html.

Collins, Patricia Hill. *Black Feminist Thought: Knowledge, Consciousness, and the Politics of Empowerment.* New York: Routledge, 2008.

Conrad, Peter. "Medicalization and Social Control." *Annual Review of Sociology* 18 (1992): 209–32.

Conrad, Peter, and D. Potter. "From Hyperactive Children to ADHD Adults: Observations on the Expansion of Medical Categories." *Social Problems* 47, no. 4 (November 2000): 559–82.

Cookson, Peter, and Caroline Persell. *Preparing for Power.* New York: Basic Books, 1985.

Coontz, Stephanie. *The Way We Never Were: American Families and the Nostalgia Trap.* New York: Basic Books, 1992.

———. *The Way We Really Are: Coming to Terms with America's Changing Families.* New York: Basic Books, 1997.

Cooper, Marianne. "'Doing Security' in Insecure Times: Class and Family Life in Silicon Valley." PhD diss., Sociology, University of California at Berkeley, 2008.

Corsaro, William A. *We're Friends, Right? Inside Kids' Culture.* Washington, DC: Joseph Henry Press, 2003.

Crawford, Louise. "Helicopter Moms vs. Free-Range Kids." *Newsweek,* April 21, 2008. http://www.newsweek.com/id/133103.

Cross, Gary. *Men to Boys: The Making of Modern Masculinity.* New York: Columbia University Press, 2008.

Cunningham, David. "Surveillance and Social Movements: Lenses on the Repression-Mobilization Nexus." *Contemporary Sociology* 36, no. 2 (2007): 120–25.

Cunningham, Laura Shaine. *Sleeping Arrangements: A Memoir.* New York: Knopf, 1989.

DeFao, Janine. "Parents Turn to Tech Toys to Track Teens." *San Francisco Chronicle,* July 9, 2006.

De Graaf, Nan Dirk, Paul M. De Graaf, and Gerbert Kraaykamp. "Parental Cultural Capital and Educational Attainment in the Netherlands: A Refinement of the Cultural Capital Perspective." *Sociology of Education* 73 (2000): 92–111.

Deleuze, Gilles. "Postscript on the Societies of Control." *October* 59 (Winter 1992): 3–7.

Demo, David H., and Martha J. Cox. "Families with Young Children: A Review of Research in the 1990s." *Journal of Marriage and the Family* 62 (November 2000): 876–95.

DeNavas-Walt, Carmen, Bernadette D. Proctor, and Cheryl Hill Lee. *Money Income in the United States: 2005.* Current Population Reports P60-231, U.S. Census Bureau. Washington, DC: U.S. Government Printing Office, 2006.

Devitt, Kerry, and Debi Roker. "The Role of Mobile Phones in Family Communication." *Children & Society,* 2008.

Dillon, Sam. "A Great Year for Ivy League Colleges, but Not So Good for Applicants to Them." *New York Times,* April 4, 2007.

DiMaggio, Paul. "Cultural Capital and School Success: The Impact of Status Culture Participation on the Grades of U.S. High School Students." *American Sociological Review* 47 (1982): 189–201.

"Do 'Helicopter Moms' Do More Harm than Good?" *ABC News,* October 21, 2005. http://abcnews.go.com/2020/print?id=1237868.

Edin, Kathryn, and Maria Kefalas. *Promises I Can Keep: Why Poor Women Put Motherhood before Marriage.* Berkeley: University of California Press, 2005.

"Editorial: Binge Drinking on Campus." *New York Times,* July 1, 2009. http://www.nytimes.com/2009/07/01/opinion/01wed3.html?pagewanted=print.

Ehrenreich, Barbara. *Fear of Falling: The Inner Life of the Middle Class.* New York: HarperCollins, 1990.

Eichenwald, Kurt. "Through His Webcam, a Boy Joins a Sordid Online World." *New York Times,* December 19, 2005.

EscapeHomes.com. "Martha's Vineyard." http://www.escapehomes.com/main.aspx?Tabid=46&EscapeTownID=102.

Farley, Tom. "The Cell-Phone Revolution." *AmericanHeritage.com,* 2007. http://www.americanheritage.com/events/articles/web/20070110-cell-phone-att-mobile-phone-motorola-federal-communications-commission-cdma-tdma-gsm.shtml.

Finder, Alan. "Elite Colleges Reporting Record Lows in Admission." *New York Times,* April 1, 2008.

Fotel, Trine, and Thyra Uth Thomsen. "The Surveillance of Children's Mobility." *Surveillance & Society* 1, no. 4 (2004): 535–54.

Foucault, Michel. *Discipline and Punish: The Birth of the Prison.* Translated by A. M. Sheridan. New York: Pantheon, 1977.

Furedi, Frank. *Paranoid Parenting: Abandon Your Anxieties and Be a Good Parent.* London: Allen Lane/Penguin Press, 2001.

Furstenberg, Frank F., Jr. *Destinies of the Disadvantaged: The Politics of Teenage Childbearing.* New York: Russell Sage Foundation, 2007.

Garey, Anita Ilta. *Weaving Work and Motherhood.* Philadelphia: Temple University Press, 1999.

Garland, David. "The Culture of High Crime Societies: Some Preconditions of Recent 'Law and Order' Policies." *British Journal of Criminology* 40 (2000): 347–75.

Giddens, Anthony. *The Consequences of Modernity.* Palo Alto, CA: Stanford University Press, 1990.

———. "Risk and Responsibility." *Modern Law Review* 62, no. 1 (1999): 1–10.

Giroux, Henry A. *Stealing Innocence: Corporate Culture's War on Children.* New York: Palgrave, 2001.

Gitlin, Todd. *The Sixties: Years of Hope, Days of Rage,* rev. ed. New York: Bantam, 1993.

Glassner, Barry. *The Culture of Fear: Why Americans Are Afraid of the Wrong Thing.* New York: Basic Books, 1999.

Goode, Erich, and Nachman Ben-Yehuda. *Moral Panics: The Social Construction of Deviance*. New York: Wiley-Blackwell, 1994.

Greene, Jay P., and Greg Forster. "Sex, Drugs, and Delinquency in Urban and Suburban Public Schools." Education Working Paper 4, Manhattan Institute, January 2004. http://www.manhattan-institute.org/cgi-bin/apMI/print.cgi.

Guryan, Jonathan, Erik Hurst, and Melissa Schettini Kearney. "Parental Education and Parental Time with Children." Working Paper 13993, National Bureau of Economic Research, Cambridge, MA, May 2008.

Haddon, Leslie. "The Social Consequences of Mobile Telephony: Framing Questions." Paper presented at the Sosiale Konsekvenser Av Mobiltelfoni, Oslo, Telenor, June 16, 2000.

Hall, G. S. *Adolescence: Its Psychology and Its Relation to Physiology, Anthropology, Sociology, Sex, Crime, Religion and Education*. New York: Appleton, 1904.

Hansen, Karen V. *Not-So-Nuclear Families: Class, Gender and Networks of Care*. New Brunswick, NJ: Rutgers University Press, 2004.

Harmon, Amy. "Lost? Hiding? Your Cellphone Is Keeping Tabs." *New York Times*, December 21, 2003.

Hart, Betty, and Todd R. Risley. *Meaningful Differences in the Everyday Experience of Young American Children*. Baltimore: Paul H. Brookes, 1995.

Hays, Sharon. *The Cultural Contradictions of Motherhood.* New Haven, CT: Yale University Press, 1996.

Heath, Shirley Brice. *Ways with Words: Language, Life and Work in Communities and Classrooms*. New York: Cambridge University Press, 1996.

Hertz, Rosanna. *Single by Chance, Mothers by Choice: How Women Are Choosing Parenthood without Marriage and Creating the New American Family*. New York: Oxford University Press, 2006.

Hochschild, Arlie Russell. *The Second Shift*. Updated ed. New York: Penguin Books, 2003. First published 1989.

———. *The Time Bind: When Work Becomes Home and Home Becomes Work*. New York: Metropolitan Books, 1997.

Hodgkinson, Tom. *The Idle Parent: Why Less Means More When Raising Kids*. London: Hamish Hamilton, 2009.

Hofer, Barbara, Constance Souder, Elena K. Kennedy, Nancy Fullman, and Kathryn Hurd. "The 'Electronic Tether': Communication and Parental Monitoring during the College Years." In *Who's Watching? Daily Practices of Surveillance among Contemporary Families*, edited by Margaret K. Nelson and Anita Ilta Garey, 277–94. Nashville, TN: Vanderbilt University Press, 2009.

Hoffman, Jan. "I Know What You Did Last Math Class." *New York Times*, May 4, 2008.

Holland, Alyce, and Thomas Andre. "Participation in Extracurricular Activities in Secondary School: What Is Known, What Needs Be Known?" *Review of Educational Research* 57, no. 4 (Winter 1987): 437–66.

Holson, Laura M. "Text Generation Gap: U R 2 Old (JK)." *New York Times*, March 9, 2008.

Honore, Carl. *Under Pressure: Rescuing Our Children from the Culture of Hyper-Parenting*. New York: HarperOne, 2009.

Hulbert, Ann. *Raising America: Experts, Parents and a Century of Advice about Children*. New York: Knopf, 2003.

Ingraham, Chrys. *White Weddings: Romancing Heterosexuality in Popular Culture*. New York: Routledge, 1999.

Jacobs, Jerry A., and Kathleen Gerson. *The Time Divide: Work, Family, and Gender Inequality*. Cambridge, MA: Harvard University Press, 2004.

Jenks, Chris. "Editorial: Children at Risk?" *Childhood* 10, no. 1 (2003): 5–8.

Jenness, Valerie, David A. Smith, and Judith Stepan-Norris. "Editor's Note: Taking a Look at Surveillance Studies." *Contemporary Sociology* 36, no. 2 (2007): vii–viii.

Johnson, Heather Beth. *The American Dream and the Power of Wealth: Choosing Schools and Inheriting Inequality in the Land of Opportunity*. New York: Routledge, 2007.

Johnson, Julia Overturf. *Who's Minding the Kids? Child Care Arrangements: Winter 2002*. Current Population Reports P70-101, U.S. Census Bureau, Department of Commerce, Washington, DC, October 2005.

Johnston, Lloyd D., Patrick M. O'Malley, Jerald G. Bachman, and John E. Schulenberger. *Monitoring the Future: National Survey Results on Drug Use, 1975–2006*. NIH Publication No. 07-6206, U.S. Department of Health and Human Services, National Institutes of Health, National Institute on Drug Abuse, 2007. http://monitoringthefuture.org/pubs/monographs/vol2_2006.pdf.

Jones, Owen. "Naturally Not! Childhood, the Urban and Romanticism." *Human Ecology Review* 9, no. 2 (2002): 17–30.

Kadison, Richard, and Theresa Foy DiGeronimo. *College of the Overwhelmed: The Campus Mental Health Crisis and What to Do about It*. New York: Wiley, 2004.

Kadlec, Dan. "Making Flexible Retirements Work." *Time*, May 10, 2008. http://www.time.com/time/magazine/article/0,9171,1619545,00.html.

Kantrowitz, Barbara, and Peg Tyre. "The Fine Art of Letting Go." *Newsweek*, May 22, 2006.

Katz, Cindi. "The State Goes Home: Local Hyper-Vigilance of Children and the Global Retreat from Social Reproduction." *Social Justice* 28, no. 3 (2001): 47–56.

Kearns, R. A., D. C. A. Collins, and P. M. Neuwelt. "The Walking School Bus: Extending Children's Geographies?" *Area* 35, no. 3 (2003): 285–92.

Kennedy, Tracy L. M., Aaron Smith, Amy Tracy Wells, and Barry Wellman. "Networked Families." Report, Pew Internet & American Life Project, October 19, 2008. http://www.pewinternet.org/~/media/Files/Reports/2008/PIP_Networked_Family.pdf.pdf.

Kincaid, James. *Erotic Innocence: The Culture of Child Molesting*. Durham, NC: Duke University Press, 1998.

King, Ryan S. "Disparity by Geography: The War on Drugs in America's Cities." Report, The Sentencing Project, Washington, DC, May 2008.

Kofman, Yelizavetta. "Preschool and the PMC: How Professional Middle Class Parents Negotiate Advantages for Their Children in the Early Education Market." Senior thesis, Department of Sociology/Anthropology, Middlebury College, Middlebury, VT, 2007.

Kohn, Melvin. *Class and Conformity: A Study in Values*. Homewood, IL: Dorsey, 1969.

Kurz, Demie. "'I Trust Them but I Don't Trust Them': Issues and Dilemmas in Monitoring Teenagers." In *Who's Watching? Daily Practices of Surveillance among Contemporary Families*, edited by Margaret K. Nelson and Anita Ilta Garey, 260–76. Nashville, TN: Vanderbilt University Press, 2009.

———. *For Richer, for Poorer: Mothers Confront Divorce*. New York: Routledge, 1995.

Lajewski, Henry C. *Child Care Arrangements of Full-Time Working Mothers*. Washington, DC: Children's Bureau, 1959.

———. "Working Mothers and Their Arrangements for Care of Their Children." *Social Security Bulletin,* August 1959.

Lareau, Annette. *Home Advantage: Social Class and Parental Intervention in Elementary Education*. Lanham, MD: Rowman & Littlefield, 2000.

———. *Unequal Childhoods: Class, Race, and Family Life*. Berkeley: University of California Press, 2003.

Laurant, Darrell. "The Re Generation." *Science & Spirit,* 2008. http://www.science-spirit.org/printerfriendly.php?article_id=676.

Lee, Valerie E., and David T. Burkman. *Inequality at the Starting Gate*. Washington, DC: Economic Policy Institute, 2002.

Leff, Lisa. "Teen's Ticket Hinges on GPS vs. Radar." Associated Press, October 25, 2007.

Lesko, Nancy. *Act Your Age! A Cultural Construction of Adolescence*. London: RoutledgeFalmer, 2001.

———. "Denaturalizing Adolescence: The Politics of Contemporary Representations." *Youth and Society* 28, no. 2 (December 1996): 138–61.

Levine, Barry. "Meet the Cell-Phone Tracking Parents." *NewsFactor Network,* June 5, 2006. http://www.newsfactor.com/story.xhtml?story_id=01100000A9QB.

Levine, Judith. *Harmful to Minors: The Perils of Protecting Children from Sex*. New York: Thunder's Mouth, 2003.

Levine, Madeline. *The Price of Privilege: How Parental Pressure and Material Advantage Are Creating a Generation of Disconnected and Unhappy Kids*. New York: Harper, 2008.

Levy, Sharon, Shari Van Hook, and John Knight. "A Review of Internet-Based Home Drug-Testing Products for Parents." *Pediatrics* 113, no. 4 (April 2004): 720–26.

Leyner, Mark. "Tinker, Tailor, Toddler." *Esquire*, July 1997, 120–21.

Loh, Sandra Tsing. "Let's Call the Whole Thing Off." *Atlantic Online*, July–August 2009. http://www.theatlantic.com/doc/print/200907/divorce.

Lomardi, Kate Stone. "High Anxiety of Getting into College." *New York Times*, April 8, 2007.

Long, Jane. "Be [Net] Alert, but Not Alarmed? Regulating the Parents of Generation MSM." *Media International Australia Incorporating Culture and Policy*, 2005, 122–34.

Lugaila, T. "A Child's Day: 2000 (Selected Indicators of Child Well-Being)." U.S. Census Bureau, 2003. http://www.census.gov/prod/2003pubs/.

Lupton, Deborah, and John Tulloch. "'Risk Is Part of Your Life': Risk Epistemologies among a Group of Australians." *Sociology* 36, no. 2 (2002): 317–34.

Lyon, David. "Sociological Perspectives and Surveillance Studies: 'Slow Journalism' and the Critique of Social Sorting." *Contemporary Sociology* 36, no. 2 (2007): 107–11.

———. *Surveillance Society: Monitoring Everyday Life*. Philadelphia: Open University Press, 2001.

———. *Surveillance Studies: An Overview*. Cambridge, UK: Polity, 2007.

Maccoby, E. D., and J. A. Martin. "Socialization in the Context of the Family." In *Handbook of Child Psychology*, vol. 4, *Socialization, Personality and Social Development*, 4th ed., edited by P. H. Mussen and E. Hetherington. New York: Wiley, 1983.

Magid, Larry. "GPS Chips in Cellphones Track Kids and Help Navigate, Too." *International Herald Tribune*, July 19, 2007.

Marano, Hara Estroff. "A Nation of Wimps." *Psychology Today*, November–December 2004.

———. *A Nation of Wimps: The High Cost of Invasive Parenting*. New York: Broadway Books, 2008.

Martens, Lydia. "Gender, Power, and the Household (Book Review)." *Sociology* 35, no. 1 (February 2001): 241.

Marx, Gary T. "Desperately Seeking Surveillance Studies: Players in Search of a Field." *Contemporary Sociology* 36, no. 2 (2007): 125–30.

———. "What's New about the 'New Surveillance'? Classifying for Change and Continuity." *Surveillance & Society* 1, no. 2 (2002): 9–29.

Matthews, Jay. "New Study Gives Hovering College Parents Extra Credit." *Washington Post,* November 5, 2007. http://www.washingtonpost.com/wp-dyn/content/article/2007/11/04/AR2007110401754.html.

Maynard, Joyce. "My Secret Left Me Unable to Help." *New York Times*, July 26, 2009, Sunday Styles: 8.

McDonough, Patricia M. *Choosing Colleges: How Social Class and Schools Structure Opportunity*. Albany: State University of New York Press, 1997.

McPherson, Miller, Lynn Smith-Lovin, and Matthew E. Brashears. "Social Isolation in America: Changes in Core Discussion Networks over Two Decades." *American Sociological Review* 71 (June 2006): 353–75.

McPherson, Miller, Lynn Smith-Lovin, and James M. Cook. "Birds of a Feather: Homophily in Social Networks." *Annual Review of Sociology* 27 (2001): 415–44.

Melby, Todd. "See No Evil: Internet Filters Block More than Porn." *Contemporary Sexuality* 37, no. 2 (2003): 1, 4–5.

Mitchell, Kimberly J., David Finkelhor, and Janis Wolak. "Protecting Youth Online: Family Use of Filtering and Blocking Software." *Child Abuse & Neglect* 29 (2005): 753–65.

Monahan, Torin. *Surveillance and Security: Technological Politics and Power in Everyday Life*. New York: Routledge, 2006.

Moore, Dawn, and Kevin D. Haggerty. "Bring It on Home: Home Drug Testing and the Relocation of the War on Drugs." *Social & Legal Studies* 10, no. 3 (2001): 377–405.

Nagy, John, and Tiffany Danitz. "Parental Fears Heightened by Columbine, Poll Shows." *Stateline.org*, April 20, 2000. http://www.stateline.org/live/ViewPage.action?siteNodeId=136&languageId=1&contentId=13994.

Nasar, J., P. Hecht, and R. Wener. "'Call If You Have Trouble': Mobile Phones and Safety among College Students." *International Journal of Urban and Regional Research* 31, no. 4 (2007): 863–73.

National Bureau of Economic Research. "U.S. Business Cycle Expansions and Contractions." 2008. www.nber.org/cycles/main.html.

National Center for Education Statistics. "Parent Expectations and Planning for College: Statistical Analysis Report." April 2008. http://nces.ed.gov/pubsearch/pubsinfo.asp?pubid=2008079.

———. "Student Effort and Educational Progress: Transition to College." In *The Condition of Education*. 2007. http://nces.ed.gov/programs/coe/2007/section3/indicator25.asp.

National Resource Center Listservs. "'Helicopter' Parents at Orientation." http://www.sc.edu/fye/listservs/archives/HelicopterParentsatOrientation.html.

National Survey of Student Engagement. "Experiences That Matter: Enhancing Student Learning and Success; Annual Report 2007." 2007. http://nsse.iub.edu/NSSE_2007_Annual_Report/docs/withhold/NSSE_2007_Annual_Report.pdf.

Nelson, Margaret K. "'I Saw Your Nanny': Gossip and Shame in the Surveillance of Child Care." In *Who's Watching? Daily Practices of Surveillance among Contemporary Families*, edited by Margaret K. Nelson and Anita Ilta Garey, 109–34. Nashville, TN: Vanderbilt University Press, 2009.

———. "Watching Children: Describing the Use of Baby Monitors on Epinions.com." *Journal of Family Issues* 29, no. 4 (April 2008): 516–38.

Nelson, Margaret K., and Anita Ilta Garey. "Who's Watching? An Introductory Essay." In *Who's Watching? Daily Practices of Surveillance among Contemporary*

Families, edited by Margaret K. Nelson and Anita Ilta Garey, 1–16. Nashville, TN: Vanderbilt University Press, 2009.

Nelson, Margaret K., and Rebecca N. Schutz. "Day Care Differences and the Reproduction of Social Class." *Journal of Contemporary Ethnography* 36 (2007): 281–317.

Newman, Susan. "When Does Mothering Become Smothering? Part 1." *Psychology Today,* April 23, 2009. http://www.psychologytoday.com/blog/singletons/200904/when-does-mothering-become-smothering-part-1.

———. "When Does Mothering Become Smothering? Part 2." *Psychology Today,* April 23, 2009. http://www.psychologytoday.com/blog/singletons/200905/when-does-mothering-become-smothering-part-2.

Pain, Rachel. "Paranoid Parenting? Rematerializing Risk and Fear for Children." *Social & Cultural Geography* 73, no. 21 (April 2006): 221–43.

Pascoe, C. J. *Dude, You're a Fag.* Berkeley: University of California Press, 2007.

Pattilo-McCoy, Mary. *Black Picket Fences: Privilege and Peril among the Black Middle Class.* Chicago: University of Chicago Press, 1999.

Paul, Pamela. *Parenting, Inc.* New York: Times Books, 2008.

Phelan, Thomas W. *1-2-3 Magic: Effective Discipline for Children 2–12.* Glen Ellyn, IL: ParentMagic, 2004.

Postman, Neil. *The Disappearance of Childhood.* New York: Delacorte, 1982.

Public Agenda. "A Lot Easier Said than Done." 2002. http://www.publicagenda.org/files/pdf/easier_said_than_done.pdf.

Pugh, Allison J. *Longing and Belonging: Parents, Children, and Consumer Culture.* Berkeley: University of California Press, 2009.

Putnam, Robert D. *Bowling Alone: The Collapse and Revival of American Community.* New York: Simon and Schuster, 2001.

Rainwater, Lee, and Timothy M. Smeeding. *Poor Kids in a Rich Country: America's Children in Comparative Perspective.* New York: Russell Sage Foundation, 2003.

Ray, Diana. "Big Brother Is Watching You." *Insight on the News,* July 23, 2001, 18.

"Readers Respond: Taking the Child Out of Childhood." *New York Times,* January 14, 2006. http://www.nytimes.com/2006/01/14/nyregion/14towns-readers.html.

Rideout, Victoria. "Parents, Children & Media: A Kaiser Family Foundation Survey." Kaiser Family Foundation, June 2007. http://www.kff.org/entmedia/upload/7638.pdf.

Rimer, Sara. "For Girls, It's Be Yourself, and Be Perfect, Too." *New York Times,* March 31, 2007.

Rose, Nikolas. *Governing the Soul: The Shaping of the Private Self.* London: Free Association Books, 1989.

———. "Government and Control." *British Journal of Criminology* 40 (2000): 321–39.

———. *Powers of Freedom: Reframing Political Thought.* Cambridge: Cambridge University Press, 1999.

Salamon, Julie. "The Rating Says PG, but Is That Guidance Enough?" *New York Times,* January 17, 2005.

Sasson, Theodore, and Margaret K. Nelson. "Danger, Community, and the Meaning of Crime Watch: An Analysis of the Discourses of African American and White Participants." *Journal of Contemporary Ethnography* 259, no. 21 (1996): 171–200.

Sayer, Liana C., Suzanne M. Bianchi, and John P. Robinson. "Are Parents Investing Less in Children? Trends in Mothers' and Fathers' Time with Children." *American Journal of Sociology*, July 2004, 1–43.

Schachter, Jason P. *Geographical Mobility: 2002 to 2003*. Current Population Reports P20-549, U.S. Census Bureau, U.S. Department of Commerce, Washington, DC, March 2004.

Scott, Marvin B., and Lyman M. Stanford. "Accounts." *American Sociological Review* 33, nos. 1–2 (1968): 46–62.

Shalit, Ruth. "Defining Disability Down: Why Johnny Can't Read, Write, or Sit Still." *New Republic*, August 25, 1997.

Shallenbarger, Sue. "Helicopter Parents Go to Work: Moms and Dads Are Now at the Office." *Wall Street Journal* (Eastern edition), March 16, 2006, D1.

Shapiro, Laura. "The Myth of Quality Time: How We're Cheating Our Kids, What You Can Do." *Newsweek*, May 12, 1997, 64–69.

Skenarzy, Lenore. *Free-Range Kids: Giving Our Children the Freedom We Had without Going Nuts with Worry*. New York: Jossey-Bass, 2009.

Spock, Benjamin. *Dr. Benjamin Spock's Baby and Child Care*. New York: Pocket Books, 1959.

Spring, Joel. *American Education,* 13th ed. New York: McGraw-Hill, 2007.

Stack, Carol. *All Our Kin: Strategies for Survival in a Black Community*. New York: Harper and Row, 1974.

Staples, William G. *Everyday Surveillance: Vigilance and Visibility in Postmodern Life*. Lanham, MD: Rowman & Littlefield, 2000.

Starr, Alexandra. "'Security Moms': An Edge for Bush?" *Business Week*, December 1, 2003, 60.

Stearns, Peter N. *Anxious Parents: A History of Modern Childrearing in America*. New York: NYU Press, 2004.

Stephenson, Michael T. "Anti-Drug Public Service Announcements Targeting Parents." *Southern Communication Journal* 67, no. 4 (Summer–Fall 2002): 335–50.

Stone, Pamela. *Opting Out: Why Women Really Quit Careers and Head Home*. Berkeley: University of California Press, 2007.

Strauss, Valerie. "Putting Parents in Their Place: Outside Class; Too Much Involvement Can Hinder Students' Independence, Experts Say." *Washington Post,* March 21, 2006. http://washingtonpost.com/wp-dyn/content/article/2006/03/20/AR2006032001167.html.

Swartz, Teresa Toguchi. "Family Capital and the Invisible Transfer of Privilege: Intergenerational Support and Social Class in Early Adulthood." In *New Directions for Child and Adolescent Development, 119*, edited by J. T. Mortimer, 11–24. New York: Wiley, 2008.

Thorne, Barrie. *Gender Play*. New Brunswick, NJ: Rutgers University Press, 1983.

Timothy. "GPS Tracking Device Beats Radar Gun in Court." *Slashdot*, July 18, 2009. http://tech.slashdot.org/article.pl?sid=08/07/18/0318228.

Tonn, Jessica L. "Online Monitoring." *Education Week*, January 19, 2005, 12.

Tonry, Michael. *Malign Neglect: Race, Crime, and Punishment in America*. New York: Oxford University Press, 1996.

Torpey, John. "Through Thick and Thin: Surveillance after 9/11." *Contemporary Sociology* 36, no. 2 (2007): 116–19.

Tutelian, Louise. "Following the Kids to College." *New York Times*, August 22, 2008.

Tyler, Kathryn. "The Tethered Generation." *HRMagazine*, 2007. http://www.gendiff.com/docs/TheTetheredGeneration.pdf.

University of Texas at Austin. "Mom Needs an 'A.'" 2007. http://www.utexas.edu/features/2007/helicopter/.

U.S. Department of Justice, FBI. "A Parent's Guide to Internet Safety." 2006. http://www.fbi.gov/publications/pguide/parentsguide.pdf.

Uttal, Lynet. "Custodial Care, Surrogate Care, and Coordinated Care: Employed Mothers and the Meaning of Child Care." *Gender & Society* 10, no. 3 (June 1996): 291–311.

Valentine, Gill. "'My Son's a Bit Dizzy.' 'My Wife's a Bit Soft': Gender, Children and Cultures of Parenting." *Gender, Place and Culture* 4, no. 1 (1997): 37–62.

———. "'Oh Yes I Can.' 'Oh No You Can't': Children and Parents' Understandings of Kids' Competence to Negotiate Public Space Safely." *Antipode* 29, no. 1 (1997): 65–89.

Valentine, Gill, and John McKendrick. "Children's Outdoor Play: Exploring Parental Concerns about Children's Safety." *Geoforum* 28, no. 2 (1997): 219–35.

Vandewater, Elizabeth A., Seoung-Eun Park, Xuan Huang, and Ellen A. Wartella. "'No—You Can't Watch That': Parental Rules and Young Children's Media Use." *American Behavioral Scientist* 48, no. 5 (January 2005): 608–23.

Vossler, Don, Jack Schmit, and Nick Vesper. *Going to College: How Social, Economic, and Educational Factors Influence the Decisions Students Make*. Baltimore: Johns Hopkins University Press, 1999.

Walkerdine, Valerie. "Safety and Danger: Childhood, Sexuality, and Space at the End of the Millennium." In *Governing the Child in the New Millennium*, edited by Kenneth Hultquist and Gunilla Dahlberg, 15–34. New York: RoutledgeFalmer, 2001.

Wang, Rong, Suzanne M. Bianchi, and Sara B. Raley. "Teenagers' Internet Use and Family Rules: A Research Note." *Journal of Marriage and Family* 67 (December 2005): 1249–58.

Warner, Judith. *Perfect Madness: Motherhood in the Age of Anxiety*. New York: Riverhead Books, 2005.

Wechsler, Henry, Jae Eun Lee, Meichun Kuo, Mark Seibring, Toben F. Nelson, Hang Lee. "Trends in College Binge Drinking during a Period of Increased Prevention Efforts: Findings from 4 Harvard School of Public Health College Alcohol Study Surveys: 1993–2001." *Journal of American College Health* 50, no. 5 (2002): 203–17.

Weeks, Linton. "How'd You Do in School Today? With Edline Online, the Report Card Goes 24/7 and Every Test Is an Open Book." *Washington Post,* April 30, 2008.

Welsh, S., A. Hassiotis, G. O'Mahoney, and M. Deahl. "Big Brother Is Watching You: The Ethical Implications of Electronic Surveillance Measures in the Elderly." *Aging & Mental Health* 73, no. 5 (September 2004): 372–75.

White, Amanda M., and Constance T. Gager. "Idle Hands and Empty Pockets? Youth Involvement in Extracurricular Activities, Social Capital, and Economic Status." *Youth and Society*, September 2007, 75–111.

White, Joseph B. "Technology Allows Monitoring of Teen Drivers, Raising Questions." *Wall Street Journal*, December 3, 2007.

White, Linda Feldmeier. "Learning Disability, Pedagogies, and Public Discourse." *College Composition and Communication* 53, no. 4 (2002): 705–38.

Whitlow, Brittany. "Helicopter Parents Limit, Stunt Student Growth." *Webster University Journal,* March 6, 2008. http://media.www.webujournal.com/media/storage/paper245/news/2008/03/06/Opinioneditorial/helicopter.Parents.Limit.Stunt.Student.Growth-3253679.shtml.

Wikipedia. "Helicopter Parent." http://en.wikipedia.org/wiki/Helicopter_parent.

Wilson, Jamie. "Girl to Get Tracker Implant to Ease Parents' Fear." *Guardian,* September 3, 2002, 2.

Wilson, Robin Fretwell. "Keeping Women in Business (and Family)." *Social Science Research Network,* April 1, 2008. http://ssrn.com/abstract=1115468.

Winerip, Michael. "Young, Gifted, and Not Getting into Harvard." *New York Times,* April 29, 2007.

Wise, J. Macgregor. "Assemblage." In *Gilles Deleuze: Key Concepts*, edited by Charles J. Stivale, 77–87. Montreal: McGill-Queen's University Press, 2005.

Wrigley, Julia. "Hiring a Nanny: The Limits of Private Solutions to Public Problems." *Annals, AAPSS* 593 (May 1999): 162–74.

———. *Other People's Children: An Intimate Account of the Dilemmas Facing Middle-Class Parents and the Women They Hire to Raise Their Children.* New York: Basic Books, 1995.

Zelizer, Viviana A. *Pricing the Priceless Child: The Changing Social Value of Children.* New York: Basic Books, 1985.

Zureik, Elia. "Surveillance Studies: From Metaphors to Regulation to Subjectivity." *Contemporary Sociology* 36, no. 2 (2007): 112–15.

INDEX

1-2-3 Magic (Phelan), 94–95
1960s counterculture, 42–44, 65–66, 69, 176–177

abduction, preying on fears of, 218n10
adolescents: immaturity of, 2, 35–36; as parent's "best friend," 9, 67; youthful indiscretions, 63–65. *See also* teenagers
adult solidarity, erosion of, 17
adults, respect for authority of, 53, 99
anxiety: about children's safety, 18–19; from using baby monitors, 114–115
AOL parental controls, 137, 140
Ariès, Philippe, 71
autonomy. *See* children's autonomy

baby monitors, 113–117; anxiety from using, 114–115; cell phones compared to, 108, 122; as connection devices, 108; facilitation of immediate responsiveness, 115–118; intrinsic fragility of babies, assumption of, 114–115, 122; normalization of vigilance, 115; ownership by social class, *196*; professional middle-class parents' use of, 10, 115–117, 166; safety concerns, 114; working-class and middle-class parents' use of, 166
Beck, Ulrich, 54, 114
Bentham, Jeremy, 171
Bianchi, Suzanne, 133, 184
Blair-Loy, Mary, 61
BrickHouse Child Locator, 109, 128

Castells, Manuel, 30
cell phones, 117–126; baby monitors compared to, 108, 122; checking children's call lists, 125; children's autonomy, 122–126; children's lying about whereabouts, 124–125; as connection devices, 108; facilitation of immediate responsiveness to "emergencies," 118–120, 121; monitoring adherence to preset limits, 126; negotiations using, 125–126, 169; not knowing who children are talking to, 125; ownership by age of child, *196*; ownership by social class, *197*; professional middle-class parents' use of, 10, 118–127, 166, 168; reasons for purchasing, 120; safety concerns, 117–118, 120; working-class and middle-class parents' use of, 120, 126, 166, 168
ChemTrac Inc., 219n17
child care: categories of, 59; familial assistance with, 209n1; "othermother" support, 210n3; paid, 209n1; poor parents, 20; primary *vs.* secondary, 58; professional middle-class parents, 209n1; U. S. Census Bureau on, 71; working-class and middle-class parents, 209n1; working-class parents, 20. *See also* child rearing
child locators, 128–133; advertisements for, 218n10; BrickHouse Child Locator, 109, 128; as devices of "constraint," 108–109; future of, 185; negative reactions to, 10, 128–131; professional middle-class parents' rejection of, 10, 128–131, 166; use of by social class, *197*; uses, 109; working-class and middle-class parents' use of, 128, 131–133, 166

child rearing: devotion to, 6; private/individual responsibility for, 54, 56–57; resentment of effort needed to raise children, 102–103; shortcuts making it easier, 6, 7, 132, 160; time spent with children, 58, 59, 61–62, 183–184
Childer, Mary, 71
childhood, stages of, 71–72
children: as the new companions for women, 183–184; time spent with, 58, 59, 61–62, 183–184; value placed on, 183
children's autonomy: cell phones and, 122–126; of children of "helicopter parents," 179; effect of parenting out of control on, 11; measures of emotional autonomy, 178–179; of professional middle-class children, 178–179; stages of childhood and, 71–72; of working-class and middle-class children, 178–179
children's future, parents' ideas about their, 23–47; education, aspirations for, 23, 33–35, 37–38; extracurricular activities, encouragement of, 26, 28–30, 77; flexibility, planning for, 30–31, 46; goals for, 6, 38–43, 45–46; impact of 1960s on attitudes toward, 42–44; launching point into adulthood, 35–38; learning disabilities, testing for, 26–27; middle-class parents' ideas, 33–34; professional middle-class parents' ideas, 24–31, 32, 34–43; talents, nurturing of, 28–30; working-class and middle-class parents' ideas, 31–32, 37–38, 45–46; working-class parents' ideas, 23, 32, 33, 38; worries about class reproduction, 23–24, 76, 96; worries about competition for entrance into elite colleges, 25; worries about downward mobility, 24; worries about economic stability, 23; worries about economic uncertainty, 42; worries about educational future, 26–28; worries about squeezing out of the middle class, 25, 42
children's safety: anxieties about, 18–19; baby monitors, 114; cell phones, 117–118, 120; nostalgic view of, 54–57; parenting out of control, 6; parenting with limits, 7; responsibility for, 6, 7, 54, 56–57; in a "risk society," 54; surveillance technologies, 145–148, 162, 166
class reproduction, worries about, 23–24, 76, 96
class status: acceptance of technology and, 132–133; child locators, response to, 128; cultural attitudes and, 4; downward mobility, worries about, 24; education and, 4–5, 26; income and, 4; occupation and, 4; parenting, intensity of, 19–20, 62–63; parenting styles, 20–21; social attitudes and, 4; worries, foremost, 18
Coben, Harlan, 185
college: competition for entrance into elite colleges, 25; educational aspirations for, 33–35; as launching pad to independent adulthood, 7, 34, 37–38, 45–46. *See also* undergraduates
communication: as a control mechanism, 12; intimacy and, 121; between parents and undergraduates, 2–3, 14, 112, 163, 179
community: loss of, 48–49, 51–53; Rose on, Nikolas, 203n25
Computer.Blogspot.com, 218n12
computers: in open places at home, 158; television compared to, 138. *See also* keystroke monitoring systems; software filters for television and Internet

"concerted cultivation": middle-class parents and, 20, 175; by professional middle-class parents, 20, 76, 90, 166
control, inclusionary *vs.* exclusionary, 170–173. *See also* parenting out of control
control mechanism *vs.* discipline techniques, 11–13
Couric, Katie, 70, 133
"culture of fear," 54
Cybersitter, 143

dangers confronting children, parent's views of, 70–86; access to pornography, 70, 138, 140; effects of ongoing pressure on children, 78; homework, amount of, 78; influences from outside the home, 76; material overindulgence, 79–80; middle-class parents' views, 74, 83–84; overscheduling of children, 32, 76–78; professional middle-class parents' views, 70, 72–82, 83–84, 86; psychological overindulgence, 80–82; seductive technologies, 75; self-centeredness, 80; sexual activity, 84–86; sexualized media images, 9, 70, 74, 86; threats to childhood innocence, 72–76; violence, images of, 75, 86; violence in the neighborhood, 82–84, 86; working-class and middle-class parents' views, 84–86; working-class parents' views, 82–85
discipline techniques *vs.* control mechanisms, 11–13
divorce rates, 183
Dr. Spock (Benjamin Spock), 9
drug abuse, signs of, 224n4. *See also* home drug tests
drug use, professional middle-class parents' attitude toward, 148–152
drugtestyourteen.com, 110–111
Duracell batteries, 128, 185

Edin, Kathryn, 183
education: class status and, 4–5, 26; educational success, seizing opportunities for, 8, 27; learning disabilities, testing for, 26–27; length of, 8; parenting out of control, 8; parenting with limits, 7; parents' aspirations for their children's, 23, 37–38; parents' expectations for their children, *195*. *See also* college; extracurricular activities; schools; undergraduates
educational attainment: parents' aspirations for their children's, 33–35, 38; sports and, 77; usage of software filters for television and Internet, 133
Ehrenreich, Barbara, 203n12
Epinions.com, 113, 165
Everyday Surveillance (Staples), 107–108
exclusionary control, 170–173
extracurricular activities, encouragement of, 26, 28–30, 77, 225n6. *See also* sports

Facebook, 156, 157–158
families: changes when mothers work, 57–52; criminal justice system compared to, 13; desire to contain deviance within the family, 172–173; in discussion of surveillance technologies, 13; government support for, 54; inclusionary and exclusionary control exercised by, 172; isolation of individual families, 49; "opting out" by professional middle-class parents, 181; "quality time" for, 58–59, 61; romantic ties as foundation of, 182; single-parent households, concerns about, 50, 52, 54
Foucault, Michel, 11–12, 171

generational divide, 68–69
Gerson, Kathleen, 44

Giddens, Anthony, 54, 114
GPS tracking systems: functions, 109–110; insurance industry promotion of, 185; professional middle-class parents' rejection of, 10, 151–152, 153, 159; SafeTrak GPS System, 110; use of by social class, *198*; Vehicle Tracker, 109–110; working-class and middle-class parents' use of, 143–144, 146–147, 162

Haggerty, Kevin, 108, 172, 219n17
Hays, Sharon, 166, 184
"helicopter parents": children of, 179; definition, 2. *See also* hovering
Hertz, Rosanna, 182, 183
Hilton, Paris, 70, 74
Hofer, Barbara, 10, 179, 180
home drug tests: drugtestyourteen.com, 110–111; extent of, 219n17; future of, 185; inclusionary control strategy, 172–173; market for, 108; professional middle-class parents' rejection of, 151–152, 225n6; referral to family physician as alternative to, 149; use of by social class, *198*; uses for, 111; working-class and middle-class parents' use of, 143–144, 145, 162
hovering: as alternative to surveillance technologies, 133–136, 151–152, 157; by elite parents, 1–2; future of, 186; intimacy as, 10; material resources, dependence on, 177; over undergraduates, 2–3; by professional middle-class parents, 10; technological assistance for, 10; technology, dependence on, 3; as tracking consequences of parenting out of control, 9. *See also* parenting out of control
"hypervigilance," 2. *See also* hovering; parenting out of control

IamBigBrother, 143
inclusionary control, 170–173
income, class status and, 4
"intensive mothering," 19–20, 166

Jacobs, Jerry, 44

Katz, Cindi, 108
Kefalas, Maria, 183
keystroke monitoring systems: function, 110; professional middle-class parents' rejection of, 151–152; use of by social class, *198, 199*; working-class and middle-class parents' use of, 143–144, 145–146, 162

Lareau, Annette, 76, 90, 100–101, 166
learning disabilities, testing for, 26–27
Lyon, David, 12

MacArthur, Douglas, 179
marriages: effect of parenting out of control on, 181–182; irrelevance of spouses compared to importance of children, 183
media images: concern with, 9, 70, 74, 86; professional middle-class parents, 9, 70, 74, 134–136; working-class and middle-class parents, 9
middle-class parents: "concerted cultivation" and, 20, 175; definition, 5; "intensive mothering" by, 20; media images, concern with, 74; their children's educational attainments, aspirations for, 33–34; their children's future, ideas about, 33–34; their past, ideas about, 52–53, 55; time spent with children, 59
Milkie, Melissa, 184
Monahan, Torin, 219n18
Moore, Dawn, 108, 172, 219n17

mothers/mothering: changes to families when mothers work, 57–62; "intensive mothering," 19–20, 166; labor force participation of mothers, 57; motherhood as center of families, 183; stay-at-home moms, 23, 57–58, 61
MySpace, 156, 157–158

Nation of Wimps (Marano), 178
National Center for Education Statistics, 33
National Survey of College Graduates, 182
National Survey of Student Engagement, 2, 179
neighborhoods: concern about, 9; schools in choosing, 28, 78; violence in, 82–84, 86
NetNanny, 143
New York Times (newspaper), 179, 185

occupation, class status and, 4

panopticon, 11–12
parenting: "1-2-3 maybe" approach, 94–95, 123; "concerted cultivation," 20, 76, 90, 166; increased difficulty of, 49–51; intensity of, 19–20, 62–63; "intensive mothering," 19–20, 166; mission of, understanding of, 62–63; private responsibility for raising children, universal assumption of, 54; shared concerns of, 58–59, 164; single parenting, 50, 52, 54, 102; taken-for-granted activities of, 56. *See also* parenting styles
Parenting, Inc. (Paul), 178
"parenting out of control" (the phrase), 11–12, 62, 165
parenting out of control, 6–9, 34–44, 54, 59–60, 87–98, 116, 121, 126, 170–173; avoidance of shortcuts to make child rearing easier, 6, 160; belief in adolescent children as parent's "best friend," 9, 67; belief in ambitious goals for children's achievements, 6, 38–43; belief in being constantly available to their children, 90–91; belief in flexibility, 87–88; belief in intense involvement with their children, 6, 20, 26, 36, 87–88, 92, 97, 126–127; belief in lengthy period of children's dependency, 6, 175; belief in their children's boundless potential, 6, 8, 26, 28–29, 88–89; belief in trusting their children, 89–90, 154–155; belief that their children are good kids, 150–151, 160–161, 170; belief that they are carving out a new mode of parenting, 91–92; commentators view of, 178–179; commitment to trust while not being trusting, 159–160; consequences for marriages, 181–182; consequences for women, 181; contradictions in, 6–7, 97; control mechanisms, dependence on, 12; difficulties in, 103, 104; doubts about child-rearing approach, 177; effect on independence and autonomy of young adults, 11; effect on parents adopting the strategy, 11; encouragement for delayed launching point into adulthood, 6, 8, 34–36, 38; encouragement for developing broad range of skills, 8, 30–31; parental authoritativeness and authoritarianism, rejection of, 62, 68, 87–88, 94, 95–96; as parenting style, 3; parenting with limits compared to, 166–167, 174–175, 177; parents' mode of parenting, rejection of (*see* rejection of parent's mode of parenting by professional middle-class parents); reliance on discussion and negotiation, 6, 88, 90, 93–94, 96–97, 126, 134–135, 137;

parenting out of control (*continued*): reliance on personal rather than technological vigilance, 136–137; responsiveness to children's individual needs and desires, 6, 115–120, 121, 129; satisfactions, rewards of, 91–92, 94, 104; sneakiness in, 161; time-consuming nature of, 61–62, 91, 181; worries associated with, 177–178; worrying about being too involved in their children's lives, 93

parenting styles: adult solidarity, erosion of, 17; belief systems, differences in, 21; child-centeredness, differences in, 19–20; children's psychological well-being, anxieties about, 18; children's safety, anxieties about, 18–19; class status, differences in, 20–21; cultural capital supplied to children, differences in, 21; discipline, differences in style of, 20–21; discipline techniques *vs.* control mechanisms in, 11–13; influences on, 7–8; language patterns, differences in, 21; lenses for examining, 5–6; lessons of the past, 67–68; material conditions and, 175–176; parents' ideas about their children's future (*see* children's future, parent's ideas about their); parents' ideas their own past (*see* past, parent's ideas about their); parents' views of dangers confronting their children (*see* dangers confronting children, parent's views of); predators, fear of, 18, 185; of professional middle-class parents (*see* parenting out of control); "risk society," emergence of, 17; shifts in, causes of, 7–8, 17–18, 69; technology and, 119, 165–170; of working-class and middle-class parents (*see* parenting with limits). *See also* parenting out of control; parenting with limits

parenting with limits, 7–9, 34, 54, 98–104; ability to say no, confidence in, 98; acceptance of the likelihood of misbehavior by their children, 169; acceptance of their children as they are, 100, 131–132, 169; assumption that college is launching pad to independent adulthood, 7, 34, 37–38, 45–46; awareness of difference between being a parent and being a friend, 9, 98–99, 100, 104; belief in achievements and accomplishments as signs of progress, 45, 101, 103; belief in improving behavior through correction, 88; belief in time limits on active parenting, 37–38; belief that children are "predestined" to be who they will be, 100, 131–132, 169; concern with developing skills to ensure their children's self-sufficiency, 7; confidence in child-rearing approach, 177; contradictions in, 7; difficulties in, 104; disciplinary techniques, dependence on, 12, 65, 68; encouragement for clear career goals, 8, 45–46; encouragement for early launching point into adulthood, 8, 166; parenting out of control compared to, 166–167, 174–175, 177; as parenting style, 3; parents' mode of parenting, similarity to, 7; reliance on clear rules and physical punishments, 88, 104, 126; resentment of effort needed to raise children, 102–103; satisfactions, rewards of, 101, 103, 104; strictness in, 98–100, 104; temporal and financial constraints, effects of, 7, 102, 164–165; trusting technology more than their children, 139, 147, 162; welcoming of shortcuts to make child rearing easier, 7, 132 past, parents' ideas about their, 48–69; adult authority, respect for, 53, 62, 99; community, disappearance of, 48–49, 51–53; middle-class parents, 52–53, 55; nostalgia for what might have been, 59–62; parents' mode of parenting, adaptation of, 7, 49, 63–65; parents' mode of parenting, rejection of (*see* rejection of parent's mode of parenting by professional middle-class parents); professional middle-class parents' ideas, 28–30, 35–36, 42, 43–44, 49–51, 53, 55–56; safety and security, nostalgic view of, 54–57; violence in neighborhoods, lack of, 83–84; working-class and middle-class parents' ideas, 49–50, 83–84; working-class parents' ideas, 51–52, 53–54

Perfect Madness (Warner), 178

permissiveness, 95–96

Pew Internet & American Life Project, 117

Phelan, Thomas, 94–95

playpens, 1–2

pornography, 70, 138, 140

Postman, Neil, 73

predators, fear of, 18, 185

Price of Privilege (Levine), 178

private schools, 27–28

professional middle-class children: abandonment of an acceptable path, 44–45, 96; autonomy of, 178–179; delayed maturity among, 35–36; parents' goals for, 6, 38–43, 46; rates of drinking, smoking, drug use and sexual activity, 151; self-centeredness of, 80; working-class and middle-class children compared to, 164

professional middle-class parents: 1960s, impact of, 42–44, 65–66, 69, 176–177; age of, 65, 176–177; awareness of personal costs of their own success, 8, 46–47; baby monitors, use of, 10, 115–117, 166; cell phones, use of, 10, 118–127, 166, 168; child locators, rejection of, 10, 128–131, 166; "concerted cultivation" by, 20, 76, 90, 166; definition, 5, 203n12; drug use, attitude toward, 148–152; Ehrenreich on, Barbara, 203n12; feminist movement, impact of, 43; generational divide, 68–69; GPS tracking systems, rejection of, 10, 151–152, 153, 159; guilt for not providing a stay-at-home mother, 61; home drug tests, rejection of, 151–152, 225n6; hovering by, 10; inclusionary control exercised by, 171–172; "intensive mothering" by, 20, 166; keystroke monitoring systems, rejection of, 151–152; labor force participation of mothers, 57; media images, concern with, 9, 70, 74, 86, 134–136; mobility of, 69, 177; nostalgia for what might have been, 59–60; parenting style (*see* parenting out of control); private schools, preference for, 27–28; "quality time" for family, creation of, 58–59, 61; software filters for television and Internet, rejection of, 133, 141; surveillance technologies, 142, 148–162, 169–170, 172–173, 174–175, 185; technology, 10, 13; television, dislike of, 138; their children, drive for connection with, 69; their children, view of dangers confronting, 70, 72–82, 83–84, 86; their children as site of friendship and fun, 61; their children's educational attainments, aspirations for, 34–35; their children's educational success, seizing opportunities for, 8, 27; their children's extracurricular activities, encouragement of, 26, 28–30, 77, 225n6;

professional middle-class parents (*continued*): their children's flexibility, planning for, 30–31, 46; their children's future, ideas about, 24–31, 32, 34–43; their children's general well-being, confidence securing, 24; their children's learning disabilities, testing for, 26–27; their children's schools, choosing a neighborhood based on, 28, 78; their children's talents, nurturing of, 28–30; their mission, understanding of, 62–63; their past, ideas about, 28–30, 35–35, 42, 43–44, 49–51, 53, 55–56; time spent with children, 59, 61–62; V-chip, rejection of, 133
Promises I Can Keep (Edin and Kefalas), 183
Public Agenda, 18
Pugh, Allison, 79

"quality time" for families, 58–59, 61

Raley, Sara, 133
RAND Corporation, 70, 133
rejection of parent's mode of parenting by professional middle-class parents: conscious awareness of, 7, 8–9; for being self-centered, 91–92; for being shocked by 1960s counterculture, 65–66; for distancing themselves from them, 9, 67; for failing to act on the potential for intimacy with them, 59–60; for failing to apply themselves seriously to parenting, 35–36; for failing to convey the pleasures of parenting, 66–67; for failing to love their children as much as they love theirs, 67, 91; for failing to nurture their unique talents, 28; for failing to prioritize happiness over economic success, 42; for having narrow goals/ambitions for them, 28–30, 42–43, 63; for relying on authority and fixed rules rather than connection and communication, 66, 87–88; for having narrow goals/ambitions for them, 93–94
"risk society," 17, 54
Robinson, John, 184
Roosevelt, Franklin Delano, 179
Rose, Nikolas, 170–171, 203n25

SafeEyes, 143
SafeTrak GPS System, 110
safety. *See* children's safety
schools: choosing a neighborhood based on, 28, 78; concern with, 9; private schools, 27–28; working-class and middle-class parents, 9
self-discipline, 12
Single by Chance, Mothers by Choice (Hertz), 182
single parenting, concerns about, 50, 52
smart cards, 174–175
social attitudes, class status and, 4
software filters for television and Internet, 133–138; AOL filters, 137, 140; children's age and acceptance of, 134–136; function and operation, 218n12; ownership by social class, *197*; professional middle-class parents' rejection of, 133, 141; usage nationwide, 133; working-class and middle-class parents' use of, 11, 76, 133, 136–137, 138–141. *See also* V-chip
Spock, Benjamin (Dr. Spock), 9
sports: competitive pressure in, 78; drug testing and, 225n6; educational attainment and, 77
spyware. *See* surveillance technologies
Staples, William, 107–108
surveillance technologies, 142–162; categories of, 108–110; commitment to trust while not being trusting,

159–160; connection devices, 108 (*see also* baby monitors; cell phones); consequences of, 219n18; as control mechanisms, 12; deterrence effects, 162; devices of "constraint," 108–109 (*see also* child locators; software filters for television and Internet; V-chip); family in discussion of, 13; future of, 185; hovering as alternative to, 133–136, 151–152, 157; information gathering devices, 109 (*see also* GPS tracking systems; home drug tests; keystroke monitoring systems); "meticulous rituals of power" and, 107–108; privacy rights, 148, 152; professional middle-class parents, 142, 148–162, 169–170, 172–173, 174–175, 185; safety concerns, 145–148, 162, 166; smart cards, 174–175; social relations in evaluating, 111–112, 122; "surveillance creep," 107; as violation of parental norms, 153; working-class and middle-class parents, 143–148, 161–162

technology: class status and acceptance of, 132–133; hovering, assistance for, 10; hovering's dependence on, 3; parenting styles and, 119, 165–170; professional middle-class parents, 10, 13; "technological determinist" *vs.* "social determinist" views of, 122, 219n18; trusting technology more than children, 139, 147, 162; working-class and middle-class parents, 10–11, 13. *See also* surveillance technologies
Teen Driver Tracking Device, 110
teenage pregnancy, 70, 133
teenagers, 21, 63–65
Telecommunications Act (1996), 218n11
television: computers compared to, 138; professional middle-class parents' dislike of, 138; ratings scale, 185, 218n11; sexuality and violence on, 185. *See also* software filters for television and Internet; V-chip
terrorism, 18, 56
The Time Divide (Jacobs and Gerson), 44
trust: academic grades, relationship to, 155, 161; belief in trusting children, 89–90, 154–155; commitment to trust while not being trusting, 159–160; essentialist approach to, 153–154, 161; parenting out of control, 89–90, 154–155, 159–160; parenting with limits, 101, 139, 147, 162; pro-forma nod to, 89–90; professional middle-class children's attitudes toward, 153–154; professional middle-class parents' attitudes toward, 89–90, 154–155, 159–160; trusting technology more than children, 139, 147, 162

undergraduates: depression among, 36; hovering over, 2–3; parents, academic assistance provided by, 180; parents, communication with, 2–3, 14, 112, 163, 179; troublesome behavior (e.g., binge drinking), 36, 229n13
Unequal Childhoods (Lareau), 76
U.S. Cellular study, 117
U.S. Census Bureau, 71
U.S. News & World Report (magazine), 25

V-chip: as a device of "constraint," 109; function, 3, 218n11; mandate for, 218n11; professional middle-class parents' rejection of, 133; usage nationwide, 222n4; working-class and middle-class parents' use of, 11, 139–140. *See also* software filters for television and Internet
Vehicle Tracker, 109–110

Wang, Rong, 133
Welfare Brat (Childer), 71
Wilson, Robin, 182
women, effect of parenting out of control on, 181
work: flexibility, need for, 30; future of, 30; labor force participation of mothers, 57; "opting out" of careers by professional middle-class women, 181
working-class and middle-class children: autonomy of, 178–179; parents' goals for, 45–46; professional middle-class children compared to, 164; wheedling and whining by, 164
working-class and middle-class parents: age of, 65, 176–177; baby monitors, use of, 166; cell phones, use of, 120, 126, 166, 168; child locators, use of, 128, 131–133, 166; disciplinary techniques, dependence on, 12, 65, 68; distinctions between, 5; generational divide, attitudes toward, 68–69; GPS tracking systems, use of, 143–144, 146–147, 162; home drug tests, use of, 143–144, 145, 162; keystroke monitoring systems, use of, 143–144, 145–146, 162; labor force participation of mothers, 57; media images, concern with, 9; neighborhoods, concern with, 9; parenting style (*see* parenting with limits); schools, concern with, 9; software filters for television and Internet, use of, 11, 76, 133, 136–137, 138–141; surveillance technologies, 143–148, 161–162; technology, 10–11, 13; their children, view of dangers confronting, 84–86; their children's education, aspirations for, 37–38; their children's future, ideas about, 31–32, 37–38, 45–46; their mission, understanding of, 62–63; their parents' mode of parenting, adaptation of, 49, 63–65; their past, ideas about, 49–50, 83–84; time limits on active parenting, belief in, 37–38; V-chip, use of, 11, 139–140
working-class parents: child care, 20; definition, 5; stay-at-home moms, 23; their children, view of dangers confronting, 82–85; their children's education, aspirations for, 23; their children's educational attainments, aspirations for, 33, 38; their children's future, ideas about, 23, 32, 33, 38; their past, ideas about, 51–52, 53–54
workweek, length of: educational attainment, 209n27; growth in, 44; professional middle-class parents, 44, 176; working-class and middle-class parents, 176
Worried All the Time (Anderegg), 178

◈ ABOUT THE AUTHOR

MARGARET K. NELSON is the A. Barton Hepburn Professor of Sociology at Middlebury College. She is the author of numerous books, including *The Social Economy of Single Mothers: Raising Children in Rural America* and is the coeditor, with Anita Ilta Garey, of *Who's Watching? Daily Practices of Surveillance among Contemporary Families.*